C in Plain English

Brian Overland

A Subsidiary of
Henry Holt and Co., Inc.

First Edition—1995

IPrinted in the United States of America.

10 9 8 7 6 5 4 3 2 1

MIS:Press books are available at special discounts for bulk purchases for sales promotions, premiums, fund-raising, or educational use. Special editions or book excerpts can also be created to specification.

For details contact: Special Sales Director
                              MIS:Press
                              a subsidiary of Henry Holt and Company, Inc.
                              115 West 18th Street
                              New York, New York 10011

Library of Congress Cataloging-in-Publication Data

Overland, Brian R.
        C in Plain English / Brian Overland.
            p.   cm.
        ISBN 1-55828-430-3
        1. C (Computer program language)   I. Title.
    QA76.73.C15094 1995
    005.13'3--dc20   95-18697
                                                                  CIP

Trademarks

Throughout this book, trademarked names are used. Rather than put a trademark symbol after every occurrence of a trademarked name, we used the names in an editorial fashion only, and to the benefit of the trademark owner, with no intention of infringement of the trademark. Where such designations appear in this book, they have been printed with initial caps.

Associate Publisher: Paul Farrell

Managing Editor: Cary Sullivan

Series Editor: Debra Williams Cauley

Editor: Michael Sprague

Technical Editor: Scott Robert Ladd

Copy Editor: Betsy Hardinger

To Purrly, the world's finest cat, whom I stepped over many times late at night on my way to the computer, and Farrah, the world's finest dog.

Contents

Contents

Contents

Acknowledgments

The drawback of working on the west coast has been that I've only gotten to know a few people on a truly first-rate editorial/production team. The In Plain English series editor, Debra Williams Cauley, has created a set of books adhering to the highest standards in the computer-press field, one in which an author—this one, at least—feels he has arrived by becoming a part of. Special thanks go to Michael Sprague, the driving force behind getting me to write this book, as well supplying much of its quality; and Stephanie Doyle who deftly managed all my last-minute changes.

And my special thanks go to my colleague at work, Ken Requa, who graciously made the whole project possible.

Preface

For years the argument raged, but in the end the C programmers won. The C programming language—especially when considered together with its offspring, C++—owns the present and future of serious programming. COBOL and FORTRAN continue to be useful for maintaining old programs (legacy code), but that's a job most people fresh out of a computer science course don't want. BASIC lives on successfully in its incarnation as Visual Basic, but most hackers wouldn't be caught dead running BASICA these days.

C has become the language to know. It's what will get you in the door, or at least taken seriously for a while. More than knowing any operating system, programming language, or jargon, the ability to program in C is what most quickly divides people who consider themselves real programmers from curious end users. And *end user*, a term that slides off a programmer's tongue like the word *peasant*, is a name you probably don't want to be called.

It's worth considering why all this is so. Back in the 1980s, languages such as Pascal and LISP had their passionate advocates, and each of these languages can still be an excellent choice for certain kinds of projects. What makes C exceptional is its universality: it's used every day to write software ranging from operating systems and device drivers (the most low-level software you can write) to navigational systems for interactive television to game programs to financial business programs.

I attribute C's universal adoption to two simple factors: power of expression and economy of expression. By power of expression, I mean this: what can you make the computer do, given the right set of instructions? In hindsight, it's easy to see why this is a critical factor. People who own computers tend to fall into one of two groups: those who want to use the computer to accomplish a limited task with as little fuss as possible, and those who want to master the computer, to figure out everthing they could possibly do with it. Most people who have at least a passing interest in programming fall into the latter camp. And it's these same people who, by and large, don't want to be told what they can't or shouldn't do—certainly not when it comes to their computers. For example, we might justify certain design elements of other languages as follows: "Pascal doesn't let you do arithmetic with an address variable; you could shoot yourself in the foot that way." But it turns out that hard core users, students, and professional programmers all want this ability. It's a jealously guarded right. Because if you do it cleverly enough, you may not be shooting yourself in the foot at all. You may come up with a better or more efficient way to do something than anyone has thought of.

In theory, anything can be done by writing machine language or assembly language (which is basically machine language in a more readable form). Because machine language is the processor's native language, we can say that, by definition, anything that can't be done in machine language can't be done at all. Period. The existence of machine language and assembly language always helped make up for gaps and limitations in high-level languages such as BASIC. If you wanted to do something badly enough, it was reasoned, you could always write an assembly-language routine and call it from the high-level language. If you didn't have the skill or the patience, then you shouldn't be doing it at all; and if you did something catastrophic, such as cause the computer to crash (a feat rather easy to do with assembly language), you could hardly blame the providers of the high-level language. That rationale was nice for the vendors of high-level languages because it left them blameless. Most popular programming languages provide some form of assembly-language interface. Many go so far as to provide *in-line* assembly, which means that you can mix assembly instructions with your other program statements without even having to change text editors or files.

But assembly language (which, not coincidentally, has a some features similar to C) falls down badly on the second criterion I mentioned: economy of expression. It takes a lot of work to tell the computer how to do anything in assembly language. And time—*programmer* time—is money. Even a simple program to add two numbers and print the result (essentially one line in BASIC or C) calls for an assembly-language programmer to write quite a few instructions—laboriously moving data into and out of temporary memory locations (registers)—rather than focusing on the functional purpose of the program. The situation is even worse with RISC chips, which introduce additional headaches related to low-level timing issues.

Power and Economy

As you might suspect, there is a bit of a trade-off between power and economy of expression. To get a programming language to automate tiresome and routine sequences of common actions (such as adding one 32-bit number to another), you have to hand over control of certain resources, such as registers. Yet the C language does a marvelous job of providing a high degree of both power and economy. Moreover, the compromise it strikes between pure power and pure ease-of-coding is a good one—one that turns out to be appealing to people who program for a living. C denies very few possibilities to the programmer—it's almost as easy to crash the machine with C as with assembly!—but it tends to hide tasks that are of little interest to anyone but a chip designer.

None of this is surprising when you consider the origins of C. C is the successor of a nearly forgotten language, B (I'm not joking), and *its* predecessor, BCPL—all of them designed for writing operating systems. An operating system is perhaps the most difficult kind of software to write.

3

The authors of such a system must be able to do just about everything possible with the chip. If programmers had to call assembly-language subroutines to do most tasks, then they might as well write everything in assembly; you should be able to do almost everything in your principal language. Furthermore, authors of an operating system must be able to create software that runs as efficiently as possible, because an operating system that is fat and slow will cripple all future use of the computer. At the same time, authors of an operating system must write and test a phenomenal amount of code. Having a tool such as C to work in, rather than assembly language, can mean completing the project years sooner. In short, defining a language for writing systems software creates a pressing need for both power and economy of expression. To this we might add a third criterion—efficiency—but this is closely related to power of expression.

What few people predicted was how useful these characteristics would prove to be for writing all kinds of software and not just operating systems. For example, the author of a commercial spreadsheet application may not need to do everything that the author of an operating system needs to do, but making efficient use of memory—accounting for every byte, if you will—turns out to be critical, especially in these days when systems having four or even eight megabytes of RAM can barely run certain programs. And when you're writing native code for systems such as Microsoft Windows (native code consists of programs that can run without an intervening layer such as an interpreter or other expensive overhead), most languages are cumbersome-to-impossible. They lack C's flexible data structures.

But the benefits of C come at a price. The same two factors that make C so dominant—power and economy of expression—are the very things that make C difficult for the person who is programming for the first time. A BASIC IF, FOR, or PRINT statement is much more limited in its capabilities than its C counterpart, but for this very reason it's always easy to look at the BASIC version and understand immediately what it does. After all, there's only so much

you can do with a BASIC IF statement. In C, such a statement can do something strange or unexpected; and certain
kinds of programming constructs are almost guaranteed to
be unreadable or (worse yet) misinterpreted, unless you are
savvy or have made the same mistake 13 times before.
Debugging—examining your program and looking for what
went wrong—can be frustrating at such times. This is the
dark side of C.

Conquering C

This brings us to the central question: why another book on
C? There are a number of books on C that do an excellent
job of summarizing the language for someone who already
has a good grasp of what's going on. The best example I
know is *The C Programming Language* by Kernighan and
Ritchie. This is the original classic and still an essential
book to have, especially once you have a basic command of
the language.

Such a book is a wonderful resource, especially if you
have a computer science degree, have spent years writing
assembly language, and aren't the slightest bit intimidated
by the ins and outs of programming-language grammars.
The problem is that most people are intimidated, at least at
first. Certain aspects of C are almost certain to trip you up
if your principal background is BASIC or FORTRAN and
you try to read C code the same way. The potential rewards
of C are substantial, but you have to steer around certain
pitfalls first. Few books focus sufficiently on the pitfalls.

Again, it's the power and economy of C that get people
into trouble. C programs look even less like English than
BASIC programs do, and C programs need more explanation.

Every so often, a C programmer produces what appears—
even to another programmer—to be a long paragraph of complete nonsense and sends it around in electronic mail. The
nonsense turns out to be a valid program, and a prize goes to

the first person who figures out what it does. This is the kind of program that gives C a bad name. You couldn't create something quite that baffling in BASIC, FORTRAN, Pascal, or even assembly language, no matter how hard you tried. But C is not intrinsically so much harder to understand. It can be abused because it provides greater freedom in how you structure programs and manipulate the computer. With that freedom comes greater responsibility and a greater need to understand the nuances of the language.

There are any number of C books for beginners. Some are useful as a first introduction. What I often see neglected is the great middle ground of the language: features that are a bit beyond the scope of a beginner's course but that, properly understood, can become some of your most useful tools. For example, there's a lot more to be said about pointers (the dreaded P-word) than that you need them for passing by reference. More than other languages, C has large areas that people tend not to master until they've spent years programming with the language. Many books define what unions are in C, for example, but for a long time it wasn't clear to me why anyone would use them. Then one day I faced a practical problem—the need to reuse a data structure efficiently for different purposes—and I realized that unions were extremely useful.

This book was written to address some of these needs, to introduce C not just as a set of rules but as a particular mindset and collection of techniques. I want people to "get" C, to think like a C programmer, to enjoy the process with somewhat less frustration than I encountered the first few times I tried.

Thinking Like a Programmer

The greatest challenge, in general, is the need to think like a programmer. This has a lot to do with communication style and approach to problem solving.

6

As a class of people, programmers are probably more concerned about being misunderstood than others are. They don't like to rely on intuition and mind reading on the part of others. (Writers share this trait, and writers of books on programming probably have more of it than anyone else.) The archetypal programmer would like to be listened to very closely and precisely and then have every word understood exactly—not what the listener guessed the speaker intended, but what in fact was said. This is why the computer is such a great friend to programmers. The computer will do precisely what you tell to it do and nothing else. Human beings tend to be good at making assumptions and leaping to conclusions, often (as in the case of double negatives) deciding that someone intended the exact opposite of the literal meaning. If you say your arms are tired because you just flew in from Chicago, the typical human will assume you are telling a joke, because otherwise the statement would be too implausible. A human will likely assume a joke was being told even if it was spoken with an utterly straight face. A computer lacks this facility and so would attempt to interpret the statement seriously.

This difference is particularly apparent with the C programming language. It is easy to write an infinite loop, for example, because you misapplied the syntax and wrote something that's legal in theory but stupid in practice. The language won't stop you from doing that. BASIC, in contrast, is so limited in structure that there aren't as many possible errors to make. C gives you the freedom to write strange programming constructs, and it doesn't provide you the luxury of an intelligence speaking back to you saying, "Hey, you don't really want to do that, do you? That would cause the computer to crash." Some compilers can be set to watch for certain common causes of errors (null pointer assignments, for example), but at a certain point you have to take responsibility for what you do.

But, as I suggested at the beginning of this preface, if you can master C, you're ready to play with the big kids. It used to be that assembly language occupied this position. It was a macho thing—or at least a very adult thing—to be an assembly language programmer. Now, at least in the personal-computer world, assembly language programming is almost an anachromism. If you say you wrote something in assembly, people will look at you as if to say, "Why did you take all that extra time by doing it that way?" Even at Microsoft, Valhalla of hard core programmers, people in most departments must justify why they should be allowed to write something in assembly language rather than C.

The benefits of C go beyond the ability to impress your friends and dominate your enemies. Apart from any practical consideration, C benefits from a grace and elegance of design. It has a cleanliness of expression that comes from the fact that it lets you control directly what you're doing. At the same time, the language hides machine-level details that would merely be an annoyance. Once you master C, you'll find that other programming languages aren't difficult to learn, and even the computer itself will seem less mysterious. But you'll probably want to continue to write most of your programs in C rather than use another language, unless of course it's C++. With a little patience, you'll find that learning C has increased your confidence and your sense of what you can do. Welcome to the major leagues.

Plan of This Book

This book is intended to take you through many levels of C programming, from complete innocence of C to refined aspects that people sometimes take years to understand.

If you've never written a line of C before, start with Part I. This part is designed to give you a general feeling for the language so that when you later encounter advanced features, you'll know how to write a program in which to take advantage of those features. I apologize if this is slow for readers who are already accomplished programmers. If you are, then you may want to skim through Part I.

In Part I, I assume some familiarity with another popular language, especially BASIC, FORTRAN, or Pascal. But it should be possible to follow Part I even without such a background. BASIC is most frequently used for comparison and contrast, so it's helpful if you've looked at BASIC first.

Part II provides an alphabetically organized encyclopedia of C programming topics, including particular keywords (for example, **if**, **switch**, and **case**) and more general topics (pointers, loops, and declarations). Where appropriate, these topics start with a summary of syntax. More important, they attempt to provide context and background for the feature being discussed. You should be able to start programming in C after reading Part I and then consult individual topics in Part II to add to your knowledge of advanced C topics over time.

A Note on Versions of C

To cover as much of C as possible in relatively small book, I made some simplifying assumptions, the main one being that you're using an ANSI-compliant C compiler. Unfortunately, there is a small chance that if you're using an old compiler, it might not be ANSI-compliant. It's as though I'm writing a Driver Training manual and assuming that your car was built in 1950 or later, although there are a few people driving around in Model T's.

ANSI stands for the American National Standards Institute, and it has a committee that draws up a standard specification for the C language. This specification mandates a few features which were not in the very first C compilers but which most C vendors added early in the game. Most significant is the function-definition style. I use the ANSI-standard "prototype" style for all functions, because of its compactness:

```
int funct(int a, int b, double x)
{
        x = a/b;
        ...
```

C in Plain English

In a non-ANSI C compiler, you would have to rewrite this as follows:

```
int funct(a, b, x)
int a;
int b;
double x;
{
        x = a/b;
        . . .
```

In the unlikely case you have a non-ANSI compiler, you'll have to revise all the function examples in the book in a similar way.

The ANSI specification also includes a few advanced features (such as the **enum** keyword), although the core of the language—including expressions, operators, loops, conditions, and the semi-colon—is the basically the same for ANSI and non-ANSI versions of C.

Syntax Conventions

To aid understanding, this book includes a number of syntax displays that show how something is supposed to be used in a program. Wherever something is to be typed in as shown, I have put it in bold. Wherever something is to be replaced with an item you supply, I have put it in italics. I use brackets to show optional items; unfortunately, brackets are also part of the C language. So pay close attention to the text and whether or not the brackets are in bold font. For example:

if (*condition*)
    statement
[**else**
    statement]

Here, the **if** keyword, **else** keyword, and parentheses are all in bold, so you type them in as shown. The *condition* and the two *statements* are italicized, so you replace them by your own expressions or statements. The brackets are neither bold nor italicized, so you don't type them in. The brackets show that **else** and the *statement* that follows it are optional. If you include either of them, however, you must include everything inside the brackets.

In the text itself, I only place C keywords in bold for the most part, although occasionally I carry over fonts from syntax displays.

Don't let syntax get in the way, though; quite often, you'll grasp syntax most easily from examples. The syntax display is often helpful later, as a way of generalizing upon what you're doing. Learning a programming language has many parallels to learning a natural (human) language, and foremost among them is the importance of examples and constant practice. I wish you success.

1

Looking at C for the First Time

There's something to be said for starting with simple examples. A lawyer, explaining a concept to a person with no knowledge of the law, would do well to begin with an elementary example rather than hitting the layperson with years of legal training at once. The layperson doesn't pay to be impressed, but to understand his or her problems better.

Learning about programming is no different. That's why we'll start with the simplest example you can imagine. To make it even easier, let's look at the BASIC version first:

```
PRINT "Here I am!"
```

This statement, in case you haven't seen it before, constitutes a complete program in BASIC. Moreover, it actually prints something, so you can verify that it worked.

Here's how the same program looks in C:

```
main () {
     printf("Here I am!");
}
```

If you're relatively new to programming (though I assume you've probably seen BASIC before), the first thing you need to know is that these examples suggest a larger pattern of simple programs. Within these patterns are, believe it or not, vast possibilities. The pattern for the simple BASIC program is:

PRINT *"your_text_here"*

Here I'm introducing a convention I'll use throughout the book: words in italics represent something that you provide. You could type any combination of characters you wanted where *your_text_here* is indicated.

The C version is:

main () {
    printf(*"your_text_here"***);**
}

So, for C, another example that follows this pattern is:

```
main(){
    printf("Programming, it sounds like fun.");
}
```

When you type in this short program, you should be careful about the following matters:

- Capitalization counts. Or rather, in this case, lack of capitalization counts. BASIC programmers, for some reason no one understands, often leave the CAPS LOCK key on, but it would make no difference if they always left capitalization off. With C, you'll quickly find that typing "PRINTF" or "Printf" instead of "printf" results in an unfriendly error message.

- Punctuation also counts. The first mistake that awaits you if you're coming from BASIC or FOR-TRAN is to forget the semicolon (;) at the end of a statement. At least C is simpler in this respect than Pascal: you always terminate a statement with a semicolon; you don't have to guess whether or not to use one. However, this rule doesn't mean that you put one after the terminating brace (;). (We'll spend more time with semicolons and statements later, in case you're thirsting for more knowledge on these esoteric subjects.)

- Remember also that double-quotation marks ("), not single, are required.

- Spacing does not count. You can put any number of extra spaces around the parentheses and braces, if you want, or even type everything on the same line. Of course, you can't put spaces in the middle of individual words, turning "printf" into "pr int f," for example. And spacing matters to some extent in the text inside the quotation marks, because the text you enter there will be printed as you entered it, letter for letter.

Here's the program one more time, with slightly different spacing:

```
main( ) {
     printf( "Programming, it sounds like fun." );
}
```

If all goes well when you enter and run the program, it will print the text string sans quotation marks:

```
Programming, it sounds like fun.
```

Assuming that this works, you might try redoing the program with different strings. If you have problems, review the preceding paragraphs for possible mistakes in entering the program. You also might need to make sure that you're using your compiler to correctly build an application.

A Few Words about Compiling, Building, and Warning Mesages

Although it may sound hard-hearted, in this book I'll offer only limited help in using a C compiler—that is, the software you buy to translate and run your program. Each C package has its own commands and idiosyncrasies, and each comes with its own instruction manual that ought to be the best guide to use of commands. Fortunately, the language itself (how you actually write the program) has a standard that is more or less universally adhered to aside from occasional extensions. So most of this book will stick to the issues in standard C and let you worry about how to use your own compiler or development environment.

However, there are a few things that can be said about the process of compiling. Together with linking, the process of compiling a program and getting it ready to run is called *building*.

If you're using Microsoft Visual C++, which I refer to because it is one of the standard compilers in use today, the steps you take are shown in the list that follows. You would follow roughly the same steps with other compilers, although the menus and exact command names may be different. Note that although "C++" is in the product name, the compiler is perfectly capable of acting as a straight C compiler—just make sure you give your source files a .C extension, and the compiler will use the rules of the C language rather than C++. I would expect other C/C++ packages to behave in a similar way.

Another thing I recommend, if you are using Visual C++ in the Windows environment, is to select **Console application** (if running Windows NT) or **QuickWin** (if running in the 16-bit environment) as the project type. Both of these types of applications print directly to the screen without forcing you to worry about all the extra details of managing a Windows application. (That's a subject for another book.)

The steps for compiling and linking are:

1. After entering a program, save it as a source file with a .C extension (for example, HI.C).

2. Create a new project and select **Console** or
    QuickWin as the application type. Add the source
    file (HI.C) to the project.

3. From the Project menu, choose **Build**.

4. From the Project menu, choose **Run**.

If you got stuck on step 3, you encountered either a compiler error or a linker error or both. A compiler error indicates that something was wrong in the way you typed in the program; perhaps you forgot to type in the semicolon (;) or one of the quotation marks ("). A linker error, at this point, probably indicates that something in the development environment was not set up correctly. Check your manual to make sure that you installed the product correctly.

If, however, you typed in the program and followed all the steps correctly, instead of error messages you probably received a couple of warning messages. At this point, don't panic if you got warning messages; there's a big difference between warnings and errors. Warning messages don't stop you. As long as you got only warning messages, you can run the program.

But you may want to get rid of the warning messages anyway, and for a good reason: warning messages are there to alert you that something unexpected may be happening. Not much can go wrong with this particular program, but in a larger program, a warning can easily catch the source of a potential error. You may as well get in the habit of trying to eliminate causes of warnings. In the world of professional development, testers don't certify that a build is correct unless it completes with zero warnings and zero errors.

If you're running Visual C++, version 1.0, with the standard environment settings, you got these warnings:

```
warning C4013: 'printf' undefined; assuming extern
returning int
warning C4035: 'main' : no return value
```

The first warning message tells you that the printf function has no return value, so the compiler assumes an integer (**int**) return value by default. Two things about this fact may be surprising. First, C has no concept of a statement or subroutine the way that BASIC and FORTRAN do. All routines are functions, and every function returns a value. In this program, printf is a function whose return value is ignored. (In C, you can always ignore return values if you choose.) The following directive, added to the beginning of the program, clears up the problem:

```
#include <stdio.h>
```

The **#include** directive causes the compiler to read in a file that properly declares printf. At this point, you may be protesting that it shouldn't be necessary to declare such a function before using it. After all, it isn't necessary with the PRINT statement in BASIC. But C is different. The number of keywords in C is kept quite small, and printf is not a keyword; it's just another function with no special status. As it happens, printf is extremely useful and is therefore provided in every standard C library. But you could freely rewrite or redefine printf if you choose to, and the compiler itself doesn't know anything about it. This aspect of C may be a slight inconvenience for now, but it ultimately makes C much more compact and flexible. For all these reasons, the compiler expects you to declare printf before you use it. As mentioned, the stdio.h header file takes care of this declaration.

 A directive is not quite the same thing as a statement, although they may look similar. One critical difference
NOTE is that a directive does not end with a semicolon (;).

There is exactly one function with special status to C itself: the **main** function. You must have a **main** function somewhere for your program to actually do anything, but except for that, **main** obeys all the basic C principles applying to functions.

So **main** should return a value too, shouldn't it? This is true, and it explains the second warning: **main** has no return value. The way to clear up this problem is to precede **main** with the keyword **void**, which tells the compiler not to expect the function to return a value:

```
void main() {
```

Earlier I stated that every function must return a value, but **void** functions are the exception. The complete warning-free program is now:

```
#include <stdio.h>

void main(){
     printf("Programming, it sounds like fun.");
}
```

Some Theory of Compiling and Linking

It would be nice if programs ran by magic, but first they have to be compiled and linked. This is true for a number of reasons, which I'll take some time to explore here. If you're already comfortable with the concept of language translators, you can safely skip to the next section. You can also skip this section if you don't like theory.

There is no available way to write programs directly for most computers, using their native language. Programs have to first be translated into binary code that the computer can execute. Even assembly language, which conceptually is nearly the same thing as machine language, has to be translated. For example, the assembly language instruction JMP LABEL1 must be translated into the binary code that the processor recognizes as a jump (JMP) instruction.

19

These facts seem to create a couple of chicken-and-egg problems that puzzled me for the first several years I had anything to do with computers. The first is an immediate problem. If the computer understands nothing but ones and zeros, who or what does the translating between C, BASIC, and assembly language, on the one hand, and machine language, on the other hand? What forms the bridge between the computer and me, considering that neither speaks the other's language? (As an analogy, if you understand only English and I understand only German, neither of us can translate for the other.) The answer is that a special *program* understands both languages. This special program has itself already been compiled, so it consists of instructions in binary code—it can therefore run on the computer. At the same time, the *logical structure* of the program enables it to recognize statements in a language such as C, BASIC, or assembler.

The underlying principle is something like a Zen koan. Don't worry if you don't get it right now, but it's worth understanding eventually. The processor is unsophisticated in terms of its behavior. It can respond only to a finite set of instructions. But a whole series of instructions, properly ordered, creates rich and complex behavior that the chip designer couldn't even imagine. Such a series of instructions is a program. As an analogy, I can translate between any languages if I have a comprehensive instruction book that tells me how to do it. The instruction book must be written in my native language, but I don't need to know anything else (assuming I have enough time and patience to follow the instructions, a quality computers have in abundance). A program plays the role of this instruction book. The processor carries out the instructions, one at a time.

This special program is called a *language translator*, of which there are three main kinds: compilers, interpreters, and assemblers. In effect, these are programs that help you create your own programs. (Yes, you can write your own language translator if you want, although this requires quite a bit of specialized knowledge.) With C, the translator is nearly always a compiler, meaning that it waits until you are finished writing a program file and then translates the whole thing. Visual Basic, which is a cross between an interpreter and a compiler, translates a little bit of code every time you enter a statement. The former approach (that of C) takes more time to prepare your program after you finish writing it, but this approach is necessary for higher-quality code. The resulting program runs faster and takes up less space. You'll have to wait while the compiler translates your program, but the wait is for a good reason.

The second chicken-and-egg problem is this: how can anyone create a translator in the first place, if no one ever writes directly in machine language? This problem is similar to the following problem in economics: if nothing can be built from scratch and if every tool requires the existence of another tool in order to be built, then how did our industrial society ever come to exist? This is the familiar Bootstrap problem: how do you get started? But the Industrial Revolution did happen, and a similar revolution has been going on with computers. Essentially, whenever a new chip is introduced, the manufacturer makes sure that a rudimentary assembler and systems software are available. This initial software may be generated on another previously existing computer. (This is called *cross-platform development*.) Ultimately, you can trace the lineage of all software back to a time when people really did write in machine code and fed it into a dinosaur in the form of punch cards.

The final stage in building a program is usually linking. *Linking* is the process of bringing together your program module with code from libraries; this is what makes it possible for you to call the printf function. In addition, if you break your program into multiple modules—especially useful for multiprogrammer projects—the process of linking connects these modules and completes function calls between the modules. *Linker errors* tend to occur when a function referred to in one module is not defined anywhere else or is defined in a way that is inconsistent with how it was used. (Chapter 3 explores function definitions.) Often, you clear up a linker error by making sure that a library is in the right directory or that environment variables are correctly set.

The bottom line is that after you write a program, there is a wait while the compiler examines your program for correctness and translates it. But there are good reasons for having to wait. Now it's time to get back to creating programs.

Printing More than One Line

The ability to print only one line is much too limiting, so let's add the ability to print multiple lines. First, I'll introduce you to a funny character, the newline. In C notation, it looks like this:

```
\n
```

 Don't forget that this sequence uses a backslash (\), not a forward slash (/). That's the mistake I made the first 10 times I tried writing a C program.

The backslash is C's way of representing a special character inside a string of text. Some of the special characters include the newline (\n), the tab (\t), and embedded quotation marks (\"). A backslash indicates that the character to follow has special meaning. So what do you do if you want to print an actual backslash? The answer is: use two backslashes (\\). Two backslashes result in printing one backslash, four backslashes result in printing two, and so on.

By putting \n inside a string, you cause the printf function to advance to the next line where indicated. For example, the following program starts a new line after each line of text is printed:

```
#include <stdio.h>

void main (){
     printf("Line 1\n");
```

```
        printf("Line 2\n");
        printf("Last line");
}
```

One thing that may surprise you is that because \n is a character like any other, you can freely embed it inside a text string. The following program prints the same results:

```
#include <stdio.h>

void main() {
        printf("Line1\nLine2\nLast line");
}
```

You can even double-space, if you want to:

```
#include <stdio.h>

void main() {
        printf("Line1\n\nLine2\n\nLast line");
}
```

It should be clear what is going on at this point. As the printf function reads each character that is not a backslash, it outputs the character to the terminal as is. If, however, it reads a backslash, it interpets the next character as a special character. When an "n" follows the backslash, it causes output to start on a new line. (Another way of saying this is to say that printf generates a carriage return.) If there is text remaining in the string, printf continues reading characters normally.

By the way, it's common practice to terminate every line—even the last—with a newline (\n), unless you know that the next input or output is to continue on the same line. With this approach, the first example in this section would be rewritten as:

```
#include <stdio.h>

void main (){
```

```
    printf("Line 1\n");
    printf("Line 2\n");
    printf("Last line\n");
}
```

Data Declaration and Number Crunching

To do anything useful in C, you need to define variables. If you have ever used any other programming language, you know that a variable is just a place in memory that stores a value for you.

Any variable you use must first be declared, because C needs to know what kind of data you're storing and how much space to allocate in memory. Most programming languages require explicit declaration, although a few (such as BASIC) let you declare variables by default; if you use a variable without declaring it, BASIC makes assumptions about the type and attributes of the variable.

But in computer programming, as in life, relying on assumptions is dangerous. C has no default declarations, and C programmers usually don't mind the small amount of additional work that this makes necessary.

The following three lines of code gives examples of C data definitions (for now, don't worry about the difference between definition and declaration):

```
double x;
int count;
int i, j, employee_num;
```

These statements, like any other C statements, are each terminated by a semicolon (;). The keywords **double** and **int** specify data types—double-precision floating point and integer, respectively. (The difference between these types is that the computer can manipulate integers much more efficiently, but only floating-point variables can store fractional quantities.) The names x, count, i, j, and employee_num in the preceding example all become the names of variables created by the definition. Except for x, all the variables are integers.

An example program should help clarify this.

```
#include <stdio.h>

void main(){
      int i, j;

      i = 1;
      j = 2;
      printf("The sum of i and j is %d", i + j);
}
```

This example introduces a very useful feature of printf: formatted number output. The first argument to printf is the format string:

```
"The sum of i and j is %d"
```

This is a quoted string of text in which most characters are printed literally but some sequences of characters have special meaning. Two-character sequences starting with a backslash (\) are one kind of special sequence, as we've seen. Another kind of special sequence consists of those starting with the percent sign (%). Such sequences print numbers. Specifically, the meaning of %d is, "Print the integer value of the next argument." In this case, that argument is the result calculated by adding the value of i to the value of j:

```
i + j
```

The practice of computer languages varies from standard English here. Note the placement of the comma (,) in the complete statement:

```
printf("The sum of i and j is %d", i + j);
```

The comma must appear after, not before, the second quotation mark ("). The role of the comma is to separate the two arguments, and it must appear *between* those arguments. In this case, at least, the rule imposed by the programming language is a good deal more logical than English is. You don't place the comma inside the quotation marks unless you intend for it to be printed.

Commas can be used in both ways, of course. You could place a comma inside the quotation marks because you actually did want to print it. You'd still need to place another comma outside the quotation marks so that the arguments would be separated.

You can experiment with much more interesting calculations here, such as the following floating-point calculation. Note that almost all floating-point calculations assume that data types and return values are **double** (double precision), which provides greater accuracy than single precision (**float**). Another thing to keep in mind is that to print a floating-point value, you must use %f, not %d. For example:

```
#include <stdio.h>
#include <math.h>

void main(){
    double a = 3.0;
    double b = 4.0;
    double c;

    c = sqrt(a * a + b * b);
    printf("The hypotenuse = %f", c);
}
```

This example introduces a couple of new features worth commenting on. First, the program calls another function, sqrt. Like printf, sqrt is provided by the standard library. The math.h header file properly declares the sqrt function, so math.h is included at the beginning of the program. If sqrt is not declared, C assumes that the function returns an integer value, which in fact it does not (like most math functions, sqrt returns a double-precision floating-point result). This would be a serious problem because it would cause the computer to make a mistake about what kind of data to pass.

 The sqrt function takes the square root of its argument, but C programmers affectionately refer to this function as the "squirt" function.

It's always good to declare all functions before using them. If the function is from the standard C library, there's a header file available with the appropriate declaration. Documentation on library functions indicates which header file to include.

Another feature introduced here is the use of definition and assignment of values in the same statement. This assignment is actually *initialization*, and it has some important restrictions:

```
double a = 3.0;
double b = 4.0;
double c;
```

The variables a and b are properly intialized with constant values. When you combine variable definition with the equal sign (=) this way, the value assigned must be a constant; the compiler must be able to determine what this value is at the time the compiler reads the program. The next statement, which assigns a value to the variable c, cannot be combined with a declaration, because the value on the right is not a constant:

```
c = sqrt(a * a + b * b);
```

This may seem like a lot of rules, but it stems from the fact that the C language reuses operators very efficiently. When you define a variable (such as a, b, or c), you can give it an initial value, but make sure it is a constant. The use of the equal sign (=) in other kinds of statements is much more flexible. You can place any variable on the left side and any valid expression on the right. The previous line of code, which calcalates the value of c, is an example.

NOTE Initialization does just what the word suggests; it provides an initial value. After being initialized, a variable can be assigned a new value. This is why an expression such as (a * a + b * b) is not a constant. There's no guarantee that the values of a and b won't change during the running of the program.

Some Comments about Comments

No programming language would be complete without a facility for placing comments in the program.

It bothers me when programming manuals say things such as "Comments explain the purpose of the code you write." Well, that's not automatically true. The comment facility gives you the capability to include such explanations, but you have to write them yourself. If you wanted to, you could go crazy and place any words in comments, even the words to "Mary Had a Little Lamb."The compiler absolutely does not care. However, it's certainly in your interest to place information in comments that may be helpful to someone reading the program.

Technically speaking, a comment consists of text that the compiler ignores. Period. The text you put there won't be evaluated as part of the C program itself. Yet you really ought to use comments because humans—as well as computers—often have to read programs. As a program grows in complexity, you may not understand the purpose of a declaration or statement written earlier, even if you wrote it yourself. The solution to this problem is to use a healthy dose of comments and to say things that will be helpful for someone looking at the code.

C comments consist of text between the symbols /* and */. This text may occur on a single line or can span multiple lines. For example, the last example in the preceding section could profitably be commented as follows:

```
#include <stdio.h>
#include <math.h>

void main(){
/* Declare a, b, and c as three sides of a triangle,
      in which a and b are 3 and 4 units long. */

      double a = 3.0;
      double b = 4.0;
      double c;

/*Find hypotenuse and print result. */

      c = sqrt(a * a + b * b);
      printf("The hypotenuse = %f", c);
}
```

Again, the compiler ignores all the text between /* and */. The exact wording and spelling are therefore unimportant.

For more discussion of the complete rules related to comments, see the topic "Comments" in Part II.

2

Anatomy of a C Program

Part I: Grammar

Programming, if you think about it, is all about patterns. A programming-language grammar is a set of patterns for putting words and symbols together to form meaningful actions. When you understand the patterns well enough, you can use them to get the computer to do anything you want, within limitations.

But without some kind of easy introduction to C, looking at a pure, comprehensive summary of C's grammar would be overwhelming. For this reason, we'll start with patterns around which you can build simple programs and then gradually add to their complexity.

The simplest programs follow this pattern:

include_directives

```
void main () {
    data_declaration_statements
    executable_statements
}
```

include_directives use the **#include** keyword to read header files (the effect is the same as if you typed the entire file right into your program code). As mentioned in Chapter 1, such header files are necessary because C doesn't know anything about library functions. It doesn't know, for example, whether the square root function (sqrt) returns an integer or a floating-point result. Nor does it know how many arguments to expect. The header files, such as stdio.h and math.h, provide this information. Examples of **#include** directives are:

```
#include <stdio.h>
#include <math.h>
#include <string.h>
```

When you use a library function, such as printf, consult C standard-library documentation to determine the corresponding header file to include. A header file needs to be included no more than one time, regardless of how many different functions require it.

You may be wondering why these lines of code are called "directives" and why they don't end with a semicolon. This is the kind of distinction that can drive a novice crazy, although experienced C programmers grow used to it. The easiest, most practical rule to remember is that any line beginning with a pound sign (#) is a directive, and, unlike statements, directives are not terminated with semicolons.

 In case you're curious, a directive is an instruction to the **compiler that controls a general condition during compi-**
NOTE **lation. For example, there are directives that affect** **reporting of error and warning messages. A C statement,** **in contrast, either declares data or is translated directly** **into an action that is performed when the program is** **actually running. The distinction between statements** **and directives may seem arbitrary, especially because** **there are some directives that can have important effects** **on program behavior. It may be easiest for now just to** **remember that if something begins with a pound sign** **(#), it's a directive.**

By *data_definition_statements*, I refer to variable definitions you place in your program. Although technically you don't have to have variables, virtually any program that does any-thing useful has at least a few. In C, variable definitions are statements, and each must be terminated by a semicolon (;). The simplest data definitions declare one variable each. The type name—**int**, **long**, or **double** in the following examples—precedes the variable name:

```
double x;
double y;
double hypotenuse;
int total;
int c;
```

Variable declarations in C enable you to define as many variables on the same line as you choose—as long as you separate the names by using commas. For example, the fol-lowing example defines the same double-precision floating point variables and integers that the preceding example does. In the first line, x, y, and hypotenuse are all defined as having type **double**, meaning that each variable stores dou-ble-precision floating-point data. The variables total and c are integers.

```
double x, y, hypotenuse;
int total, c;
```

You can also combine muliple data definitions with initial-ization:

```
double weight = 3.5, height = 1.0;
int i, j, k = 1;
int a = 0, b, c = 27;
```

Finally, by *executable_statements* I refer to the rest of the program. These statements take some sort of action during run time. Data definitions, in contrast, don't cause any actions while the program is actually running; they just reserve space.

The distinction between data definitions and executable statements is important, because you must place all data definitions ahead of all executable statements—the two kinds cannot be intermingled. In Chapter 3, I'll mention ways around this rule.

Executable statements can do a lot of things, but nearly all of these things fall into one of three major categories of actions:

- Call a function.

- Assign a value to a variable (or other memory location).

- Transfer program control to a new location or perform an action conditionally.

The last category involves control structures, which we'll start to examine later in the chapter. Aside from control structures, nearly all actions in C boil down to either calling a function or assigning a value. Many statements do both, as in the following statement, which uses the result of the sqrt function to help calcuate the new value of c:

```
/* Calculate c as the square root of a squared plus b
   squared. */

c = sqrt(a * a + b * b);
```

This list of action categories shouldn't be too surprising if you've looked at other programming languages. All the processor can do, really, is move data, perform calcuations, or jump to a new instruction.

As with all other high-level languages, C lets you combine assignment to a variable with calculation. C is no different from any other language in this respect except that it combines two kinds of routines (functions and procedures in BASIC) into one: the C function. About the only innovation here is that C uses just one type of subroutine: the function. You can use a function's return value for calculation, as was done in the preceding example. But you can also throw away the return value, just as you would with a BASIC procedure or a FORTRAN subroutine. For example:

```
printf("The value of c is %f\n", c);
```

C has a great many more innovations when it comes to the details of how some actions are performed, as we'll see.

Putting It Together: Some Program Examples

Let's look at these three basic syntax elements—directives, declarations, and executable statements—in a couple of complete examples. Figure 2.1 shows a simple program that takes a number as input and prints the double of that number.

```
                                  Include directive
#include <stdio.h> ]

void main() {                              Data declaration
        int n; ]

        printf("Enter a number here: ");
        scanf("%d", &n);                          Executable
        n = n * 2;                                statements
        printf("Twice the number is %d\n", n);
}
```

Figure 2.1 *A simple program that prints the double of an imput number.*

The first part is the data directive, which causes the compiler to read the contents of the header file stdio.h. This directive is necessary for providing correct declarations for the functions used in the program: scanf and printf.

```
#include <stdio.h>
```

Note that this line of code is not terminated by a semi-colon, although most lines are.

After the beginning of the **main** function, the next part contains the data definition of the integer variable n. Data declarations, as well as executable statements, are each terminated by a semicolon.

```
int n;
```

The variable can have any name you choose as long as it does not conflict with a C keyword and it follows a few simple naming rules. (See the topic "Identifiers" in Part II for more information.) For example, the name could be "my_number," in which case it would be defined by the following statement:

```
int my_number;
```

The name "n" is shorter and easier to type, so let's stick with that name for now.

The last part of the program consists of executable statements. These statements do the following: print a prompt message, get numerical input, perform a calculation, and print the result. In BASIC and some other languages, the first two steps could be combined into one statement, but in C they are carried out in two separate function calls.

```
printf("Enter a number here: ");
scanf("%d", &n);
n = n * 2;
printf("Twice the number is %d\n", n);
```

The first statement does *not* include a newline character (\n) in the prompt message. So when a user runs the program, he or she types input on the same line where the prompt ("Enter a number here:") is displayed. It's always valid to omit the newline; doing so just means that intput and output continue on the same line.

It's characteristic of C to make things more explicit than BASIC does. C causes you a little more work but also gives you more control. In the case of printing output, C never assumes that you want a carriage return except where you explicitly indicate one with a newline.

But the line of code that really introduces a new twist here is scanf, which gets input. Scanf waits for the user to type a number and press ENTER.

```
scanf("%d", &n);
```

The scanf call looks suspiciously like a call to printf, but, unlike a printf call, this call has a strange-looking character in front of n. This is not a typo. It's an ampersand (&), which serves as the address operator in C. This operator has a lot to do with pointers, a topic covered in a later chapter. If you've heard the horror stories surrounding pointers, you may already be panicking. But don't worry. For now, all you need to remember is that to get integer input, use statements with the following pattern:

scanf("%d", &integer_variable**);**

(The "d" stands for decimal number.)

To get double-precision (**double**) floating point, use the following statement. Note that two characters—"lf", which stands for long floating-point number—follow the percent sign.

scanf("%lf", &_double_prec_variable_**);**

 Already you may be getting exasperated with C. The character "d" stands not for double but for integer; double is "lf", which is an extra character, and scanf requires an ampersand—what is all this? It's probably easiest to remember just to use these characters, but there are sound technical reasons for them. For example, integer input and output can use other bases ("o" for octal, "x"

NOTE

37

for hexadecimal), so it really is logical to use "d" for decimal integer. By the way, you can use "i" if you want. There is usually a good reason for something in C, but it's not always immediately apparent the first time you use the feature.

With printf, you can also use "d" and "lf" or just stick with "d" and "f". For reasons that are technically complicated, printf is a good deal more forgiving than scanf and will successfully print a floating-point number in either "f" or "lf" format.

This simple program can be optimized in one or two ways. One possibility is to replace the multiplication and assignment with a single assignment that does the same thing:

```
n *= 2;                 /* Does the same as n = n * 2*/
```

The multiplication-assignment operator (*=) is part of a family of such operators that do the same thing: combine a calculation on a variable with assignment to that same variable. These operators include +=, /=, -=, and others.

However, the best optimization in this case is to simply calculate the desired value (twice of n) on the fly—simply feed the expression "n * 2" right into printf. The revised program is then:

```
#include <stdio.h>

void main() {
    int n;

    printf("Enter a number here: ");
    scanf("%d", &n);
    printf("Twice the number is %d\n", n * 2);
}
```

But this program is not particularly interesting, because all it does is calculate what twice a number is, something you could probably do yourself without exceptional strain. The next example is a little more interesting. It prompts the user for two numbers and then calculates a hypotenuse (see Figure 2.2).

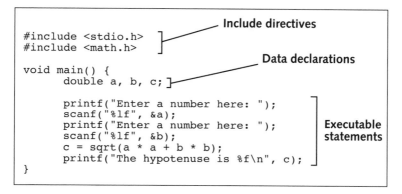

```
                                Include directives
#include <stdio.h>
#include <math.h>
                                Data declarations
void main() {
    double a, b, c;

    printf("Enter a number here: ");
    scanf("%lf", &a);
    printf("Enter a number here: ");    Executable
    scanf("%lf", &b);                   statements
    c = sqrt(a * a + b * b);
    printf("The hypotenuse is %f\n", c);
}
```

Figure 2.2 *This program calculates a hypotenuse from two input numbers.*

This program looks similar to Figure 2.1 in most respects, but there are a few differences. One difference is that the math.h header file is included to provide a declaration for the sqrt function.

Another difference is that three floating-point variables are defined rather than one integer:

```
double a, b, c;
```

This statement could have been rewritten as three separate statements, but why do all that extra typing?

```
double a;
double b;
double c;
```

As before, floating-point variables are defined as **double** rather than **float**. Why? C converts all floating-point values to double precision when doing calculations. It's therefore inefficient to define variables as single precision floating-point (**float**) except in special situations, such as structures, where space is at a premium. One drawback of C is that it doesn't use "single" as a keyword to match "double," but this is one of the things you just have to live with.

The executable-statement portion of the program does the following: read the value of a, read the value of b, calculate the result, and print the result. As with the previous example, the last two steps—calculatation and printing results—can certainly be combined, eliminating the need for the variable c. Whether you take this approach is a matter of programming style, because the result is admittedly a little harder to read.

Here's the revised version with comments added to clarify what's going on at each stage.

```c
#include <stdio.h>
#include <math.h>

void main() {
    double a, b;

    printf("Enter a number here: ");
    scanf("%lf", &a);
    printf("Enter a number here: ");
    scanf("%lf", &b);
    printf("The hypotenuse is %f\n", sqrt(a * a + b *
        b));
}
```

Time Out for a Few Definitions of Terms

Until now, I've assumed that you know some of the standard terms from math and computer programming. In case I've assumed too much, here are definitions for terms that come up a lot in this chapter and in others.

Argument

This is a term that comes up a lot in this book. Many people use *argument* interchangeably with *parameter*. Although there is a difference, I don't think it's worth worrying about too much here.

An argument is a value that you pass to a function. For example, in the following line of code, angleA and angleB are arguments to the Calculate_Angle function, and angleC is a variable that stores the result:

```
/* angleA and angleB are arguments */

angleC = Calculate_Angle(angleA, angleB)
```

As you'll see in Chapter 3, you can use the same or different variables within the function definition—the code that defines what Calculate_Angle does. Some purists insist on calling the values actually passed *arguments* and the variables used in definitions *parameters*—or alternatively, actual arguments vs. formal arguments—but we'll stick with using *arguments* except where the distinction is critical.

Integer

You may recall from high-school math that an integer is a whole number (no fractional portion) that can range into negative values as well as zero or positive. This corresponds exactly with the concept of integer (**int**) in C and other languages.

Generally speaking, floating-point variables can hold any value that an integer can, so why use integers at all? The reason is that floating-point math is much more complex. A CPU can operate far more efficiently on an integer. Moreover, there are many cases in which a variable needs to hold a number that will never be a fraction. Ever. An example is a variable used to count trips through a loop. Integers are a much better choice for data representation in such cases.

Floating-Point Values

Floating-point values can hold fractions. Other languages often refer to floating-point values as *reals* (for real numbers), and, realistically speaking, the terms can be used interchangeably. To provide maximum flexibility, floating-point values are represented with a kind of scientific notation involving sign, exponent, and mantissa. If you don't remember these terms from school, that's OK, because it's all supposed to be hidden from you anyway. The only thing to remember is that it requires more computing power for the poor little CPU to handle floating point, although modern-day math coprocessors do help. For optimal results, stick to integers as much as possible.

Single-Precision Values

A single-precision value in C is a floating-point value stored in four bytes. Strangely, variables of this type are declared with the **float** keyword.

Double Precision Values

A double-precision value (**double**) in C is a floating-point value stored in eight bytes. These values require more space but provide substantially more range and accuracy. Because of the necessary conversion between decimal (for display) and binary (for internal storage), there's usually a loss of precision whenever fractions are involved. For this reason, if you are going to do floating-point calculations, double precision is much better.

Hypotenuse

The long side of a right triangle. It's not really essential to C; it's just used as an example here. The Pythagorean theorem makes for a nice little program.

Expressions

An expression is a single number or variable, or a combination of variables, numbers, and operators (such as +) that evaluates to a single value. The numeral 5 is an expression; so is x + y. In C, expressions have an interesting relationship to statements (the basic unit of execution) as described in the next section.

Expressions and Statements

One of the areas in which C most strongly departs from other languages is in its concept of expressions. There are some points here that aren't obvious, and you need to understand them to fully take advantage of C or to read C code.

In BASIC or FORTRAN, which are typical of most computer languages, you can only assign a value to only one variable at a time. For example, the following is a complete statement in either BASIC or FORTRAN:

```
i = j + 1
```

BASIC and FORTRAN use a single equal sign (=) to show assignment. C does the same. In Pascal, you'd use the := symbol instead:

```
i := j + 1
```

43

Pascal also uses semicolons in its own perverse fashion, but let's not get into that.

With all three languages—BASIC, FORTRAN, and Pascal—you can look at this expression and know that it forms a complete statement. But with C, the equal sign (=) is an operator like any other, and it returns a value just as operators such as +, −, *, and / do. This means that assignment may be performed in the middle of a larger expression.

An example should help clarify. You can write the same expression in C as you can in BASIC or FORTRAN, but the C version returns a value—namely, the value that was assigned:

```
i = j + 1     /* Value of this expression is j + 1 */
```

And here's where we can see the big difference. Because this assignment returns a value (namely, j + 1), you can place the whole thing inside a more complex expression:

```
k = i = j + 1;
```

What is this funny-looking construct? To understand it, you first have to understand that the associativity of assignment is right-to-left, which means that when more than one assignment operator (=) is involved, the rightmost assignment is evaluated first. Consequently, the preceding example is equivalent to:

```
k = (i = j + 1);
```

The subexpression i = j + 1 does two things: it assigns the value of j + 1 to i and then it returns the value that was assigned—namely, j + 1. Replacing the right side with j + 1 creates the following expression:

```
k = j + 1;
```

In other words, after i is assigned the value j + 1, that value is then assigned to k. So *both* k and i are assigned the value of j + 1.

Let's look at another example, which uses a common coding technique. This example assigns the value 0 to all four variables: a, b, c, and d.

```
a = b = c = d = 0;
```

Again, associativity is right-to-left. Therefore, this expression is equivalent to:

```
a = (b = (c = (d = 0)));      /* Assign 0 to d */
```

The subexpression d = 0 obviously assigns 0 to d. The return value of d = 0 is 0, which means that the program acts as though d = 0 were replaced with 0. The program then evaluates the statement as if it were:

```
a = (b = (c = 0));    /* Assign 0 to c */
```

This causes 0 to be assigned to the variable c. The process continues, by successive steps:

```
a = (b = 0);          /* Assign 0 to b */
a = 0;
```

So a, b, c, and d all get the value 0.

The statement isn't really being rewritten. The program statements always remain intact and can be executed repeatedly (which can happen when you write a loop). What's going on is that the C compiler interprets the statement as though it were a series of smaller statements.

Let's look at one more example. Because the equal sign (=) is an operator like any other, it can be combined with other operators, such as addition (+). For example, assume that a, b, and c are all integer variables:

```
a = 1 + (b = 1 + (c = 30));  /* Assign 30 to c */
```

The program first evaluates c = 30, which places 30 into c and returns the value 30. The program then proceeds as if the subexpression c = 30 were replaced by its return value, 30:

```
a = 1 + (b = 1 + 30);        /* Assign 31 to b */
```

Now the program evaluates b = 1 + 30, which places 31 into b and returns the value 31. The program proceeds as if the subexpression b = 1 + 30 were replaced by the value 31:

```
a = 1 + 31;                  /* Assign 32 to a */
```

Finally, a is assigned the value 32.

In the preceding example, parentheses are necessary. Although you can freely mix the assignment operator (=) with other operators, the assignments must make sense. C language expressions are governed by C's rules of precedence, which dictate that addition (+) is evaluated before assignment (=). Consider what would happen if the preceding example had no parentheses:

```
a = 1 + b = 1 + c = 30;
```

Because addition (+) has higher precedence than assignment (=), this statement is equivalent to:

```
a = (1 + b) = (1 + c) = 30;
```

This in turn places the subexpression (1 + c) on the left side of an assignment:

```
(1 + c) = 30
```

This last expression clearly makes no sense and is explicitly disallowed by rules of C syntax. (See the topic "L-values" in Part II.) Therefore, when you mix assignment with other operations, be sure to use parentheses to clarify order of evaluation.

This flexibility in the use of assignment has important implications for C syntax. Assignments are just one of the building blocks of expressions—assignments don't automatically form complete statements as they do in other languages.

When does an expression become a statement? That's simple: when it's terminated by a semicolon. An expression terminated by a semicolon is the most common type of statement in C:

expression;

This syntax has some interesting consequences. It implies that any expression can be terminated with a semicolon to form a complete statement. Such expressions don't even have to involve assignment. Here's an example:

```
x;
i + j;
total * sum + 2;
5;
27.0;
```

You will likely never see these statements in a real C program, for the good reason that they don't actually do anything. But they are legal just the same. As with all expressions, each of these returns a value. But when a statement is terminated by a semicolon, the overall value of the expression is thrown away.

What you will see, and often, are expressions in which a function's return value is ignored. For example, both of the following are legal constructs:

```
result = Calc(a, b, c);
Calc(a, b, c);
```

You could write either statement depending on whether you wanted to save the result of the function. This is a nice convenience, because some times you may care about the result of the function and other times you may not.

47

NOTE The first statement in the preceding example is not legal if the function is declared void, although the second statement is always legal.

Many functions (of which printf is a prominent example) have side effects: they do more than just return a value. When a function has side effects of some kind, a function call can be useful even though it has no return value or that value is ignored.

Returning a Value to the System

The **main** function can return a value just as other functions can, depending on how you declare it. The value returned by **main** is passed back to the system or calling process. An example of where such a return value might be used is in an MS-DOS batch file. The value returned by the program (its return code) can cause a jump to a new location within the batch file, assuming that the file is written to test the program's return code.

As a rule, a return code of 0 indicates that the program detected no problems. By convention, a nonzero return code indicates an error.

The revised syntax for a program is:

include_directives

int main () {
       data_declaration_statements
       executable_statements
       return *expression;*
}

Strictly speaking, this syntax isn't absolutely precise, but it gives you an idea of what's possible. Actually, the **return** statement can occur any number of times within *executable_statements*, and it doesn't necessarily have to occur on the last line.

As a first example, the following program prints out a message and returns 0 unconditionally, to indicate sucess:

```
#include <stdio.h>

int main() {
    printf("Hello, there.\n");
    return 0;
}
```

More typical is the next example, which tests for an error condition (a zero divisor) before deciding whether to return an error code:

```
#include <stdio.h>
#include <math.h>

int main() {
    double divisor, quotient;

    scanf("%f", divisor);
    if (divisor == 0)
        return -1;
    quotient = 100.0 / divisor;
    printf("The quotient is %d\n", quotient);
    return 0;
}
```

This example introduces the use of the C **if** statement, which in this case tests the value of divisor before deciding whether to return an error code. Note carefully the use of double equal signs (==) to test for equality.

```
    if (divisor == 0)
        return -1;
```

We'll see a lot more of the **if** statement in later chapters. The simplest form of the **if** statement has the following format:

if (*condition*)
    statement

I should clarify that *condition* is just an integer expression. An expression evaluating to zero means false—statement is not executed—whereas everything else means true. This implies that any integer expression is valid in this context. So you can write this:

```
if (1)
    return -1;
```

But this code would mean return –1 unconditionally, which is silly, if you think about it, because it would be easier just to type:

```
return -1;
```

The **if** statement looks harmless, but it has a few pitfalls that await you. By far the worst is the possibility of mistaking the assignment operator (=) for the test-for-equality operator (==). Be careful! These two operators are very different, in ways to be explained later. For now, just make sure that you double check all tests for equality within an **if** condition to make sure that double equal signs (==) are in use. There *are* times when you will want to use the assignment operator (=) within a condition, but they are much less common. For now, consider a single equal sign (=) within a condition as a sure-fire indicator of a bug.

The **if** statement is the first example of a control structure in this book. A *control structure* is a place at which the program may skip ahead or back instead of going to the next statement. In the case of **if**, a condition that evaluates to false causes the program to skip over the statement immediately following the **if**. A condition evaluating to true lets the program execute that statement.

We'll return to the subject of control structures in detail, but first let's move to the all-important topic of functions in C.

3

Anatomy of a
C Program

Part II: Functions

One of the greatest aids in programming is the use of functions. They can save you from having to type common sequences of code over and over. They also let you organize your program into logical and coherent units.

A *function* defines how to carry out a specific task. Once the task is defined, you can have it carried out wherever you want, simply by calling the function. If you've been following the earlier chapters, you've seen examples of function calls:

```
printf("Hi there!\n");
scanf("%d", &number);
x = sqrt(2.0);
```

The words printf, scanf, and sqrt refer to functions, although only in the last case is the value returned by the function actually used. In C, a function is a function whether or not it returns a value and whether or not the value is used. There is no separate terminology such as *procedure, subroutine,* or *subprogram.*

Of course, "subprogram" is a good way to suggest what functions do. When a function is called, control passes to the function as if it were a separate program. The computer then executes each statement in that function until it either comes to the end of the function or encounters a **return** statement. In either case, the function is said to *return*. At that point, control returns to the place in the program where the function was called.

Return is an appropriate term. It means that the program goes back to where it was before the function was called.

Calls to functions such as printf, scanf, and sqrt work because these functions are defined in the standard library. You don't need to supply definitions for the functions. In this chapter, we'll take a look at functions that are defined in the program itself.

Approach 1: Top-Down

Most C programmers usually place the **main** function first, followed by the functions that **main** calls directly, followed by other functions. This style of program organization is the *top-down* approach. The basic pattern for these programs is shown in Figure 3.1.

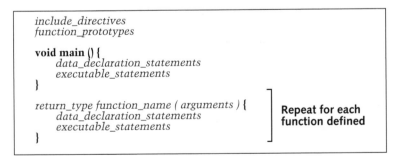

Figure 3.1 *The basic pattern for top-down programs.*

The new syntax element here is *function_prototypes*. A function prototype provides type information to the compiler.

You can call a function without first providing a prototype, but the compiler would have to assume a default return type (**int**), and it would not be able to check argument types. As a rule, you should always include function prototypes for each function you call.

Here's the general form for a function prototype:

return_type function_name(arguments);

The *arguments* consist of a list of argument declarations; they are separated by commas if there are more than one. The declarations, in turn, consist of a data type followed by an argument name:

type name, type name, ...

Here are some examples of prototypes:

1. Double-precision result, integer argument.

   ```
   double FindReciprocal(int n);
   ```

2. Double-precision result, three double-precision arguments.

   ```
   double Quadratic(double a, double b, double c);
   ```

3. Integer result, two integer and one double-precision argument.

   ```
   int ResetVars(int NewStart, int Delta, double
       Ratio);
   ```

The argument names have little purpose in a prototype except for documentation. If you want to, you can omit argument names from prototypes. The following declarations are equivalent to the ones you've just seen:

```
double FindReciprocal(int);
double Quadratic(double, double, double);
int ResetVars(int, int, double);
```

Defining the Function

Once again, here's the function-definition part of the syntax:

return_type function_name (arguments) {
        data_declaration_statements
        executable_statements
}

The *executable_statements* can include one or more **return** statements (assuming *return_type* is not **void**):

return *expression;*

Two things may strike you about this syntax. First, it looks very similar to the syntax for the **main** function. It should, because the **main** function is like any other function except for a few key differences (mainly, that it gets executed first). Second, the first line is almost the same as a function prototype. For example, here is a possible first line of a function definition:

```
double FindReciprocal(int n) {
```

In fact, the beginning of a function definition is so close to the syntax for a prototype that you can save work by copying the prototype and pasting it into the definition.

But there are a couple of important differences between prototypes and definitions:

- A prototype ends with a semicolon (;), but in a function definition, an opening brace ({) follows the argument list. Function definitions are not terminated by semicolons at all, not even after the final brace (}). Individual statements inside the braces will have semicolons, however.

- The argument name is not optional in a function definition even though it is optional in prototypes.

54

Figure 3.2 shows a complete function definition. The only semicolons are inside the braces.

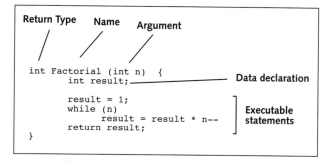

Figure 3.2 *A complete function definition.*

Most of the syntax in this function should be familiar, but some parts are probably new to you. Here's a synopsis of what the function does.

The first line of the function definition (its "heading," if you will) features **int n** in the argument list. This means that the value passed to the function is stored in the variable n. For example, suppose that the main program calls the function as follows:

```
x = Factorial(5);
```

The result is that the function-definition code is executed, with the value 5 assigned to n at the beginning of the function.

The function contains another variable, result. Like "n" the word "result" is not a keyword. Any valid names could have been chosen for either variable. The variable named "result" is used to temporarily hold a value that is ultimately passed back when the function returns. The first statements in the body of the function declare result as a variable and initialize it to 1:

```
int result;

result = 1;
```

The next statement is a **while** statement. Its structure is similar to the **if** statement introduced in the previous chapter, but the statement following **while** can be executed repeatedly.

Another expression that may be new to you is "n--". This expression gives the same value as n, but the variable is decremented by 1 after the statement is executed. So this statement:

```
while (n)
      result = result * n--;
```

means the following in English:

> While n is not equal to zero,
>   Multiply result by n
>   Decrease n by 1

Finally, the function returns whatever value is left in result:

```
return result;
```

To see how all this works together, first assume that the function is called with a value of 4:

```
my_number = Factorial(4);
```

The function-definition code for Factorial is then executed, with 4 passed as the value for n. Then result is assigned the value 1 and repeatedly multiplied by n, until n is equal to 0. Remember that n starts at 4 and is decremented each time by 1. The calculation is shown in Figure 3.3.

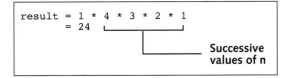
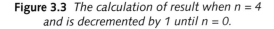

Figure 3.3 *The calculation of result when n = 4 and is decremented by 1 until n = 0.*

Now consider the case in which the value 6 is passed to n:

```
my_number = Factorial(6);
```

The same process occurs except that n starts at 6:

```
result  = 1 * 6 * 5 * 4 * 3 * 2 * 1
        = 720
```

You may see a possible optimization here. The last part of the multiplication, in each case, involves the value 1. However, multiplication by 1 has no effect. Mathematically, it's valid, but in terms of computer time, it's a wasted operation. We can easily drop the wasted calculation by specifying that the **while** loop continue as long as n *is greater than 1*. The resulting loop is:

```
while (n > 1)
     result = result * n--;
```

If passed the value 6, the function does the following:

```
result  = 1 * 6 * 5 * 4 * 3 * 2
        = 720
```

In C, there are often many ways to write the same thing, and some are more compact than others. Such code compacting is not really the same as optimization—it doesn't necessarily improve the efficiency of the running program—but it saves typing. What's more, it helps convince people that you're a "real" C programmer, so you can impress your friends and mystify your rivals.

You can use two code compacting techniques here. First, result can be initialized as it's being defined; second, you can use the multiplication-assignment operator (*=). An expression of the form

*variable = variable * another*

can be replaced by

variable *= *another*

The revised, more optimal function definition is therefore:

```
int Factorial(int n) {
    int result = 1;

    while (n > 1)          /* While n > 1,
        result *= n--;     /*   multiply by n
                                 decrement n   */
    return result;
}
```

Here I've added comments to clarify what some of the statements do.

 If you test this function with a good range of values, you'll quickly find that the factorial function produces results that exceed the maximum range for the two-byte integer type (32,768 to – 32,767). An easy way to extend this range is to rewrite the function so that it uses the four-byte integer type, **long**, rather than **int**. This is left as an exercise for the reader. The range of **long** is approximately plus or minus two million. Note, however, that the size of an **int** varies from one implementation to another. If you are running in a 32-bit environment, **int** may be the same as **long**.

A Complete Example

Functions don't do anything until called by an executing program. Even **main** has to be called before it can execute— although in the case of **main**, the caller is the operating system.

Once written, a function can be called any number of times. The following example builds on the Factorial example of the previous section to show repeated function calls in the context of a program (see Figure 3.4):

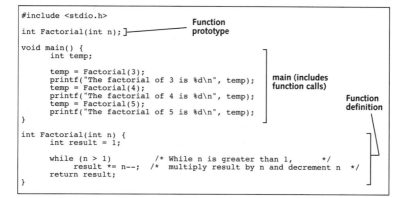

```
#include <stdio.h>
                                    Function
int Factorial(int n);                prototype

void main() {
      int temp;

      temp = Factorial(3);
      printf("The factorial of 3 is %d\n", temp);     main (includes
      temp = Factorial(4);                            function calls)
      printf("The factorial of 4 is %d\n", temp);                      Function
      temp = Factorial(5);                                             definition
      printf("The factorial of 5 is %d\n", temp);
}

int Factorial(int n) {
      int result = 1;

      while (n > 1)          /* While n is greater than 1,      */
            result *= n--;   /*  multiply result by n and decrement n  */
      return result;
}
```

Figure 3.4 *Example program showing repeated function calls.*

Each reference to Factorial within **main** results in a function call. Consider what happens when a statement within **main** has this form:

temp = Factorial(*input*);

The following things happen when this statement is executed:

1. Control is passed to the Factorial function.

2. The value of *input* is passed to n within the function definition.

3. After the function is finished executing—in this case, because of the **return** statement—control returns to the place in the program that called Factorial.

To be more accurate, in step 3 control returns to the statement following the statement that called the function. Once the function has executed and returned, the function call is complete and control should pass to the next task (see Figure 3.5).

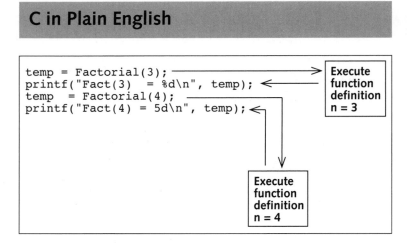

Figure 3.5 *Function calls and returns.*

Yet even this doesn't tell the whole story. As you can see, Factorial is not executed in isolation but is part of a larger expression. Consider the following statement:

```
Factorial(3);
```

This statement is perfectly legal but is pointless. A value is calculated—namely, the factorial of 3—only to be ignored. The following statement is much more useful:

```
temp = Factorial(3);
```

But notice what's happening here. After the function executes, the return value is assigned to temp. So it's most accurate to say that after a function call is evaluated, the rest of the statement, if any, is executed.

The important point here is that a function call such as Factorial(3) is an expression just like any other—even though it involves temporarily transferring execution to something very much like a subprogram. Because a function call is an expression, you can nest it inside another function call, such as printf. You can use this technique to create a more compact version of the program:

```
#include <stdio.h>

int Factorial(int n );

void main() {
    printf("The factorial of 3 is %d\n", Factorial(3));
    printf("The factorial of 4 is %d\n", Factorial(4));
    printf("The factorial of 5 is %d\n", Factorial(5));
}

int Factorial(int n) {
    int  result = 1;

    while (n > 1)            /* While n > 1,
        result *= n--;    /*  multiply by n
                                decrement n  */
    return result;
}
```

Arguments and More Arguments

The Factorial function takes a certain amount of liberty with its argument, n:

```
while (n > 1)            /* While n > 1,
    result *= n--;    /*  multiply by n
                            decrement n  */
```

These statements cause n to change during execution of the function: n is continually decremented until it is no longer greater than 1. So n is finally reduced to 1.

Now, what do you think the following statements do?

```
int Temp1, Temp2 = 3;

Temp1 = Factorial(Temp2);
printf("The value of Temp2 is still %d.\n", Temp2);
```

61

If you put this code into a program and run it, you'll find that it produces the following:

```
The value of Temp2 is still 3.
```

How can this be? The value of Temp2 was passed to the argument n, and the function changed the value of n to 1. Why didn't Temp2 change?

The answer is that the function gets a copy of Temp2's value but not the right to alter it. The argument, n, is initialized to the same value as Temp2. The function then goes on its merry way without having any further interaction with Temp2. What happens to n later doesn't matter; the value of n is thrown away as the function returns.

This is called *pass by value*. (The other principal method for passing arguments—*pass by reference*— requires pointers in C and is the subject of Chapter 7, "Pointers and Other Sharp Instruments".)

As a consequence, any valid expression can be passed as an argument as long as it is the right type. You aren't limited to passing variables. The following function calls are all legal:

```
temp = Factorial(1 + 2 + (3 - 1) );
temp = Factorial(3 + diff);
result = sqrt(1.0 + Factorial(thing));
```

Functions can have multiple arguments. For example, here is a prototype for the Pythagoras function:

```
double Pythagoras(double a, double b);
```

And here's the function definition:

```
double Pythagoras(double a, double b) {
    return sqrt(a * a + b * b);
}
```

Once Pythagoras is properly declared and defined, you can pass any two valid arguments. The first argument in the function call is assigned to a; the second, to b:

```
/* Pass 3=>a, 4=>b  */
hyp1 = Pythagoras (3,4);

/* Pass 4.0=>a, 5.0=>b */
hyp2 = Pythagoras (4.0, 5.0);

/* Pass temp1=>a, x+3=>b*/
hyp3 = Pythagoras (temp1, x+3);
```

Here, of course, the order doesn't matter. But it usually does matter with most functions. For example, the Quadratic function treats its arguments differently:

```
double Quadratic(double a, double b, double c) {
    double temp;

    temp = sqrt(b * b - 4 * a * c);
    return ((-b + temp) / (2 * a));
}
```

 Mathematically, this function is incomplete because it returns only one of the two roots of a quadratic equation. However, the function can return only one value. In Chapter 7, you'll see how to return more than one value.

A function can even have no arguments. A trivial example is a function that prints a standard message. The prototype uses the **void** keyword in the argument list, as does the function definition. In this context, **void** simply means "no arguments."

```
int Print_message(void);
...
int Print_message(void) {
    printf("Fatal error: stop the program.");
    return 0;
}
```

The function is then called with an empty argument list, but the parentheses must still be used:

```
temp = Print_message();
```

If the function has no need to return a value, the return value may also be **void**. This means that no value is returned at all; in that case, no **return**_expression_ statement may appear within the function definition, and the function, when called, cannot be used as part of a larger expression. Instead, a **void** function can be called only directly:

```
Print_message();
```

It's not very common to see a function with both a **void** return type and a **void** argument list, but such a function would be perfectly valid. Note the absence of a **return** statement in the function definition:

```
void Print_message(void);    /* function prototype */
...
void Print_message(void) {
    printf("Fatal error: stop the program.");
}
```

If you have a philosophical turn of mind, you might think of **void** as C's contribution to the concept of being and nothingness. (To what entity does the word _nothing_ refer?) The **void** keyword can mean an empty argument list, or—more paradoxically—a return value that is not a return value, but is instead an indicator of the _absence_ of return value. Ultimately, though, **void** is practical rather than philosophical. It serves a number of miscellaneous—and only loosely related—purposes. See "**void** Keyword" in Part II for a fuller discussion.

The Joy of Recursion

Simply stated, _recursion_ occurs when a function calls itself. This is legal in C, as it is in many other programming languages.

Recursion is an interesting logical and mathematical technique, but it's not vital to the writing of most C programs. If you are eager to understand just the basics of C syntax, you can safely skip this section.

You might think that recursion leads automatically to an infinite regress, as is the case when you point a mirror at another mirror. When recursion is properly done, this doesn't happen at all, because there is an initial condition.

Let's return to the factorial example. The factorial of a number is the product of all the integers from 1 to the number. For any number n:

```
factorial of n = 1 * 2 * 3 * ... n
```

To go from the factorial of n − 1 to n, multiply by n. For example, here are the factorials of 3 and 4:

```
factorial of 3 = 1 * 2 * 3
factorial of 4 = 1 * 2 * 3 * 4
```

Multiplying factorial of 3 by 4 produces the factorial of 4. Generalizing on this, we can say:

```
factorial of n = (factorial of n - 1) * n
```

There is one case in which this does not hold: the case of the number 1. The factorial of 1 is simply 1. So, logically, we can say:

```
If n > 1 then
        factorial of n = (factorial of n - 1) * n
else
        factorial of n = 1
```

We can code this logic in a C function very nicely by writing a Factorial function that calls itself:

```
int Factorial(int n)
{
    if (n > 1)
        return (Factorial(n - 1) * n);
    return 1;
}
```

If n is greater than 1, the first **return** statement causes the function to return immediately after calculating the value. Only if n is not greater than 1 does the second **return** get executed. The statements therefore create an "if-then-else" logic. (C does have an **else** keyword, by the way, as you'll see in Chapter 4.)

This approach results in a whole series of function calls, because, in most cases, before the function can complete execution, it must call itself. But during each call to Factorial, there is a different value of n. This is perfectly fine. C supports multiple instances of the same function, each with its own value of n.

If the main program executes Factorial(4), for example, the series of actions is:

1. Main program calls Factorial(4).

2. Factorial(4) calls Factorial(3).

3. Factorial(3) calls Factorial(2).

4. Factorial(2) calls Factorial(1).

5. Factorial(1) returns the value 1.

6. Factorial(2) multiplies this result by 2 and returns 2.

7. Factorial(3) multiplies this result by 3 and returns 6.

8. Factorial(4) multiplies this result by 4 and returns 24.

Recursion can be a useful technique for expressing a calculation succinctly. It's most often applicable in programs that involve complex math or logical relationships. However, you should be aware that recursion is almost never the most efficient way to implement something. Generally speaking, any algorithm that can be expressed through recursion also has an iterative solution—that is, an approach that uses a loop (such as a **while** loop). The recursive approach is almost always less efficient, because for each function call, there is a certain amount of overhead. Part of the function overhead stores the values of arguments and local variables, such as n, for the particular instance of the function call. The function overhead also keeps track of where the function returns when finished.

I'm not saying that you should never use recursion; but if there is an obvious alternative that uses a loop (as is the case with factorials), use the loop instead. In some cases, though, the recursive version may be much easier to write and nearly as efficient.

Why do I mention recursion, if it is rarely the best approach? Recursion is useful as a way of illustrating a basic fact of most real-world C programs: at any time, there may be many function calls pending. Only one function call can be currently executing, but there may be a number of them waiting for another function to return.

None of that would be the case if you did away with all functions except **main**. In fact, you could do just that, using complex loops and control structures to handle repeated operations. However, such code would be exceptionally difficult to write, understand, and maintain, even though in theory it might be slightly more efficient. It wouldn't be reusable; only when you write functions can you create part of a program so that it can easily be reused in another program.

Functions, after all, provide many benefits. Although machine-level efficiency is an important goal in C, the ability of a human being to write good programs is even more important. For all these reasons, functions are an invaluable tool.

Approach 2: Bottom-Up

If you want to avoid having to write prototypes, one way to do so is to define a function completely before using it. This *bottom-up* approach means putting **main** last (see Figure 3.6).

67

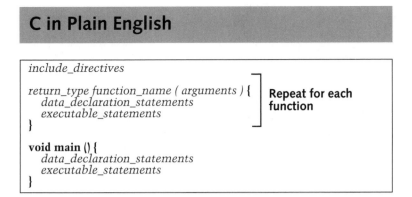

Figure 3.6 *The basic pattern of a bottom-up program.*

With this approach, the Factorial function would be rewritten as follows:

```c
#include <stdio.h>

int Factorial(int n) {
    int  result = 1;

    while (n > 1)        /* While n is greater than 1,   */
        result *= n--; /*  multiply result by n and
                            decrement n   */
    return result;
}

void main() {
    printf("The factorial of 3 is %d\n", Factorial(3));
    printf("The factorial of 4 is %d\n", Factorial(4));
    printf("The factorial of 5 is %d\n", Factorial(5));
}
```

Most C programmers don't use this approach, because they like to start with the big picture (the main program) and work downward. Moreover, if you spend enough time programming, you'll find that ultimately there is no escape from writing prototypes. In a serious program, the relationships between different functions become very complex. It is not uncommon for functions to end up calling each other (a variation on recursion), in which case it is impossible to define every function before it is called.

The bottom line is that you might as well get into the habit of putting a prototype for every function at the beginning of your program.

A Final Word on Prototypes

In many serious C programs, you won't see prototypes at the beginning of a source-code file, and for a good reason: all the prototypes are placed in a header file, which is then read in with a **#include** directive.

This is a sensible approach, especially when you have multiple source files and want all of them to get the prototypes for all the functions in the program. For example, you might place prototypes for all your functions in a file called my_prog.h. Then include my_prog.h along with the other header files:

```
#include <stdio.h>
#include <math.h>
#include "my_prog.h"
```

The syntax for the last **#include** is a little different from that of the first two; the quotation marks cause the current directory to be searched for the header file.

In the final analysis, entering prototypes may seem like unnecessary work at first, but they are just too useful to ignore—as are functions in general.

4

Decisions, Decisions: Control Structures in C

What most distinguishes a computer from other electronic equipment (a toaster, say) is its ability to make a wide variety of decisions. It would be going too far to suggest that computers have judgment—that intangible collection of experience, intuition, and character found in a subset of humans. But computers can follow directions on how to respond to different conditions as long as those directions are logically precise.

At the CPU level, a computer has a few primitive instructions that enable it to jump to a new instruction. But it takes many jumps to odd locations to produce usable program logic; when you look at assembly code and try to decipher the effect of all these jumps, you feel as if you're unwinding a ball of twine or untangling a plate of spaghetti. This gives rise to the quaint expression "spaghetti code," descriptive of assembly language and of primitive (unstructured) BASIC.

Higher-level languages, such as C, use control structures to represent this jumping around to different instructions in a readable, coherent way—so that you see more clearly the overall logic of the program. In C (as in other languages such as Pascal and Ada), the way you express decisions, conditions, and loops is not so different from the way you might express them in English.

71

C control structures roughly match those found in other "structured" languages such as Pascal. In some cases the C version is considerably more flexible. Unfortunately, this often means flexibility to get yourself into trouble. In this chapter, I'll try to steer you around the main causes of errors with control structures.

Compound Statements, or That's What Blocks are Made Of

Most of the time, you'll need to use compound statements (also called "statement blocks") when you use a C control structure. A multiple statement has the following form:

```
{
statements
}
```

In other words, put any series of C statements between an opening brace ({) and a closing brace (}), and you have a multiple statement. Here's an example:

```
{
    temp = a;
    a = b;
    b = temp;
}
```

This is useful because anywhere a statement is legal, a multiple statement is legal, too. This is consistently true everywhere in C syntax, without exception. Consider the **if** statement syntax:

if (*expression*)
    statement

Because of the principle I've just stated—that a multiple statement is always legal wherever a statement is legal—the **if** statement syntax automatically extends to support the following:

if (*expression*)
{
     statements
}

Now any number of statements can be executed in response to the condition. Spacing is flexible in C syntax, by the way, so that you can write the **if** statement this way:

if (expression) {
    statements
}

For example, let's say that if a certain condition (swap_vars) is true, then the values of a and b should be swapped. You can express this with the following **if** statement:

```
if (swap_vars) {
    temp = a;
    a = b;
    b = temp;
}
```

If swap_vars is true, then all three statements are executed. If not, then all of them are skipped.

We can extend the usefulness of the **while** keyword in the same way. From Chapter 3, you should recall that **while** repeatedly executes the statement that follows it as long as the condition is true:

while (*expression*)
    statement

Again, *statement* can be replaced by a multiple statement. Doing so extends the **while** statement to support a block of statements repeated over and over (a loop) of any size:

while *(expression)* {
    statements
}

Consider the factorial example from Chapter 3. After initializing the variables result and n, the function carried out this logic:

> While n is not equal to zero,
> > Multiply result by n
> > Decrease n by 1

In Chapter 3, I used the trick of using a special C operator (--) to collapse two of these statements into one. However, using the multiple-statement syntax, you can write the two statements on separate lines:

```
while (n) {
    result = result * n;
    n = n - 1;
}
```

This version is not the most compact, but it's easy to understand. It also most closely approximates how the code would look in another language such as Pascal or structured BASIC. C offers so much flexibility that there are often many ways to write even a simple program.

Using C's multiplication-assignment (*=) and decrement (--) operators, the code can be made a little more compact:

```
while (n) {
    result *= n;     /* Multiply result by n. */
    n--;             /* Decrement n by 1.     */
}
```

Finally, there is this version, the most compact:

```
while (n) {
    result *= n--;    /* Multiply result by n */
}                     /*  and decrement n.    */
```

In this last case, there is only one statement inside the braces. However, a multiple statement consisting of just one statement is completely legal. In fact, it's not uncommon to see single-statement blocks (braces with just one statement inside).

One reason you might use single-statement blocks is that you expect to add more statements later, even though there is only one statement in the block for now. Putting in the braces ({}) now saves the trouble of adding them later. Another reason you might see a single-statement block is that originally there were several statements, but revision of the program has left only one. (This is exactly what happened here.) There's no need to take away the braces once they're there.

In general, it never hurts to use the statement-block syntax with control structures such as **if** and **while**, even if (for now) there is only one statement in the block. Some programmers do this as a matter of course. Having the braces there makes no difference whatsoever in the run-time efficiency of the program, and the increase in compile time is insignificant.

There's another feature of compound statements that's good to know about, even if you use it only occasionally. Compound statements are blocks that define their own level of *scope*. Essentially this means that you can define variables within the statement block; these variables can be used only in the statement block. Take the variable-swapping example again. The variables a, b, and temp can be defined at the same level:

```
int a, b, temp, swap_vars;
.
.
.
```

```
if (swap_vars) {
    temp = a;
    a = b;
    b = temp;
}
```

You could define temp within the statement block:

```
int a, b, swap_vars;
.
.
.
if (swap_vars) {
    int temp;

    temp = a;
    a = b;
    b = temp;
}
```

Why would you want to do this? In this case, the only effect seems to be additional typing. You should always be aware, though, that every variable you define requires computer memory. By defining temp inside this block, you cause the program to allocate room for temp for only a few statements; then temp is destroyed and the memory is given back. You can conserve memory by restricting the scope of a variable to just a block.

There are other advantages, too. It's possible there might be another variable floating around that has the name "temp." By declaring a variable inside the statement block, you give the block its own private copy of temp. Changes to the variable inside the block have no effect on any other variable of the same name.

In practice, you might never choose to define variables inside a statement block. Yet you'll sometimes see it used in advanced programming techniques.

Direct Jumps with goto

C includes its own version of the direct-jump statement, called **goto**:

goto *statement_label;*

The target of the **goto** is the statement that has this same *statement_label*. (A label is simply a means of identifying a statement by preceding it with a name; labels are similar to line numbers.) This statement must be in the same function, and the label must be unique; no two statements in the same function can be given the same label.

statement_label:
    statement

The effect of the **goto** is to transfer program control unconditionally so that the next statement executed is the one preceded by the *statement_label*. For example, in Figure 4.1 the statement "goto the_top" causes the computer to execute the first statement in the function again:

```
void Calc(double x) {
        int n;

the_top:
        n = 0;
        x = n / 2;
        .
        .
        .
        goto the_top;
}
```

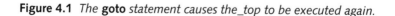

Figure 4.1 *The* **goto** *statement causes the_top to be executed again.*

One use of **goto** is to help illustrate how loops work. We can now express the workings of the **while** statement in terms of an **if** statement and a **goto**:

while (*expression*)
    statement

This code is equivalent to the code shown in Figure 4.2.

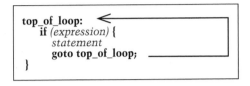

```
top_of_loop:
    if (expression) {
    statement
        goto top_of_loop;
    }
```

Figure 4.2 *A* **while** *statement works like this* **if** *and* **goto** *combination.*

This control structure can execute the *statement* an indefinite number of times. As long as *expression* is true, the *statement* is executed (the statement can be a multiple statement), and then control is transferred to the top of the loop, starting the process again. This results in a repetitious cycle, making the term *loop* so appropriate. Only when the conditional expression is not true does execution skip past the **goto** and so break out of the loop.

You can use **goto** in your own code, but usually it's not necessary. Programming with **goto** is most often useful when you have a complex nesting of control structures (control structures inside other control structures), have detected an error condition, and want to jump out of all of them quickly.

The Conditional Expression: What is Truth?

The **if** and **while** statements execute code if their conditional expression is true. But what exactly does "true" mean in computer terms—or rather, in C programming terms?

if (*expression*)
    statement

while (*expression*)
    statement

In many languages (Pascal and FORTRAN are prominent examples), a conditional expression must be of a special Boolean type, which can assume only the values TRUE or FALSE. The following expressions, or equivalent ones, are considered Boolean in those languages:

```
a > b
a < b
a >= b      // greater than or equal to
a <= b      // less than or equal to
a == b      // equal to
a != b      // not equal to
```

 In C, you do comparisons with a test-for-equality operator (==); this operator is distinct from the assignment operator (=). Confusing these operators is a common source of
NOTE   nasty errors, a problem we'll look at in the next section.

Although C supports all these comparison operations, it has no built-in notion of true and false as such. Instead, the results of these comparisons translate into 0 (if false) or 1 (if true); see Table 4.1.

Table 4.1 *These expressions evaluate to 0 if false or 1 if true.*

Expression	If FALSE, expression evalutes to	If TRUE, expression evalutes to
a > b	0	1
a < b	0	1
a >= b	0	1
a <= b	0	1
a == b	0	1
a != b	0	1

In case this isn't yet completely clear, you might want to try the following experiment, in which a program prints the actual numeric value of true and false expressions:

```
<stdio.h>

void main() {
    printf("A FALSE value is: %d\n", 4 > 9);
    printf("A TRUE value is: %d\n", 4 < 9);
}
```

When run, this program prints the following:

```
A FALSE value is: 0
A TRUE value is: 1
```

At first it may seem strange that a logical expression (an expression with a true/false value) is translated into a number. But everything works together smoothly in C, because control stuctures such as **if** and **while** respond to numeric values. Look at the basic pattern for an **if** statement again:

if (*expression*)
       statement

The C compiler interprets this as follows:

If the *expression* is not equal to zero,
       Execute the *statement*
Else
       Skip over the *statement*

So familiar-looking **if** statements work exactly as you'd expect. If a is greater than b, for example, then the expression "a > b" evaluates to 1. The **if** statement interprets 1 as "true" because it is nonzero and therefore executes the printf call in the following code:

```
if (a > b)
    printf("a is greater than b.");
```

The statement does exactly what you'd expect. But the way true and false are handled in C gives rise to a number of interesting C programming techniques:

- You can test numeric variables directly, without having to explicitly compare them to zero. In other words, "if (n)" becomes shorthand for "if n not equal to zero."

- You can assign the results of comparisons to integer variables.

- Both assignment (=) and tests for equality (==) can be used inside the conditional expression of **if** or **while**, although you must be careful not to confuse them.

You've already seen examples of the first programming technique. The Factorial function used the the following **while** loop:

```
while(n)
    result = result * n—;
```

The test could have been written to explicitly compare n to zero, in which case the code would have looked like the following:

```
while(n != 0)
    result = result * n—;
```

The behavior of the program, in either case, is exactly the same. If n is any value other than zero, (n) is considered "true" from the standpoint of the **while** statement. The expression (n != 0) is also true in those cases (see Table 4.2).

Table 4.2

Value of n	With while(n), is statement executed?	Value of (n!=0)	With while(n!=0), is statement executed?
0	No	0	No
1	Yes	1	Yes
2	Yes	1	Yes
3	Yes	1	Yes

So the conditional (n) causes the same behavior as the conditional (n != 0). All the control structures use a similar logic, interpreting nonzero values as true.

As with many other things in C, you should think of comparison operators as just another set of numeric operators, and Boolean expressions (such as n > 1) as just another kind of numeric expression. Consequently, you can assign the results of comparisons to integer variables:

```
int     Is_Proper_Age, No_Crim_Record;
.
.
.
Is_Proper_Age = (age > 21);
No_Crim_Record = (crimes == 0);

if (Is_Proper_Age && No_Crim_Record)
    Sell_Merchandise();
```

This example uses the logical AND operator (&&), which does what you'd expect: it checks both operands, and, if neither is equal to zero, it evaluates to 1; otherwise it evaluates to zero. The effect is that the function Sell_Merchandise is executed if both conditions (age > 21 and crimes == 0) are true.

 If you look at the table in the "Operators" topic of Part II, you'll see that both && and & are listed. The latter is
NOTE **the bitwise AND operator, and although it is similar to the logical AND, it is not the same. Chapter 5 discusses the differences.**

82

The C programming language puts a lot of trust in you, the programmer. Rather than assume that a certain kind of statement doesn't make sense—and therefore prohibit it—C makes relatively few assumptions about what makes sense. If an expression can be translated into something the CPU can somehow execute, C usually lets you do it. This is why C isn't picky about what is a Boolean and what is merely a number. To the CPU, all data is numeric anyway.

But this extra freedom means that you have to know what you're doing. It also opens up potential sources of errors. One of the major kinds of errors involves assignment and comparison tests, which we'll look at in the next section.

Assignment and Tests for Equality

As I've stated, a Boolean expression is a numeric expression like any other. So is assignment. Both of these kinds of expressions can be used as a conditional test for an **if** or **while** statement.

```
n == 5;  /* Compare n to 5; evaluate to 1 if equal. */;
n = 5;   /* Assign 5 to n; evaluate to 5. */
```

These are two different operations, and, in other languages, they can't be confused. BASIC uses the same symbol (=) for each operation but relies on context to determine which operation is meant. Pascal uses = for comparison and := for assignment; this makes C confusing if you come from Pascal, because comparison in Pascal looks like assignment in C! Moreover, Pascal won't let you confuse the context, because assignment is not permitted inside a conditional expression.

But in C, both of the following pieces of code are legal—the compiler will report no error:

```
while (n == 5) {                          /* CASE 1 */
    printf("n equals 5\n");
    n = n + 1;
```

83

```
}

while (n = 5) {                                    /* CASE 2 */
    printf("n equals 5\n");
    n = n + 1;
}
```

The first case (n == 5) does what you'd expect. The program tests n to see whether it is equal to 5; if it is, the statement block is executed. After printing the statement, the program increments n from 5 to 6. The **while** condition tests n for 5, but it is now equal to 6, so the loop is terminated. The text "n equals 5" is printed no more than once.

The second case (n = 5) does something strange:

1. The value 5 is assigned to n.

2. The return value of the expression "n = 5" is 5, because 5 was the value assigned. This means that the program acts as if "5" were substituted for "n = 5," as described in Chapter 2.

3. The **while** statement considers the expression true, because it is nonzero (it is equal to 5). So the statement block is executed.

In other words, the expression n = 5 will evaluate to 5 regardless of what value was previously in n. Consequently, the **while** loop will continue executing no matter what. The result is an infinite loop! It doesn't even matter that n changes during execution of the statement block. Every time the conditional is evaluated, n is reset to 5 because of the assignment.

The moral should be clear. Using assignment (=) inside a conditional test is dangerous and in a novice C programmer's code often signifies an error. If you're not careful to remember that the two operators (= and ==) are different, you're likely to stare at a conditional such as n = 5 for hours, wondering why the program is in an infinite loop.

Yet there are legitimate reasons for placing an assignment in a conditional expression. You just have to be very sure that this is what you want. For example, consider this code:

```
int c;
.

.

.
while(c = get_next_char()) {
    /* statement block... */
    /* Do some work on c */
}
```

Let's assume that the function get_next_char attempts to get another character (from a file, say, or a string of text) and returns zero if it fails. If it finds another character, it returns the ASCII value of that character.

 Individual characters (letters, spaces, and so on) are stored as numbers. ASCII is by far the most common system for encoding these characters. Other formats are available, however, such as Kanji, which is used to encode Japanese characters.

In this case, this code works correctly. After the value is assigned to c, that same value is evaluated as the **while** condition. A value of zero (no more characters) causes breaking out of the loop. If get_next_char does find another character, that value is stored in the variable c and then the statement block is executed. The assignment of the return value to c could have been done separately from testing this value, but combining them saves a good deal of extra typing.

The reason assignment works here is that the value assigned is not a constant, so the **while** statement does not execute an infinite loop. Generally, any conditional test on a constant number produces incorrect behavior, although C certainly won't stop you from doing it. The exception would be a situation in which you really do want to set up an endless loop, possibly because you break out of the loop in the middle. Here, a conditional expression that is a constant number makes sense.

```
while (1) {    /* Loop always executes */

    /* Execute some statements */

    if (no_more_characters)
        goto done;

    /* Execute some more statements */
    }
done:
```

Variations on while Loops

Sometimes you want the loop to execute at least once and then afterward test a condition before deciding whether to repeat. You can do this with a **do-while** loop:

do
> *statement*
while (*expression*);

You can easily expand the *statement* into a statement block by using braces:

do {
> *statements*
} **while** (*expression*);

Again, the only real difference between a **do-while** loop and a **while** loop, introduced earlier, is that **do-while** executes the loop at least once. There is also a subtle, purely syntactic difference: a **while** loop, if it uses multiple-statement syntax, does not end with a semicolon (;). A **do-while** loop always ends in a semicolon.

Here is an example that prompts for input, prints a factorial (calling the Factorial function from Chapter 3), and then repeats these steps unless the user entered zero. In that case, the program quits.

```
<stdio.h>

int Factorial( int n );


void main() {
    int the_number;

    do {
        printf("Enter a number: ");
        scanf("%d", &the_number);
        if (the_number)
                printf("Factorial is %d\n",
        Factorial(the_number));
    } while (the_number);
}
```

The **do-while** loop here is appropriate because you want the prompt to be printed at least once.

Some programming languages have a "repeat-until" structure, which executes a loop until a specified condition is true. C doesn't have this control structure, no doubt to keep the number of keywords to a minimum. Instead, it's easy to write the equivalent of a repeat-until structure by combining a **do-while** loop with the logical NOT operator (!).

do {
       statements
} while (! *expression*);

The logical NOT operator reverses the meaning of the condition, so that !*expression* is true only if *expression* is false, and vice versa. The result, in this case, is to execute until *expression* is true (! *expression* produces a false result).

The All-Purpose for Loop

More often than not, loops are intended to execute a specific number of times. To take a trivial example, you might write code to print all the numbers from 1 to 10. You can certainly do this with a **while** loop. Note that the increment operator (++) is used to increase the value by 1 each time.

```
int num;

num = 1;
while (num <= 10) {          /* While num is less than
    or equal 10, */
    printf("%d ", num);      /*   print the number, */
    num++;                   /*   increment num. */
}
```

This code, when executed, prints the following:

```
1 2 3 4 5 6 7 8 9 10
```

This is not very exciting. Much more useful is code that prints a table of Celsius temperatures and corresponding Fahrenheit temperatures. This table starts at 0.0 degrees Celsius and increases by 10.0 in each row.

```
double Celsius, Fahrenheit;

Celsius = 0.0;
/* while num is less than 10,
    print row of table and
    increment Celsius. */
while (Celsius <= 100.0) {
    printf("%f    ", Celsius);
    Fahrenheit = 32.0 + Celsius * 1.8;
    printf("%f\n", Fahrenheit);
    Celsius = Celsius + 10.0;
}
```

In both cases, the code follows the same general pattern of steps:

1. Set the main variable of the loop—that is, the loop variable—to an initial value.

2. Test the condition: if true (nonzero), proceed; otherwise, exit loop.

3. Execute the main action of the loop.

4. Increment the loop variable. Repeat, beginning at step 2.

It turns out that these basic steps are so common in computer programming that all programming languages have some kind of direct support for writing these loops. Often, this mechanism is called a "do loop." In C, it is a **for** loop. The C version, however, is far more flexible. Here is the basic syntax:

for (*initialize; condition; increment*)
      statement

The *initializer* generally initializes the loop variable (step 1). You can also use it to initialize any number of variables or do other kinds of initialization. For now, just consider it a way of initializing one or more variables at the beginning of a loop. The *initializer* is executed only once.

The *condition* is the loop condition (step 2). This is the same as the *expression* in a **while** loop. If this expression is true (nonzero), the *statement* is executed (step 3) and then the *increment* is executed (step 4). Then the condition is tested again.

This is easier to understand with an example or two. Figure 4.3 shows the code that prints numbers from 1 to 10.

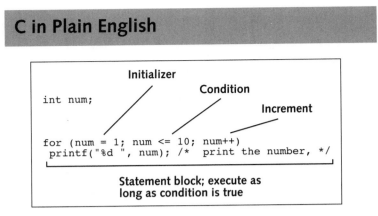

Figure 4.3 *This code prints numbers from 1 to 10.*

The expression "num = 1" is executed just once—to initialize the loop variable, num. The condition "num <= 10.0" is evaluated before every iteration of the loop, just as in a **while** statement. When "num <= 10.0" is no longer true (because 10 is exceeded), the loop terminates. The expression "num++" increases num after each time through the loop.

The expressions "Cels = 0.0", "Cels <= 100.0", and "Cels = Cels+ 10.0" serve the same purpose in the next example:

```
double Cels, Fahrenheit;

for (Cels = 0.0; Cels <= 100.0; Cels =  Cels + 10.0) {
    printf("%f      ", Cels); /*  print row of table, */
    Fahrenheit = 32.0 + Cels * 1.8;
    printf("%f\n", Fahrenheit);
}
```

In each case, the most important part of the **for** statement, in some ways, is the conditional expression—the middle of the three expressions. Usually, this expression tests the value of the loop variable. For example, Cels runs from 0.0 to 100.0, so it should continue as long as num doesn't exceed 100.0. The expression is therefore "Cels <= 100.0". Another language might express a loop as

```
DO num = 1 TO 10
```

or

```
DO Cels = 0.0 TO 100.0 STEP 10.0
```

Although the C version might seem more complex at first, it's similar to what other languages do, and the order is the same. The starting value is expressed first (Cels = 0.0). The terminating value is expressed next (Cels <= 100.0). Finally, the increment is expressed (Cels = Cels + 10.0). The difference is that in the C version, you must specify explicitly what each of these expressions does—assign a value, evaluate a conditional test, or update a variable. This syntax requires a little more work, but it makes the C **for** statement vastly more flexible than the do loops of other languages. You can enter any legal C expressions for *initialize, condition,* and *increment.*

In general, we can say that a **for** loop, using the syntax

for (*initialize; condition; increment*)
      statement

behaves precisely the same way as this code written as a **while** loop:

initialize;
    while (*condition*) {
        statement
        increment;
    }

We can even write this as an **if** statement with a **goto** (see Figure 4.4).

You can, if you choose, write programs entirely without the **for** statement. It's easy enough to create any program using only **if**, **while**, and **goto**. But the **for** statement is included in C because loops that count to a particular number are very common. In these situations, the use of **for** loops is a good code-compacting technique.

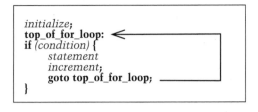

Figure 4.4 *A* **for** *statement rewritten with* **goto***.*

With any luck, you noticed that in each of the examples, the **for** loop version is a couple of lines shorter than the **while** loop version.

Extending the if Statement: Selecting from Alternatives

So far, I've been understating what the **if** statement can do. The complete syntax of the **if** statement is this:

if (*expression*)
      statement_1
  [**else**
      statement_2]

I've used brackets to indicate that the **else** part is optional.

As before, *statement_1* and *statement_2* can each be replaced by compound statements. Although visually it's a little confusing to do so, *statement_1* can be a single statement while *statement_2* is a multiple statement, and vice versa.

Here's a simple program that uses the **if-else** syntax:

```c
#include <stdio.h>

void main() {
    int a, b;

    printf("Enter a number: ");
    scanf("%d", &a);
    printf("Enter a number: ");
    scanf("%d", &b);
    if (a < b)
        printf("a is less than b.\n");
    else
        printf("a is not less than b.\n");
}
```

Incidentally, the first four executable statements of the program use an almost identical two-line sequence of code (a printf statement followed by a scanf statement). When code is repeated like this, it's generally a good candidate for being relegated to a function. The result here doesn't save any lines of code, but it would if this code sequence were used many times or if the repeated sequence were longer. Here's the revised version, using function calls:

```c
#include <stdio.h>

int get_a_number(void);

void main() {
    int a, b;

    a = get_a_number();
    b = get_a_number();
    if (a < b)
        printf("a is less than b.\n");
    else
        printf("a is not less than b.\n");
}
```

```
int get_a_number(void) {
    int num;

    printf("Enter a number: ");
    scanf("%d", &num);
    return num;
}
```

What's new here is the **if-else** structure. This code does exactly what you'd imagine it would do, printing a message telling whether or not a is less than b.

```
if (a < b)
    printf("a is less than b.\n");
else
    printf("a is not less than b.\n");
```

Here's the problem: what you'd really want to do when writing a program like this is to test for the three possible cases: a is less than b, a is greater than b, or a is equal to b. There is no "elseif" keyword, exactly, but testing for multiple alternatives in C is easy enough. All you have to do is place another **if** statement inside the **if-else** statement. You can always do this in C; any kind of syntax that takes a *statement* or *statements* can accept an **if-else**, **while**, **do-while**, **for**, or any other kind of statement.

```
if (a < b)
    printf("a is less than b.\n");
else {
    if (a > b)
            printf("a is greater than b.\n");
    else
            printf("a and b are equal.\n");
}
```

Here the braces ({}) following **else** are not necessary, but I've inserted them for clarity. In terms of C syntax, the second

else applies to the second **if** and not to the first. However, the second **if-else** is a single statement, so the braces aren't really required. The C compiler keeps the syntax straight. You can rewrite the code as:

```
if (a < b)
    printf("a is less than b.\n");
else
    if (a > b)
        printf("a is greater than b.\n");
    else
        printf("a and b are equal.\n");
```

More compact still—but equivalent to this code—is the following. Note that whether or not **else** and **if** are on the same line makes no difference to the compiler.

```
if (a < b)
    printf("a is less than b.\n");
else if (a > b)
    printf("a is greater than b.\n");
else
    printf("a and b are equal.\n");
```

Simply by changing the spacing, you create a virtual "elseif" keyword—even though, technically speaking, it's not "elseif" but two keywords: an **else** followed by an **if**. By using **else if** this way, you can test any number of alternatives.

If you find yourself often testing between several alternatives, there is another control structure that is useful: the **switch** statement. You can use the **switch** statement to execute one of several cases, as determined by a single variable.

This may sound esoteric, so here's an example. Suppose that a variable is used to represent one of the first three presidents—1 is Washington, 2 is Adams, and 3 is Jefferson. You can print the president by testing the variable with an **if-else** statement:

```
if (pres == 1)
    printf("President Washington\n");
else if (pres == 2)
    printf("President John Adams\n");
else if (pres == 3)
    printf("President Jefferson\n");
else
    printf("Not a valid president\n");
```

As you can see, the variable pres is tested repeatedly, but you'd rather test it just once. The following **switch** statement produces the same behavior as the **if-else** statement:

```
switch(pres) {
    case 1:
        printf("President Washington\n"); break;
    case 2:
        printf("President John Adams\n"); break;
    case 3:
        printf("President Jefferson\n"); break;
    default:
        printf("Not a valid president\n"); break;
}
```

This code is somewhat easier to follow, so any time you're testing alternatives that depend only on the value of a single variable, you may want to use this coding technique. For more information on how to use **switch**, see the topic "switch Keyword" in Part II.

My apologies to all presidents living and dead for this example. I didn't necessarily mean to imply that all presidents after Jefferson were "invalid," although one has to admit that they have a strong example to live up to.

And on that note, we'll leave the subject of C control structures, having covered them all at least briefly.

5

Operators:
C the Unique

Over the years, I've found it fun to look at different programming languages and characterize the personality or flavor of each one. C's personality is quite definite; it's one of the easiest languages to characterize. As programming tools go, C is like a finely tuned sports car—not very forgiving to a beginner but much faster than a station wagon if driven correctly.

At first, you might not think of C as being economical. C doesn't have built-in text string operators, for example, so some kinds of operations take longer to write in C than in BASIC. (Interestingly, the lack of string operators is easily remedied in C++, which helps to explain the popularity of this close relative of C. That's a topic for another book.)

But C has a number of operators you won't find in other languages. Some of them, such as the bitwise operators, increase your power over the computer, making C nearly as powerful as assembly language. By succinctly representing some of the most common programming tasks, other operators help you write more compact code. This means that there are often many different ways to write essentially the same program, some more compact than others.

Assignment Operators

An *operator* is a symbol (or a combination of symbols) that you use to combine variables and constants to produce a value. Here are several expressions that use an operator to combine two values:

```
a + b
my_num * 20.75
total / 3
x = 1
```

An *expression*, in turn, is something that evaluates to a single value. All the preceding lines of code are expressions, and you can turn any of them into a statement by appending a semicolon. For example:

```
x = 1;
```

An assignment (=) is the most common kind of expression to turn into a statement, although other kinds of statements are possible. An assignment can be part of an expression involving other operators:

```
x = x + 1;
```

It turns out that operations of this form are extremely common: operating on a variable and storing the result in that same variable. You might increase the value of a variable by adding a number to it. Or increase the variable by multiplying it. Or do the same with division or subtraction:

```
num = num + 10;      /* Increase num by 10. */
num = num * 2;       /* Double the value of num. */
num = num / 2;       /* Decrease num by half. */
num = num - 35;      /* Decrease num by 35. */
```

C provides special assignment operators to succinctly represent operations of this kind. The assignment operators, and their equivalent forms, are shown in Table 5.1.

Table 5.1 *The C assignment operators.*

OPERATION	SYMBOL	EXAMPLE	EQUIVALENT TO
Addition	+=	x += y	x = x + y
Subtraction	-=	x -= y	x = x - y
Multiplication	*=	x *= y	x = x * y
Division	/=	x /= y	x = x / y
Remainder	%=	x %= y	x = x % y
Left shift	<<=	x <<= y	x = x << y
Right shift	>>=	x >>= y	x = x >> y
Bitwise AND	&=	x &= y	x = x & y
Bitwise OR	|=	x |= y	x = x | y
Bitwise exclusive OR	^=	x ^= y	x = x ^ y

Some of these operators (remainder, left shift, right shift, and the bitwise operators) are ones you haven't seen before. Don't worry; we'll get to them later in the chapter. For now, all that matters is that you understand the pattern.

For example, consider an absolute-value function, which multiplies a number by –1 if it is less than zero:

```
int abs(int val) {
    if (val < 0)       /* If val is negative, */
        val *= -1;     /*   val = val * -1.   */
    return val;
}
```

Assignment operators—particularly addition and subtraction—are common in **for** statements. For example, here is the count-to-10 example of Chapter 4, "Decisions, Decisions: Control Structures in C" written with addition assignment (+=). The expression i += 1 bumps up the value of i by 1 each time through the loop.

```
for (i = 1; i <= 10; i += 1)
    printf("%d ", i);
```

You could also count *down* from 10 using subtraction assignment (-=).

99

```
for (i = 10; i >= 1; i -= 1)
    printf("%d ", i);
```

And here's the Celsius/Fahrenheit example, replacing Celsius = Celsius + 10.0 with the more succinct expression, Celsius += 10.0:

```
double Celsius, Fahrenheit;

for (Celsius = 0.0; Celsius <= 100.0; Celsius += 10.0) {
    printf("%f     ", Celsius);  /*   print row of table, */
    Fahrenheit = 32.0 + Celsius * 1.8;
    printf("%f\n", Fahrenheit);
}
```

N O T E In this section, I've suggested that an expression such as x += y is exactly equivalent to x = x + y. This is almost true. There is a difference: the expression x is evaluated only once in x += y, but it is evaluated twice in x = x + y. This makes no difference in the last few examples, but with more complex expressions, there are important consequences. First, the former expression (x += y) can potentially result in greater run-time efficiency, because the program evaluates fewer expressions. Second and more important, program behavior can be different if x has side effects. (A side effect occurs when the process of evaluating x causes one or more values to change.)

Expressions involving functions frequently have side effects. In the next section, you'll see some operators with side effects. Such operators are another aspect of C that makes it different from most programming languages.

Increment and Decrement Operators

The assignment operators represent some of the most common operations. Of these, the most common are addition and subtraction.

Let's take this one step further. What are the most common numbers to add or subtract with? The most common number to add or subtract is 1:

```
x += 1; /* Increment x by 1. */
y -= 1; /* Decrement y by 1. */
```

These operations are common, in part, because they are used frequently in loops. If you wanted to repeat a statement block 50 times, for example, the obvious way to do it is to set up a loop variable and count to 50, bumping up the variable by exactly 1 each time. C provides four operators for incrementing or decrementing by 1 (see Table 5.2).

Table 5.2 *The four C operators for incrementing or decrementing by 1.*

OPERATOR	NAME	DESCRIPTION
n++	Postfix increment	Return the value of n, then increment n by 1.
++n	Prefix increment	Increment n by 1, then return the new value of n.
n--	Postfix decrement	Return the value of n, then decrement n by 1.
--n	Prefix decrement	Decrement n by 1, then return the new value of n.

The difference between the postfix (n++) and prefix (++n) versions is whether the variable is changed before or after the value is used.

To clarify, let's turn to the factorial example one last time:

```
while (n)
    result = result * n--;   /* Postfix decrement */
```

Because the decrement operator is postfix, the decrement happens after n is used, so the example is equivalent to:

101

```
while (n) {
    result = result * n;
    n = n - 1;                   /* Change n after. */
}
```

So n is not changed until after being used to calculate result. Now consider what would happen if the code were written this way:

```
while (n)
    result = result * --n;   /* Prefix decrement */
```

This is equivalent to:

```
while (n) {
    n = n - 1;                   /* Change n first. */
    result = result * n;
}
```

 As mentioned in the previous note, the equivalence is not absolute, because in this last version n must be evaluated NOTE four times rather than two. Depending on the ability of the compiler to optimize, the run-time efficiency may be better with the shorter version. However, this is a trivial difference that we can ignore for the moment.

If you're not careful, confusing postfix and prefix can lead to the wrong results for even the simple Factorial function. Again, here's the function definition, this time with prefix decrement:

```
int Factorial(int n) {
    int result = 1;

    while (n)
        result = result * --n;      /* Prefix decrement
    */
    return result;
}
```

Assuming that n is passed the value 5, you can follow the calculation to see that it produces the result shown in Figure 5.1.

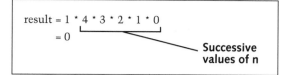

result = 1 * 4 * 3 * 2 * 1 * 0
      = 0
                              Successive
                              values of n

Figure 5.1 *Factorial function with incorrect use of prefix decrement.*

The Factorial function, rewritten this way, returns 0 for any value of n! Instead of running from n to 1, the multiplication factors run from n–1 to 0. This is because n is decremented before, rather than after, result is multiplied by n.

If you use an increment or decrement operator by itself (and not as part of a larger expression), there is no difference in the behavior of postfix and prefix. For example, the following statements result in the same program behavior:

```
total++;
++total;
```

If you want to keep your programs as easy as possible to read and debug, you might want to restrict your usage of increment and decrement operators to this kind of simple usage.

When used as just shown, the increment and decrement operators provide a nice way to save typing. They also aid the compiler in producing optimal run-time code. One of the basic characteristics of C is that it's designed to exploit common features of microprocessors. These processors have several instructions—such as ADD, SUB, INC, and DEC on Intel 80x86 chips—that closely parallel C operators. For example:

```
INC  total        ; C equivalent: total++
ADD  ax, 5        ; C equivalent: ax += 5
```

C can therefore translates such operations directly into equivalent machine instructions—one machine instruction for one C statement.

But be careful. Increment and decrement operators have side effects, which means that if you use several of them within a complex expression, it can be difficult to predict the results. Computer scientists use the term *side effects* to refer to expressions that do more than produce a value when evaluated: they cause one or more values to change. Actually, you have already seen many examples of the most common type of expression that produces side effects: an assignment. For example:

```
i = (n = 32) + 2;
```

The subexpression "n = 32" evaluates to a value: 32. But the expression "n = 32" does more than produce a value; it also changes the value of n. The effect of this statement is to set i to 34, but, as a side effect, n is set to 32.

Similarly, an expression such as "n++" evaluates to a certain number, but, as a side effect, it alters the value of n. That's fine when "n++" is used in a simple expression, but consider what happens in the following statement:

```
my_total = n++ / (thing + n++) * n-- * n++;
```

In this case, the value of n is used repeatedly, but each time, n has a different value! It becomes difficult to predict what such a statement will do when the program runs. As a general rule, never increment or decrement the same variable more than once in a statement. The C compiler is ever a faithful servant, so it won't stop you from doing that.

Logic—Bitwise and Otherwise

The word *and* normally has a single, clear-cut meaning in human ("natural") languages, although I'm sure you can find interesting exceptions. Two kinds of "and" operations are possible in computer languages—as well two kinds of "or" and two kinds of "not."

One kind of "and" operation acts on individual bits. This is a bitwise, or binary, "and." It's extremely useful in programs that analyze bit patterns or store different pieces of information within the same byte. Most high-level languages don't provide any way of doing these operations, even though they're easily translated into equivalent machine instructions. (But with C, if something can be readily implemented by the processor, C lets you go ahead and do it.)

In addition to bitwise manipulation, you can also use *logical* operations to combine true and false conditions in an optimal way. This kind of "and" and "or" operation works like a series of **if** statements, rather than testing individual bits. For example, you might want to execute code only if x is in range, which in the following example is true as long as x is between 0.0 and 100.0. Here, the logical "and" is used:

```
if (x >= 0.0 && x <= 100.0) {     /* If x >= 0 AND
                                      x <= 100, */
    process_data(x);    /*  process data, get new x. */
    scanf("%lf", &x);
}
```

What's the difference between bitwise "and" and logical (non-bitwise) "and"? First, let's look at how two such expressions are represented in C:

```
9 & 6      /* Bitwise AND */
9 && 6     /* Logical (non-bitwise) AND */
```

Assembly language and Microsoft BASIC support only the bitwise operators, although in those languages it is possible (if cumbersome) to write code to simulate what the C logical operators do.

In C, here's how the two operators work. Bitwise "and" compares each bit in one operand to its corresponding bit in the other. This is a bit-by-bit operation that works on any two integers of the same storage size. The logical "and," in

105

contrast, uses a short-circuit logic that evaluates only as many terms as it needs to: if the first operand is false (zero), the resulting expression is set to 0 and the second operand is never evaluated. This short-circuit approach helps optimize performance of programs with complex conditionals.

But it's important to understand that even with trivial operands, bitwise and logical operations frequently produce different results. Figure 5.1 illustrates how bitwise and logical operations would work on the operands 6 and 9. Note that the binary representation of 9 is 1001, and the binary representation of 6 is 0110. Here, the result is 0, not 1, because although operands both are nonzero, no single bit position contains 1 in both operands. This differs from the logical version of "and," in which the bit positions are unimportant.

The "or" operations work in a similar way. Bitwise "or" tests each bit position, and, if either operand has the bit set, the corresponding bit in the result is set. Logical "or" uses the following short-circuit logic: if the first operand is true (nonzero), the result is 1 and the second operand is not evaluated at all. Figure 5.3 shows how the "or" operations would work on the operands 9 and 6.

With more-complex expressions, the difference between bitwise and logical "or" is even more important. Logical "or" does not always evaluate the second operand; in that case, the side effects of the second operand do not happen. (With bitwise operations, both operands are always evaluated.) The operands 6 and 9 involve no side effects, but many expressions do. For example, function calls often have side effects.

The moral of the story should be clear. Don't confuse the two kinds of operators, because depending on the operands, the results can be completely different. You should know which kind of operator you're using and why.

The typical use for the logical (non-bitwise) operator is in conditional expressions. As you'll see, a bitwise operator might also appear inside a conditional expression, but unless you're sure that's what you want, a bitwise operation inside a condition may indicate an error.

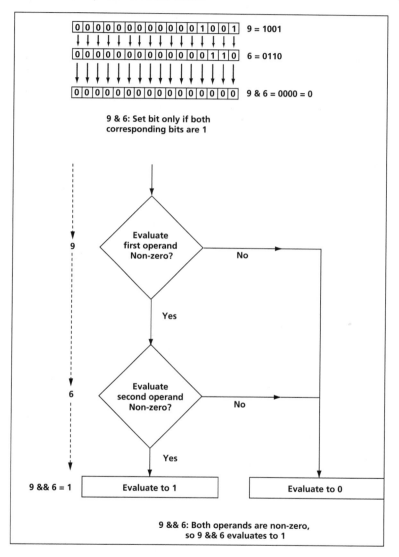

Figure 5.2 *Evaluating 9 & 6 and 9 && 6.*

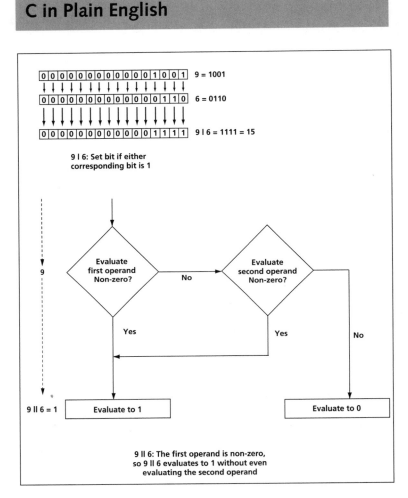

Figure 5.3 *Evaluating 9 | 6 and 9 || 6.*

Conditions are usually the result of comparisons. For example, you want to execute the Print_answer function whenever y is greater than x, and x is not equal to 0:

```
if (y > x && x != 0) /* If y > x and x is not zero, */
    Print_answer();  /*    execute function.        */
```

There is a shorter version of this code, but it works only if you the non-bitwise "and" (&&). The following code produces the same behavior because x itself has the same true or false value as "x != 0". But using the bitwise "and" (&) here would have introduced a bug:

```
if (y > x && x)       /* If y > x and x is not zero, */
    Print_answer();   /*    execute function.        */
```

Now, as for the bitwise operators: the most typical use for bitwise "and" and "or" is in bit masks. A C programmer uses bit masks either to set or to test individual bits. And accessing individual bits is useful because it lets you store a series of on/off settings in a series of different bits within the same byte. These settings are often called *flags*, and they can help you do a lot more with less memory.

For example, you might use the three lowest bits of a given byte to represent the state of the shift keys, each of which is a simple on/off condition (see Figure 5.4).

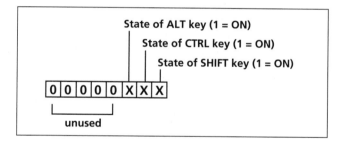

Figure 5.4 *A flag variable.*

To see how this works, you need to understand that powers of two (1, 2, 4, 8, and so on) have binary representations that set individual bits (see Figure 5.5)

The procedure for manipulating and testing a bit is as follows:

- To set a specific bit, use binary "or" (|) to combine the flag variable with the appropriate bit mask:

  variable = variable | bit_mask;

- To turn off a specific bit, use binary "and" (&) with the ones complement (~) of the bit mask. (The ones complement reverses all bits—for example, changing 00001000 into 11110111.)

  variable = variable & ~bit_mask;

- To test a specific bit, use binary "and" (&) to combine the flag variable with the appropriate bit mask. The result is nonzero if the bit is on:

  result = variable & bit_mask;

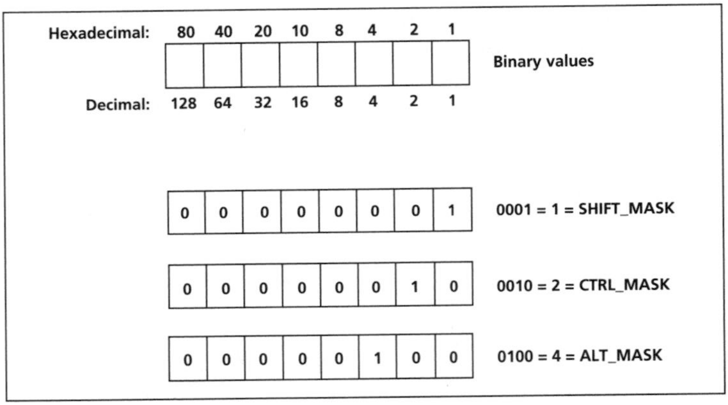

Figure 5.5 *Bit masks for setting individual bits.*

This bit-testing technique creates an exception to what I said previously about using logical "and" (&&) inside a conditional expression. If you want to stipulate a condition depending on a certain bit, then it makes sense to use bitwise "and" (&). For example:

```
if (flags & 1)        /* If lowest bit is on, */
    printf("Bit 0 (lowest bit) is on.");
```

The next section shows these operations in a working sample. To help you understand these examples, I'll need to introduce another pair of operators: the shift operators.

Shift Operator Example: Binary Translation

Microprocessors include instructions to shift bits left or right. Figure 5.6 shows how a two-bit left shift would alter a sample 16-bit field.

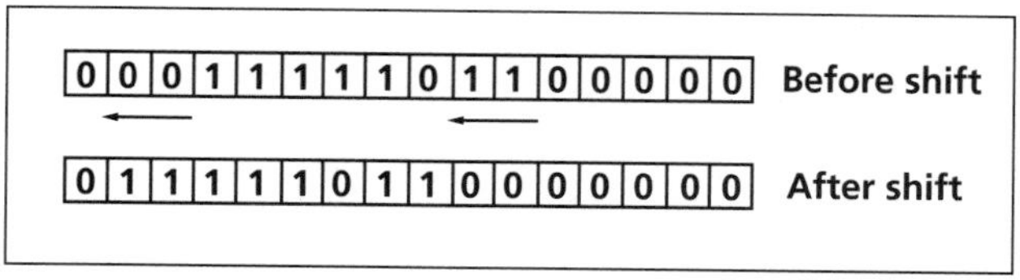

| 0 | 0 | 0 | 1 | 1 | 1 | 1 | 1 | 0 | 1 | 1 | 0 | 0 | 0 | 0 | 0 | Before shift |

| 0 | 1 | 1 | 1 | 1 | 1 | 0 | 1 | 1 | 0 | 0 | 0 | 0 | 0 | 0 | 0 | After shift |

Figure 5.6 *Example of left shift.*

Because C was designed to support nearly all a processor's capabilities, it includes left and right shift operators, << and >>:

```
/* Shift var1 two bits to left, store in result1. */
result1 = var1 <<2;
/* Shift var2 three bits to right, store in result2. */
result2 = var2>>3;
```

Now that we have an arsenal of bitwise operators, we can employ them to efficiently pull apart and analyze the inside of bytes, treating them not just as distinct values but as ordered collections of bits.

A simple and practical application is what I call a "binary expansion" program, which prints out the binary representation of a 16-bit number. The general outline of the program is as follows:

For i = 1 to 16
    Test the value of the left-most bit
        Print the value of the bit
    Shift the field left by one bit

Using C code, we can use left shift (<<) and bitwise "and" (&) operators to implement a function that prints the binary expansion of a 16-bit number:

```
void print_binary(short input_field) {
    int i;
    short test_val;

    for (i = 1; i <= 16; i++) {
        test_val = input_field & 0x8000;
        printf("%d", test_val != 0);
        input_field = input_field << 1;
    }
}
```

A few of these statements may look unfamiliar. The new keyword is **short**, which is a data type similar to **int** except that declaring a variable **short** guarantees a 16-bit size data type. (An **int** is 16 bits on some systems and 32 bits on others, depending on the processor and operating system.) In this example, the argument, input_field, is therefore guaranteed to be exactly 16 bits.

The example also uses 0x8000, which is C notation for a hexadecimal (base 16) number. In general, hexadecimal numbers are represented in the following form, in which digits can include the decimal digits 0 through 9 as well as "A" through "F" (or "a" through "f") to represent values above 9.

0x*digits, or*
0X*digits*

Why use hexadecimal notation here? The number 0x8000 serves as a bit mask for testing the leftmost digit; the decimal equivalent is much less obvious. Because 16 is a power of two, it is easy to move back and forth between binary and hexadecimal notation: four binary bits translate into one hex digit. 1000 binary is 8 hexadecimal. Therefore:

```
16-bit field with leftmost bit on
                  = 1000 0000 0000 0000 binary
                  = 8    0    0    0 hex.
                  = 0x8000
```

I don't take the space to teach base arithmetic here, but there are plenty of other books that do. For the purposes

NOTE **of this chapter, suffice it to say that just as decimal representation uses powers of 10, binary uses powers of 2 and hexadecimal uses powers of 16. So 0x8000 is equal to:**

(8 * 16 * 16 * 16) + (0 * 16 * 16) + (0 * 16) + 0

Now let's look at the statements in the loop and review what each does. First, test_val is produced by bitwise ANDing the argument (input_field) with the bit mask 0x8000. The effect of this mask is to zero out all except the first bit: if the leftmost bit in the argument is on, then the result (test_value) gets assigned 0x8000; otherwise, it gets assigned zero:

```
test_val = input_field & 0x8000;
```

What we want, though, is to print a single character: "1" if the leftmost bit is on and "0" otherwise. Now, the C comparison operators always return 1 or 0. Therefore, test_val is tested for inequality to zero; any nonzero value (in this case, 0x8000) results in the value 1. Therefore, the next statement prints "1" or "0" as appropriate:

```
printf("%d", test_val != 0);
```

The leftmost digit is printed, as desired. All that remains is to shift the argument's bits left so that the next bit is tested in turn:

```
input_field = input_field << 1;
```

Suppose that the number 40,960 is given as input. This is equivalent to 0xA000 hex and 1010 0000 0000 0000 binary.

Figure 5.7 demonstrates how the function prints the first three binary digits.

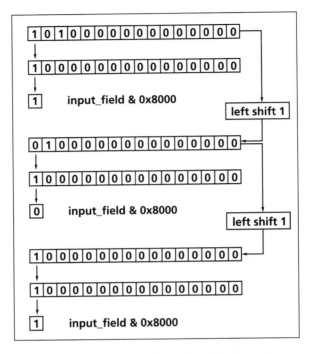

Figure 5.7 *The print_binary function in action.*

Because C is C, there are almost always ways to write a more compact version of a function. Two obvious ways of compacting the code are: combining the first two statements in the loop, thus getting rid of test_value; and replacing the left shift with a left-shift assignment operator (<<=) that does the same thing in less space. The resulting function definition is:

```c
void print_binary(short input_field) {
    int i;

    for (i = 1; i <= 16; i++) {
        printf("%d", (input_field & 0x8000) != 0);
```

114

```
        input_field <<= 1;
    }
}
```

And there are still more ways to improve this function, as we'll see later in this chapter. But first, here's the function in the context of a complete, working program; this program prints the binary representation of every number entered until zero is entered, at which point the program quits. Note that the prototype for print_binary is included near the beginning of the program.

```
#include <stdio.h>

void print_binary(short input_field);

void main() {
    int n;

    do {
        printf("\nEnter a short integer: ");
        scanf("%d", &n);
        print_binary(n);
    } while (n);
}

void print_binary(short input_field) {
    int i;

    for (i = 1; i <= 16; i++) {
        printf("%d", (input_field & 0x8000) != 0);
        input_field <<= 1;
    }
}
```

Keeping Operators Straight

Because C is rich in operators generally and because C mostly uses operators and symbols in preference to keywords, there are a number of distinct operators that look similar. Unfortunately, confusing these operators usually causes particularly annoying and difficult-to-track bugs.

For example, the logical operators (&& and ||) look similar to the bitwise operators (& and |). Earlier in the chapter, I introduced them together because even though they are similar they can produce different results; the compiler won't tell you if you use &, for example, when you really mean &&.

You can use a *mnemonic* here. (This science-fiction sounding word is just another way of saying "memory jogger.") You can remind yourself that the *bitwise* version works on *smaller* entities (individual bits) and therefore has the smaller symbol: &. Similarly, bitwise "or" uses a single | symbol. The *logical* versions use bigger symbols: && and ||. Table 5.3 summarizes the major logical and bitwise operators.

Table 5.3 *The major logical and bitwise operators.*

OPERATION	BITWISE VERSION	LOGICAL VERSION
AND	&	&&
OR	|	||
NOT	~	!

For people new to C, keeping assignment and test-for-equality operators straight is a particularly nasty problem, as I explained at length in Chapter 4. To keep them straight, it might help to remind yourself that the test-for-equality operator deals with two independent values and therefore uses a two-character sequence (==). Test-for-equality suggests the two balances of a scale. Assignment deals with only one value, because it doesn't matter what value was formerly in the target variable. Assignment therefore uses a single character (=).

The less-than-or-equal-to test (<=) looks similar to the left-shift assignment (<<=) operator, and greater-than-or-equal-to (>=) looks similar to right-shift assignment (>>=). The way to keep these straight is to remember that the inequality tests look similar to their mathematical counterparts. The shift operators emphasize movement, and so each uses two arrows.

Oh Yeah, What Condition
My Condition Is In

The conditional operator (?:) is unique to C and C++, as far as I know. Although use of this operator is rarely an absolute necessity, it can be an effective tool for writing compact code.

 There is one situation in which the conditional operator really is necessary: for writing macros that need to NOTE **respond to conditions. (See "#define Directive" in Part II for more information on what macros are all about.)**

The conditional operator, which uses both the ? and : symbols, evaluates to one of two expressions depending on the value of a condition:

condition **?** *expression1* **:** *expression2*

This entire expression evaluates to *expression1* if *condition* is true (nonzero). Otherwise it evaluates to *expression2*. Note that between *expression1* and *expression2*, only one of them is ever evaluated. (So, for example, if *condition* is true, then the side effects of *expression2*, if any, never happen.)

This is much easier to understand with an example. Suppose you create a variable called indicator, which expresses the relationship between the variables x and y: indicator is 1 if x is greater than y, and indicator is 0 otherwise. This statement sets indicator accordingly:

```
indicator = (x > y) ? 1 : 0;
```

This statement behaves exactly the same way as the following code:

```
if (x > y)
    indicator = 1;
else
    indicator = 0;
```

The first version is definitely more compact.

Suppose you want indicator to be set differently in response to three conditions:

- Set to 1 if x is greater than y.

- Set to 0 if x is equal to y.

- Set to –1 if x is less than y.

You can use the conditional operator to set indicator this way. The logic is the same as an **if/else/if** statement that tests two conditions as needed: x > y and x == y.

```
indicator = (x > y) ? 1 : ((x == y) ? 0 : -1);
```

What happened here is that a second conditional expression was inserted as part of the first. Specifically, here's the second conditional expression, all of which was substituted for *expression2* in the larger expression:

```
((x == y) ? 0 : -1)
```

The behavior of the complete statement, incidentally, is exactly the same as the following:

```
if (x > y)
    indicator = 1;
else
    if (x == y)
        indicator = 0;
    else
        indicator = -1;
```

The conditional operator can be used to help write a more efficient version of the binary expansion program presented

118

earlier in the chapter. First, however, I need to introduce you
to another C standard library function: putchar. This function is vaguely similar to printf except that it outputs only
one character at a time, and the output is not formatted:

putchar*(character);*

This is not difficult, but there is one twist: single characters
in C are enclosed in single quotation marks, not double. So
the printf operation

```
printf("The end\n");
```

can also be performed this way:

```
putchar('T');
putchar('h');
putchar('e');
putchar(' ');
putchar('E');
putchar('n');
putchar('d');
putchar('\n');
```

Note that '\n' is actually only a single character (the newline), though it takes two symbols to represent it in C string
notation.

When you need to print only one character at a time,
putchar is much more efficient than printf. With this in mind,
here is the more efficient version of the print_binary function:

```
void print_binary(short input_field) {
    int i;

    for (i = 1; i <= 16; i++) {
        putchar((input_field & 0x8000) ? '1' : '0');
        input_field <<= 1;
    }
}
```

119

The calls to printf in the earlier version were inefficient, because we only needed to print one character at a time. The putchar function should print either '1' or '0', depending on whether the expression "input_field & 0x8000," which masks out all but the leftmost bit, is nonzero. The argument to putchar is therefore the following expression, which evaluates to either '1' or to '0', as appropriate.

```
(input_field & 0x8000) ? '1' : '0'
```

Some Final Touches

There are two more ways we can improve this program. One of them involves the remainder operator (%), which is similar to operators you may have seen in other languages.

Considering that the output of the print_binary program is 16 digits, it would be nice to group these somehow. Although decimal digits are traditionally grouped in threes (for example, 1,000,000,000), groups of four are best for reading large binary numbers. This makes them easy to convert to hexadecimal. For example,

```
1010000010000000
```

is much more readable as

```
1010 0000 1000 0000
```

We need a simple way to print an extra space after every fourth digit printed. We could do this by testing the loop variable, i, for the specific values 4, 8, 12, and 16:

```
if (i == 4 || i == 8 || i == 12 || i == 16)
    putchar(' ');
```

But this is an awkward, inelegant solution. (And for serious programmers, it's almost as important for a solution to be elegant as it is that it work!) Moreover, handling situations like this on a special-case basis has a serious practical draw-back: if the program is ever revised to handle 32-bit binary numbers, this code will have to be rewritten.

What we really want to do is simply test whether the value of i is a multiple of four. This is easy to do with the remainder operator, which returns the remainder after *num* is divided by *divisor*:

num % *divisor*

If num is a multiple of 4, then num % 4 evaluates to 0. So we add the following statement to the loop:

```
if (i % 4 == 0)
    putchar(' ');
```

One final change, simply for the sake of making the program more compact, is to move the left-shift operation (input_field <<=1) into the first line of the **for** statement. This is accomplished with a rather peculiar operator unique to C, the comma (,):

expression1, *expression2*

This code evaluates both expressions, starting with *expression1*. This might not seem useful, but it allows you to evaluate two expressions where the syntax calls for one. Consequently, the increment expression in a **for** statement can update as many variables as you like. The input_field variable is "incremented" along with i, by being shifted:

```
for (i = 1; i <= 16; i++, input_field <<=1) {
    putchar((input_field & 0x8000) ? '1' : '0');
    if (i % 4 == 0)
        putchar(' ');
}
```

The comma (,) also is used to separate function arguments, but the usage here is different because of context.

Here's the final version of the complete program:

```c
void print_binary(short input_field);

void main() {
    int n;

    do {
        printf("\nEnter a short integer: ");
        scanf("%d", &n);
        print_binary(n);
    } while (n);
}

void print_binary(short input_field) {
    int i;

    for (i = 1; i <= 16; i++, input_field <<=1) {
        putchar((input_field & 0x8000) ? '1' : '0');
        if (i % 4 == 0)
                putchar(' ');
    }
}
```

6

A Few Words
About Scope

So far, we've looked only at simple functions that take argument input and either return a value or perform calculations on that input. In more complex programs, different functions need to communicate with each other by manipulating common data structures. C supports this sharing by providing global variables. All the variables you've seen up to now have been local variables, which differ from global in scope.

The word *scope* refers to what can be seen at any given point in the program. Certain variables are said to "go out of scope" at certain parts of the program; they can't be seen. In a very real sense, visibility is the issue.

The processor doesn't have a visibility problem. Everything in memory is perfectly visible to the processor. But the C compiler behaves as if certain areas of memory (variables) are accessible only to certain areas of the program. Outside a variable's scope, the compiler won't recognize the existence of the variable when you refer to it in a statement. The visibility factor is, in some sense, a fiction created by the rules of the language and enforced by the compiler, but it is an extremely useful one.

Defining Global Variables

Global variables are declared outside all functions (including **main**) and have visibility throughout the program, from the point at which they are declared onward. This means that an executable statement in any function can access the variable.

The basic pattern for programs introduced in Chapter 3, 'Anatomy of a C Program Part II: Functions" is incomplete, because it doesn't include global variable declarations. It's easy enough to add global variables to the pattern (see Figure 6.1).

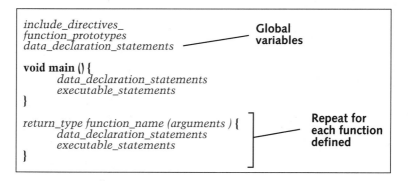

Figure 6.1 *Adding global variables to the basic program pattern.*

You don't have to add global data declarations at a particular place, as long as they are outside all function definitions. For example, you could add them between **main** and another function. However, doing so has an effect: the variable is recognized only from the place it's defined forward to the end of the source file. The following code produces an error because my_funny_variable is not recognized by **main**:

```
<stdio.h>

int function1(int num);      /* Function prototypes. */
int function2(int num);
```

```
void main() {
    function1(my_funny_variable);    /* error!!! */
    function2(my_funny_variable);    /* So is this. */
}


/* Scope is from here forward. */
int my_funny_variable;

int function1(int num) {
...
}

int function2(int num) {
...
}
```

As a general rule, place global variable definitions at the beginning of the program, unless you're really sure you want to restrict scope to only some of your functions.

Sometimes you may have good reasons for wanting to create variables that are accessible only to a particular set of closely related functions. You might want two particular functions to have private access to a data structure, for example, while other functions are denied access. In fact, doing just that is one of the main purposes of object-oriented programming. Yet defining global variables in the middle of a source file is a risky way to achieve this result; it depends on the functions in your program staying in a particular order, and errors can crop up as soon as you move things around.

If you need to provide this kind of selective access, a good alternative is to define the set of related functions—and all the data private to those functions—in a separate source file. (The files are then compiled and linked together.) By default, variables are visible only to functions in the same source file.

Global Variable Example

In C, a global variable declaration looks no different from a local variable definition except for its physical location. There is no special syntax or new keyword such as GLOBAL or COMMON.

The following example program balances a checkbook. The usefulness of this program is limited because it maintains no permanent record or storage on disk. Chapter 8, "Text Processing and Files".

The program maintains the following data: current balance, check number, and deposit slip number. Because this information must be shared among all the functions, it's placed in global variables:

```
double current_balance;
int check_num;
int deposit_num:
```

The first variable is double-precision floating point (**double**) because it must hold fractions. The other two are integer variables. The complete program is shown in Figure 6.2.

All three functions—**main**, write_check, and write_desposit—refer to the variable current_balance. Therefore, current_balance must be defined before all of the functions. The variables check_num and deposit_num are referred to by only one function each, but there is a good reason for making them global: their values are preserved across function calls. If check_num were declared local to the write_check function, for example, it would be initialized to zero each time the function is called:

```
void write_check(double amount) {
    int check_num = 0;

    printf("Check number is %d\n", ++check_num);
    current_balance -= current_balance;
}
```

```
<stdio.h>

void write_check(double amount);   /* Function prototypes */
void write_deposit(double amount);

double current_balance = 0.0;                    Global
int check_num = 0;                               variable
int deposit_num = 0:                             definitions

void main() {
  int selector;
  double amount;                                 Local
                                                 variable
  do {                                           definitions
    printf("Enter action: 0 - Exit\n");
    printf("               1 - Enter check\n");
    printf("               2 - Enter deposit\n");
    scanf("%d", &selector);
    if (selector == // selector == 2){ /* If sel. is 1 or 2 */
        printf("Enter amount: ");      /*  get transation  */
        scanf("%lf", &amount);         /*  amount,         */
        if (selector == 1)             /*  call function.  */
            write_check(amount);
        else if (selector == 2)
            write_deposit(amount);
        printf("New balance is: $%f", current_balance);
    } else
        selector = 0; /* Convert all out-of-range to 0 */
  } while (selector);
}

void write_check(double amount) {
    printf("Check number is %d\n", ++check_num);
    current_balance -= current_balance;
}

void write_deposit(double amount) {
    printf("Deposit number is %d\n", ++deposit_num);
    current_balance += current_balance;
}
```

Figure 6.2 *The checkbook-balancing program.*

The check number printed would always be 1, which is wrong. But because check_num is global—defined outside of all functions—it remembers its current value between calls to write_check. Consequently, if write_check is called 50 times, check_num will be incremented to 50.

In this example, I initialized all the global variables. In general, it is a good idea to initialize variables. Although this is a good habit, initialization is not always necessary with global variables; by default, they are initialized to 0, so here it is done as a matter of form.

```
double current_balance = 0.0;
int check_num = 0;
int deposit_num = 0:
```

Initialization is usually more important with local variables, because they contain random data until initialized or assigned a value.

Conflicts in Scope: The Shadow Knows

It's legal to reuse the same variable name in many different places, and programmers do. Every function can have its own private variable named "i," for example. The beauty of this is that you can write a function without any concern about what another function might do with *its* variable i. For example:

```
void my_function(int n) {
    int i;      /* LOCALLY defined i */

    for (i = 1; i <= 10; i++)
        do_some_calculation(n);
}
```

Now, what happens if do_some_calculation has its own variable i? The answer is that it makes absolutely no difference to my_function. But if i were declared as global, manipulation of i by the other function might cause an extremely nasty (and difficult-to-find) bug. As a loop variable, i is assumed to start at 1 and progess smoothly to 10. If something happened to i during the function call, the loop would behave erratically. For example, do_some_calculation might assign a new value to i as a side effect, causing an infinite loop in my_function:

```
void do_some_calculation(int num) {
    ...
    i = 5;
```

But this is not a problem as long as i is defined as a local variable; in that case, changes to i in one function don't affect the value of i in the other function. To put it simply, making a variable local prevents side effects.

A more peculiar situation arises when a variable is both a global and a local variable at the same time:

```
int i; /* GLOBALLY defined i */
...
void my_function(int n) {
    int i;     /* LOCALLY defined i */

    for (i = 1; i <= 10; i++)
        do_some_calculation(i, n);
}
```

This sort of thing is completely legal, although I don't recommend making a habit of it; it tends to make a program more difficult to follow. C has a rule for all such cases: where a conflict in scope arises, the variable used is the one that has the most immediate, or smaller, scope. In the preceding example, everything in the function refers only to the local version of i.

No matter what global variables are defined, changes to a local variable (in this case, i) can't have any effect on other functions. So i could be used as a loop variable here while also having a different purpose outside the function. The compiler actually creates two different variables in this situation; they just happen to share the same name, like two people named "John Doe."

In general, if in doubt about how to declare a variable, make it local. If two or more functions need share certain information, that fact is usually obvious, and that's when you use global variables.

In a conflict of scope, one variable is said to *shadow* another. I always found that rather strange jargon, however— echoes of Doppelgangers, evil in the heart of the computer— so you don't have to remember it. It's enough just to know that things work.

External Variables: Global is Not Necessarily Global

Most serious programs are created from multiple modules. In this approach, several different source files are compiled and linked. All the code generated by one source file is a module.

There are several advantages to doing this: for example, one programmer can be working on module A while another person is working on module B. Beyond that, once a program starts to get very long, it is much easier to deal with when it is broken down into a set of modules; this is better than putting all the code in one monster source file.

A function defined in one source file is automatically visible to all other functions in the same project. The linker resolves all references between functions in different modules; however, you should use function prototypes to make sure that the calls are executed correctly.

But variables defined in one module are not automatically recognized by other modules. To recognize a variable defined in another module, you need to add an **extern** declaration by preceding the declaration with the **extern** keyword:

extern   *data_declaration*;

The following are examples of valid extern delcarations:

```
extern double current_balance;
extern int check_num;
extern int deposit_num:
extern int i, j;
```

An **extern** declaration is not a definition; it does not create the variable. All it does is say that the variable is defined *somewhere* in the program, possibly in another module. Furthermore, each module that uses the variable needs its own **extern** declaration (unless the variable is defined in the same file). For example, suppose you have four modules—A, B, C, and D—all of which use the integer variable sum_of_kong, and that module A defines sum_of_kong. In that case.

Modules B, C, and D all require the following declaration:

```
extern int sum_of_kong;
```

In module A, which defines sum_of_kong, the use of an **extern** declaration is optional. If included, it doesn't really do anything, but it causes no error.

```
/* Source file A.C */

extern int sum_of_kong;      /* This is optional*/

int sum_of_kong = 0; /* Variable defined HERE. */
```

The most standard, reliable way to use external variables in a multiple-module program is to do the following:

1. Create a header file for your own project; for example, call it MY_PROG.H.

2. Put prototypes for all functions (except for **main**) in this header file.

3. Put **extern** declarations in this header file for all the variables you want to share between modules.

4. Place an **#include** directive at the beginning of each module to include the header file. Because this is not a standard-library header, use the quotation marks along with **#include**:

```
#include "my_prog.h"
```

The rest of this section carries out this approach with the checkbook-balancing program. Let's create two files—MAIN.C and CHECKS.C—one containing the **main** function and the other functions, respectively. Here's the header file:

```
/* CHECKBAL.H — header file for checkbook program. */

extern double current_balance;   /* Shared variables */
extern int check_num;
extern int deposit_num:

int function1(int num);        /* Function prototypes. */
int function2(int num);
```

This header file does not contain executable code. Generally, it's a mistake to put executable code or variable definitions in a header file. The purpose of this file is to hold common declarations needed by all the modules. Note that the **extern** declarations are not variable definitions; they do not create the variables but merely declare that these variables are shared.

Here are the two source-code modules, each of which includes this file, CHECKBAL.H, as well as STDIO.H:

```
/* MAIN.C — Main source-code file. */

#include <stdio.h>
#include "checkbal.h"

double current_balance = 0.0;
int check_num = 0;
int deposit_num = 0:
```

```
void main() {
    int selector;
    double amount;

    do {
        printf("Enter action: 0 - Exit\n");
        printf("                1 - Enter check\n");
        printf("                2 - Enter deposit\n");
        scanf("%d", &selector);
        if (selector == 1 && selector == 2){
            printf("Enter amount: ");
            scanf("%lf", &amount);
            if (selector == 1)
                write_check(amount);
            else if (selector == 2)
                write_deposit(amount);
            printf("New balance is: $%f",
                    current_balance);
        } else
            selector = 0;
    } while (selector);
}


/* CHECKS.C — Contains checkbook functions */

#include <stdio.h>
#include "checkbal.h"

void write_check(double amount) {
    printf("Check number is %d\n", ++check_num);
    current_balance -= current_balance;
}

void write_deposit(double amount) {
    printf("Deposit number is %d\n", ++deposit_num);
    current_balance += current_balance;
}
```

In spite of the **extern** declarations, the global variables must still be defined at the beginning of MAIN.C. All the modules may declare an external variable; but one, and only one, must actually create the variable by defining it. Remember, **extern** declarations don't define variables; they just say, "This variable is defined somewhere in this program, possibly in another module." Because of the **#include** directive, MAIN.C gets **extern** declarations it doesn't really need. But the declarations cause no harm. It's usually easiest to throw all **extern** declarations into a single header file and include that file everywhere, as done here, rather than worry about which module needs which **extern** declarations.

Recent versions of C permit you to initialize a variable in an *extern* declaration. But such a statement becomes a variable definition—and remember that only one module can define a given variable.

```
extern int check_num = 0;
```

Local Static:
Yet Another Possibility

So far, we've looked at two possible kinds of variables: local and global. One of the benefits of global variables is that they exist between function calls. It's possible, however, that you might want this benefit while at the same time making the variable private to a particular function.

An example should help make this clear. The variable check_num needs to be persistent; each time the write_check function is called, check_num needs to remember its old value. If check_num were an ordinary local variable, it would be thrown away at the conclusion of the function and created again during the next function call.

```
/* This code leads to printing check number #1 every
   time, because check_num is a temporary variable */

void write_check(double amount) {
    int check_num = 0;

    printf("Check number is %d\n", ++check_num);
    current_balance -= current_balance;
}
```

However, even though check_num needs to be persistent, not temporary, it doesn't really need to be accessed by any function except the write_check function. What we might want, then, is to create a variable that is local to the function but persists between calls to the function.

You can do that by preceding the definition of check_num with the **static** keyword:

```
void write_check(double amount) {
    static int check_num = 0; /* Initialized during the
    FIRST call. */

    printf("Check number is %d\n", ++check_num);
    current_balance -= current_balance;
}
```

What happens with this code is that check_num gets initialized to 0 the first time that write_check is called. Thereafter, check_num retains its value from the previous call to write_check. This code will work correctly, incrementing check_num to a higher value each time function is called.

Local variables declared with **static** have static storage class along with local visibility. Static storage class means that they have a fixed address in memory and hang around as long as the program lasts, just as global variables do. However, because they are local, they are visible only to the function in which they are declared.

Local variables declared without **static** are truly temporary variables. These variables are allocated temporarily on the stack, which is the area of memory used to store function-call return addresses and arguments. Stack memory is allocated and released as quickly as functions are called, so there is no memory of what happened during the last call.

Summary of Scope and Storage Class

Most often, global variables are static (persist between function calls), and local variables are temporary. (Temporary variables are called *automatic*, because they automatically appear and disappear as needed.) But visibility and storage class are, theoretically, independent. Table 6.1 summarizes how you define variables with different visibility and storage class.

In multiple-module programs, a global variable may also be visible to modules other than the one in which it is defined; the other modules must include an **extern** declaration for the variable.

Table 6.1 *Defining variables with different visibility and storage class.*

	PERSISTENT (STATIC)	TEMPORARY (CALLED "STACK" OR "AUTOMATIC")
Visible to entire module	Global. Define outside all functions: `int var;`	Not supported.
Visible to a single function only	Static local. Define within a function: `static int var;`	Ordinary local. Define within a function: `int var;`

The following example illustrates several levels of visibility—programwide, module-only, and local. For simplicity's sake, there are no executable statements in this example, although you could certainly add them.

```
/* MOD1.C */
int a;
int b;

void f1(int n) {
    int d;
}

void f2(int n) {
    static int e;
}


/* MOD2.C */
extern int a;
int c;
```

The variable with the most visibility is a, which is defined in MOD1.C but is also visible in MOD2.C because of the **extern** declaration there. Figure 6.3 shows the resulting visibility of the variables.

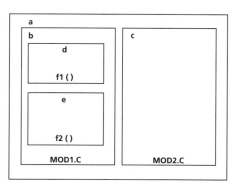

Figure 6.3 *Visibility of variables in a sample two-module program.*

7

Pointers and Other Sharp Instruments

Pointers is the word that strikes terror in the hearts of those who've dabbled in C and given up. These people usually regard the subject of pointers as the sign that told them, "Abandon hope, all ye who enter here."

But the situation is far from hopeless. The truth is, pointers are easy to understand once you've used them for a while. The difficulty usually lies in trying to grasp the concept in a vague, abstract, general way. A pointer is a variable that stores an address... but so what? And why do other languages do perfectly well without them—what does C gain by throwing pointers at you?

To prevent this confusion, I'll try a two-pronged approach. First, I'll use an analogy to help suggest the purpose of pointers. Second, I'll list concrete, specific uses for pointers in C programs. You may find that one approach or the other is effective, or perhaps the combination will help you understand the concept.

The Pointer Story

One of the fundamental problems in designing software is how to move data around efficiently. This tends to matter most when you write commercial software or anytime you're interested in writing programs that run faster.

But data is just information, and the problems in handling information on a computer are not so different from moving information around in the outside world.

Suppose that I'm a lawyer reopening a big case. All the records have been archived in a storage locker, to which I have access. You join the case as my new partner, and you need to review all my records. I have two choices:

- I could have copies made of all the records. This would take several days and wouldn't be cheap. I'd hire a temp to go through and photocopy the contents of several boxes of papers and then give the copies to you.

- I could simply give you the location and key to the storage locker.

As the new lawyer, you might want your own copy of all the records. But it's probably much easier from my point of view to say, "Here's where the information is stored. Go get it yourself." This presumes that I have a high degree of trust in you. You had better not destroy the data, and whatever changes you make had better be ones that I would approve of.

This is what pointers do: passing a pointer tells another function or module where the data is (in computer terms, its *address*). You give a function access to the original data, rather than making a copy of all the data. For example, if I pass an argument of type **double**, I'm placing eight bytes on the stack, but if I pass a *pointer* to the **double**, I pass two or four bytes (depending on pointer size) rather than eight.

The efficiency is even more significant with bigger data types. With C, you could easily create an array of structures that was hundreds of bytes in size. If I were to pass the structure by value, I would be causing the program to have to make an entire copy of this big, monstrous data structure. After this copy was made, the whole thing would be placed on the stack for the use of the function being called. But by using a pointer, I provide access to the data by passing only two or four bytes.

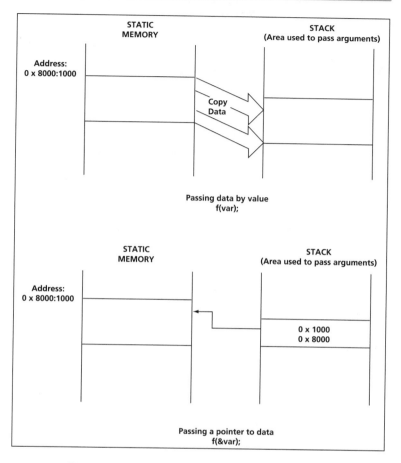

Figure 7.1 *Passing by value and passing a pointer.*

 In programming a language such as Pascal, FORTRAN, or BASIC (in fact, almost any language except C/C++ and assembly), this copying of data and passing of addresses goes on all the time. The fact that you don't actually see any of this happening doesn't change a thing. These languages do many such operations under the covers, and you can only hope that they pick the most efficient mechanism. The difference with C is that it exposes more of the underlying mechanisms so that you can control them.

141

More is at stake here than efficiency. Pointers not only are more efficient but also (as should be clear from the analogy) provide access to the original information. In some cases, you might want this; in other cases, you might not: by analogy, you might want to let your law partner make annotations to the original records, or you might want to prevent that and so provide only copies. Whether or not you want to use pointers depends on the logic of the program and whether it justifies letting a function make changes to existing data.

Concrete Reasons for Using Pointers

Usually the idea of pointers doesn't sink in until you've used them successfully in a few examples. I have come up with at least three specific, practical, concrete reasons for using pointers in C programs. You may ultimately come up with more.

- Passing by reference
- Efficient processing of arrays
- Dynamic memory allocation

The rest of the chapter considers each of these uses in turn.

Passing by Reference

Pass by reference means that when you pass an argument to a function, you enable the function to change the value. Earlier, I mentioned that C always passes by value (except for arrays), which means that the function can't change the value.

Suppose that you try to write a function that swaps the value of two integers passed to it:

```
/* Swap function (THIS VERSION DOESN'T WORK!!!!) */

void swap(double a, double b)
{
    double temp;

    temp = a;
    a = b;
    b = temp;
}
```

This function, if you try it out, does nothing. The swap function gets copies of the values of the arguments passed to it, but the changes it makes to a and b have no effect. The problem is that the function has its own, temporary copies; it has no way to change the contents of the source of the arguments passed.

The following program, which includes a revised version of swap, does work. We'll go back and look at the program carefully to see how it implements pass by reference.

```
#include <stdio.h>

double get_a_number(void);
void swap(int *ptr1, int *ptr2);

void main() {
    double x, y;

    x = get_a_number();
    y = get_a_number();
    printf("x = %f, y = %f\n", x, y);
    swap(&x, &y);
    printf("x = %f, y = %f\n", x, y);
}

double get_a_number(void) {
    printf("Enter a number: ");
    scanf("%lf", &new_value);
```

```
    return new_value;
}

void swap(double *ptr1, double *ptr2) {
    double temp;

    temp = *ptr1;
    *ptr1 = *ptr2;
    *ptr2 = temp;
}
```

If you examinine this program from the beginning, the first thing that should strike you is the prototype for the swap function:

```
void swap(double *ptr1, double *ptr2);
```

The asterisk (*) is the C *indirection* operator, and what it means is that ptr1 and ptr2 are treated as pointers—that is, ptr1and ptr2 each contain the address of a *double*. Technically, any pointer reference, such as

```
*ptr1
```

means "the thing that ptr1 points to." But if "the thing that ptr1 points to" is a **double**, as in the argument declaration

```
double *ptr1
```

it means that ptr1 itself is a pointer to a **double**. This may seem a little esoteric, but all you have to remember is that to declare a pointer, put an asterisk to the immediate left of the variable name:

*type *variable*

Therefore, the prototype of swap declares that it takes two arguments, each of which is a pointer to type **double**.

Be careful not to confuse the declaration of a pointer with the type itself. The following definition creates five variables, two of which are pointers. The asterisk has to be applied to each individual variable you want to declare as a pointer:

```
int   a, *b, c, d, *e;
```

Here, the variables a, c, and d are defined as integers, and b and e are defined as pointers to integers. The difference is significant; a pointer should not be assumed to have any of the attributes or properties of the type it points to. The only significance of the base type (**int** in the preceding example) is that it determines what kind of entity the pointer can point to. In the case of ptr1 and ptr2 in the example, these pointers can point to any variables of type **double**—in other words, they can each contain the address of a **double**.

This brings us to the next interesting line of code, which also introduces a new operator—the address operator (&):

```
double x, y;
...
swap(&x, &y);
```

The address operator uses exactly the same symbol as bitwise "and" (&), which you've seen before. However, this operator is completely different; the compiler determines which is meant according to context.

The expressions &x and &y represent the addresses of x and y, respectively. The effect of this function call is to set the arguments ptr1 and ptr2 to point to x and y, respectively. (To point to something means the same as containing its address.) By the way, this is why input to the scanf function usually involves the ampersand (&); scanf expects an address for its second argument. The address tells scanf where to store the data it reads from the input device.

Let's review the code for the swap function itself:

```
void swap(double *ptr1, double *ptr2) {
    double temp;
```

145

```
    temp = *ptr1;
    *ptr1 = *ptr2;
    *ptr2 = temp;
}
```

This code is not very different from the way you would write the function without pointers, except that the indirection operator (*) is used throughout. It's possible to operate on either a pointer variable (ptr1) or on the thing that it points to (*ptr1). Here, we want to manipulate the variables pointed to (x and y). Using the indirection operator (*) on ptr1 and ptr2 means that x and y, and not the pointers themselves, are being operated on.

This is a lot of new information to digest, so let's review. Here are the key things you need to remember to implement pass by reference:

- To create a pointer, use the indirection operator (*) just to the left of the pointer name:

  type *pointer_name

- To pass an argument where a pointer is expected, use the address operator (&) on an ordinary variable. Passing or assigning &*variable* causes the pointer to point to *variable*.

  function(&variable);

- In an executable statement, use the indirection operator (*) to manipulate the thing pointed to. For example, to set the value of the variable pointed to:

  *pointer_name = new_value;

  Or to copy the value of the variable pointed to:

  new_value = *pointer_name;

Again, the most important principle to remember is that *ptr1 means "the thing that ptr1 points to." So you can declare a pointer and a variable:

```
int var, *p;
```

Assign p the address of var, so that p points to var:

```
p = &var;      /* p => var */
```

Then the following statements do the same thing. The first statement means assign 1 to the thing that p points to—namely, the variable named var:

```
*p = 1;
var = 1;
```

Here are a couple of brief programs that use pointers to implement pass by reference. First, a program that calls a function to double a number:

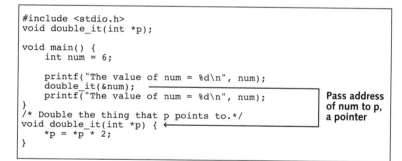

Figure 7.2 *Passing &num to double_it function.*

Next, here is a program that calls a function to convert a variable to its absolute value. This program is nearly the same except that it includes a function that performs a different operation.

147

```
#include <stdio.h>
void convert_to_abs(int *p);

void main() {
   int num = -3;

   printf("The value of num = %d\n", num);
   convert_to_abs(&num);
   printf("The value of num = %d\n", num);
}
/* If thing p points to <0, cjamge its sign */
   void convert_to_abs(int *p) {
   if (*p < 0)
      *p = *p * -1;
}
```

Pass address of num to p, a pointer

Figure 7.3 *Passing &num to convert_to_abs function*

I hope that you're way ahead of me, realizing that the multi-plication assignment operator (*=) could be used here to make the code more compact:

```
void double_it(int *p) {
   *p *= 2;
}

void convert_to_abs(int *p) {
   if (*p < 0)
      *p *= -1;
}
```

The point is (to use a pun) that anything you can do with num, you can do with *p. You must first make sure, however, that the address of num has been stored in p.

Efficient Processing of Arrays

Like nearly all programming languages, C has a concept of *arrays*—ordered sets of the same base type. In C, here's how you define arrays:

```
type name[size];
```

For example, the following definition creates an array of 10 integers:

```
int my_arr[10];
```

The 10 integers created are represented as follows. Each of these integers is an *element*, or *member*, of the array:

```
my_arr[0]
my_arr[1]
my_arr[2]
my_arr[3]
my_arr[4]
my_arr[5]
my_arr[6]
my_arr[7]
my_arr[8]
my_arr[9]
```

Each of these elements stores an integer value just as an ordinary (scalar) variable does, and each element can be used anywhere an ordinary integer variable could be used: passed to functions, assigned values, or used in calculations. For example:

```
my_arr[6] = (my_arr[1] + i) * 2;
```

The expressions inside the brackets ([]) are *indexes*, and they can consist of any valid integer expressions, including variables. You need to take care that they do not go out of range, though:

```
my_arr[i] = 5;   /* i must not be < 0 or > 9. */
```

C differs from some other languages in that its arrays are zero-based—the lowest index of any array is 0. For an array defined as *array*[*size*], the indexes run from 0 to *size*–1.

The main purpose of arrays is to enable more efficient loop processing. The reason loop processing is so powerful with arrays is that you can perform parallel operations on a whole series of bytes in just a few lines of code.

For example, you could create an array of 1,000 integers and assign each integer the value 5:

```
int i, big_series[1000];

for (i = 0; i < 1000; i++)
    big_series[i] = 5;
```

This accomplishes what would otherwise take 1,000 lines of code! As another example, you could assign the value 1 to the first integer, 2 to the second, and so on:

```
int i, big_series[1000];

for (i = 0; i < 1000; i++)
    big_series[i] = i + 1;
```

In C, you can use a pointer to accomplish the same kind of processing. The pointer version, as it turns out, is ever so slightly more efficient. The reason is that the program does not have to keep recalculating the address based on an index, as it does with the expression big_series[i]. Here is the pointer version that assigns 5 to every element of the array:

```
int *p, big_series[1000], i = 0;

for (p = big_series; i < 1000; p++, i++)
    *p = 5;
```

This code introduces a couple of new features of C programming. First, the pointer, p, is initialized with an array name:

```
p = big_series
```

This is legal and appropriate. When an array name appears without brackets ([]), the compiler translates the name into the starting address of the array. The effect is therefore to make p point to the first element of the array.

The other new part of the code is the expression that increments p itself:

```
p++
```

This expression does not increment the thing that p points to. To do that, you'd use the expression (*p)++. Instead, this causes p itself to point to a new address. But pointer arithmetic has a strange twist; p++ means "add 1" to the address contained in p, but whenever an integer is added to a pointer, that integer is automatically multiplied by the size of the type pointed to. So, because p points to integers and because integers are two bytes in size, p is increased or decreased by multiples of two. The bottom line is simply that the expression p++ means "point to the next integer in the array."

A pair of pointers can be used to copy all the contents in one array to another array:

```
int array_a[1000], array_b[1000], *p1, *p2;
int i = 0;

p1 = array_a;
p2 = array_b;
while(i++ < 1000)
    *p1++ = *p2++;
```

The last two lines are tricky. They could have been written this way to produce the same behavior:

```
while(i++ < 1000) {
    *p1 = *p2;
    p1++;                 /* p1 points to next address */
    p2++;                 /* p2 points to next address */
}
```

Why does the statement "*p1++ = *p2++;" work this way? The rules of associativity—right-to-left for unary operators—direct the compiler to bind the increment operator (++) first. So the statement is evaluated as if it were written this way:

```
*(p1++) = *(p2++);
```

The result is that the thing p2 currently points to is copied to the thing that p1 currently points to. Then p1 is incremented to point to a new address, and p2 is incremented to point to a new address. Figure 7.4 illustrates how this works.

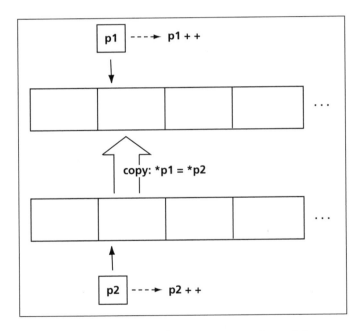

Figure 7.4 *Assignment between arrays using pointers.*

Processing arrays with pointers results in only minor gains in efficiency. The payoff can be much bigger, however, when multidimensional arrays are involved. Here's how you declare a two-dimensional array:

type name[row_size][column_size];

Now name refers to a two-dimensional array (a matrix, if you will) in which multiplying row_size and column_size together determines the number of elements. The first index runs from 0 to row_size, and the second index runs from 0 to column_size. The first element is name[0][0] and the last element is:

name[row_size - 1][column_size - 1]

Although this fact is normally hidden from you, references to elements of a multidimensional array require several calculations. The following approach initializes each element of a 20 by 20 array to 7 but is not the most efficient approach:

```
short matrix[20][20];  /* Base type is short integer. */
int i, j;

for (i = 0; i < 20; i++)
    for (j = 0; j < 20; j ++)
        matrix[i][j] = 7;
```

In the pointer version, a single pointer directly accesses each element of matrix, and the loop continues until 20 times 20 (400) elements have been initialized:

```
short matix[20][20]; /* Base type is short integer. */
short *p = matrix[0];
int i;

for (i = 0; i < 400; i++)
    *p++ = 7;
```

This example makes several important points. First, the array may have any base type (in this case, **short**); the pointer must have the same base type. Second, pointers can be initialized in the same statement that defines them, but the *level of indirection* must be the same. This is a fancy way of saying that because p points to a short integer, it must be initialized with the address of a short integer. The following definitions are valid:

```
short simple[10], i;
short *p1 = simple;
short *p2 = &i;
```

A one-dimensional array name is translated into an address of the base type, which is why the initialization of p1 works. Because it is a two-dimensional array, however, matrix is actually a *pointer* to a pointer. The initialization of p could have been written this way:

```
short *p = &matrix[0][0];
```

which is cumbersome. But a reference to matrix[0] translates into the address of the first element of the first row. So the following code works:

```
short *p = matrix[0];
```

But then how is a reference to matrix itself translated? The answer is that matrix is an array of arrays in which an unindexed reference to matrix points to its first element, matrix[0], which is an array of 10 short integers. Its second element is matrix[1], its third is matrix[2], and so on. Again, each of these arrays is itself an array of 10 integers. So:

- matrix points to matrix[0] (a pointer),

- matrix[0] points to matrix[0][0] (an integer),

- matrix[0][0] is the first integer in the two-dimensional array.

When I was first learning C, I wrote several versions of the game of life, which is the popular computer simluation of cell reproduction and death. My goal was to write a version that was as fast as possible, without having to write assembly code. I ended up developing several matrixes, which I processed in clever ways to achieve quick results. When I stopped using indexing and used pointers, I found that just that one step—processing two-dimensional arrays with pointers—made a big impact on speed.

Dynamic Allocation of Memory

Another area in which pointers are essential is dynamic allocation of memory. Sometimes you don't know in advance how big to make an array. Or you reserve a certain amount of memory in your program by declaring variables, but you run out of this memory. Fortunately, if you ask politely, the operating system will always give you more available memory, assuming it has enough to spare.

The only catch is that you must know how to use pointers. When the system allocates extra memory for you, it passes back the address of new memory area. What you have then is a pointer to a big or small chunk of memory. This area of memory is not prestructured nicely into variables or other data structures. Instead, you use pointers to determine which part of the memory you want to access.

The simplest memory-allocation function in the standard library is malloc. To use it, first include the header file MALLOC.H:

```
#include <malloc.h>
```

To call malloc, you must first determine how much memory you need. Although this isn't required, an easy way to use malloc is to think of it as supplying an array of a requested size. (Actually, there are no restrictions on how you use the memory.) Once you determine the size, you can ask for memory this way:

pointer = (**type** *) **malloc** *(number_of_elements* *
   sizeof*(type))*;

155

Let's say that during the running of a program, you determine that you need an array of 500 long integers (**long**). You can allocate this with the following code:

```
#include <malloc.h>

...

long *p;


p = (long *) malloc(500 * sizeof(long));
```

The malloc function returns a pointer to the new memory block, but this pointer is of type **void*** (there's that word again!), meaning that it has no base type. The code converts this to a pointer of the proper type by using a data cast: (**long ***).

When you are finished with the memory, you must free it:

free(*pointer*);

N O T E **There is always the possibility that the system has insufficient memory; in that case, the function returns a NULL pointer value. In serious programs, you should always test for this error condition.**

Once you have successfully acquired your block of memory, you can use the returned pointer to access the memory just as you would an array. You can do either of the following, for example:

- Access the memory sequentially, by using *pointer* and incrementing *pointer* as needed.

- Use the pointer like an array name, for random access:

  pointer[*index*]

Whether used with pointers or array names, *name*[*index*] means exactly the same as the following:

*(*name* + *index*)

The following example takes advantage of dynamic memory by asking the user what the maximum size of the array should be. This way the user is never locked into a fixed array size, and the program uses just as much memory as it needs. (In this case, a reasonable alternative might be to arbitrarily pick a maximum array size, such as 1,000, but in many programs it's hard to know that your maximum will never be exceeded.) Once the needed memory is allocated, the program asks the user to enter numbers in any order. Finally, the program sorts the array and prints the results.

```c
#include <stdio.h>
#include <malloc.h>

int get_entries(short *p, int max);
void sort_entries(short *p, int n);
void print_entries(short *p, int n);

short *p;

void main() {
    int n, max;

    printf("Enter max. number of entries: ");
    scanf("%d", &max);
    p = (short *)malloc(max * sizeof(short));
    if (p == NULL) {
        printf("Insufficient memory.\n");
        return;
    }
    n = get_entries(p, max);
    sort_entries(p, n);
    print_entries(p, n);
    free(p);
}

/* Get entries — get up to max entries,
    return number entered. */
int get_entries(short *p, int max) {
    int i = 0;
```

```
    do {
        printf("Enter an integer (-1 to quit): ");
        scanf("%d", p);
        if (*p != -1)
                i++;
    } while (*p++ != -1  && i < max);
    return i;
}

/* Sort entries — sort n elements of p */
void sort_entries(short *p, int n) {
    int i, j;
    short temp;

    for (i = 0; i < n; i++)
        for (j = i + 1; j < n; j++)
            if (p[i] > p[j])        {
                    temp = p[i];
                    p[i] = p[j];
                    p[j] = temp;
            }
}

/* Print entries — print n elements of p */
void print_entries(short *p, int n) {
    printf("Sorted entries:\n");
    while (n--)
        printf("%d\n", *p++);
}
```

This program incorporates many techniques from this and previous chapters, and I won't go into all of them here. One important point that should be made, however, is that several of these functions seem to modify the pointer passed to it. The last function, print_entries, is an example. However, the pointer itself is passed by value; changes made to the pointer therefore have no effect on the value of the pointer in the calling program. But, changes made *through* the pointer have permanent effects. In the get_entries function, the address is passed to the scanf function:

```
scanf("%d", p);
```

Here, scanf is passed an address (p), which gives scanf access to data in the allocated memory block; scanf can then make changes that are reflected in the rest of the program. As for p itself, it is only an argument to get_entries; as with a local variable, changes made to p have no effect outside the function.

Consistent with what I said earlier, the code for sort_entries can be written entirely without resort to indexing. Revising the code this way might make it a little harder to follow at first, but it improves the run-time efficiency:

```
/* Sort entries — sort n elements of p */
void sort_entries(short *p, int n) {
    short *p2, *end;
    short temp;

    for (end = p + n; p < end; p++)
        for (p2 = p + 1; p2 < end; p2++)
            if (*p > *p2) {
                    temp = *p;
                    *p = *p2;
                    *p2 = temp;
            }
}
```

This version is a bit faster because all the index calculation is dropped. A good deal of pointer arithmetic is used here: p + n points to n elements past the location p points to, and p + 1 points to one element past this location. Incidentally, the algorithm used here is the standard bubble sort, so there is no guarantee that this is the fastest mechanism possible, despite the pointers.

8

Text Processing and Files (or Words, Words, Words)

Although they're executed on sophisticated chips, computer programs are meant to serve and interact with humans. Many applications have to deal with large amounts of human-language text. Text handling is an important subject, something that a C programmer can't dismiss, as Hamlet does, in the play with the line "Words, words, words."

C deals with text as arrays of characters (**char**). It uses function calls, rather than operators, to perform standard text operations. For these reasons, I deferred the topic of text processing until after discussing the other basics: functions, arrays, and pointers.

Text strings may seem harder to manipulate in C than in, say, BASIC. Some tasks take a little more work in C, but, in return for this effort, you get much more control over what the program is doing. BASIC's mechanisms for handling text strings hide so many details from you that you have no way of knowing how costly or efficient one operation is compared to another. In C, you know exactly what's going on, so you have the potential to write much more efficient algorithms.

What's a String? The C Implementation

The fundamental numeric unit of a program is an integer or a floating-point variable, which is a simple variable stored at a specific address. The fundamental unit of text is a *text string*, also called a *character string* or just a string. In C, a string is array of **char**. This use of the term *string* is probably strange if you're not used to it. The use of *string* alludes to the fact that a text string is a continuous series of characters strung out in memory, one after another. A string is not necessarily limited to a single word. It can contain any number of spaces and even new lines (\n), which represent carriage returns.

Another reason for the use of the word *string* is that text strings come in many different lengths, just as regular strings do.

With C, the final character in a string is a null byte (indicated by '\0' which means a character with a numeric code of zero (0), as opposed to a printable zero). The null byte, or *null terminator*, is used by many different functions in C. For all practical purposes, it's virtually a requirement to end your strings with a null terminating byte. The use of a null terminator enables any function to determine the length of the string by searching for the null (zero) value (see Figure 8.1).

Figure 8.1 *Basic string architecture in C.*

Although the null byte is always there, you don't necessarily see it. When you write a string literal into your program, the compiler automatically appends a null terminating byte. Except for rare situations, you won't explicitly place the null terminator into any string literal.

Yet at times you must be aware that the null terminator is there. (Examples in this chapter will help to make that fact clear.) When you write a string-handling routine, you must look for the null terminator at the end of any string or else you won't know where to stop. It is often important to determine the string's length, and this information generally isn't kept anywhere. You can get it only by counting the number of bytes before you reach the null terminator. For example, here's a generalized string-length routine:

```
unsigned strlen(char *s) {
    unsigned length;

    for (length = 0; *s; length++, s++)
        ;
    return length;
}
```

This sample strlen function, by the way, does the same thing that the C library strlen function does.

Clearly, the **for** loop here does all the work of the function. The critical part of the **for** loop, in many ways, is the condition:

```
*s
```

As you may recall from previous chapters, giving a condition like this is the same as testing the expression for inequality to zero:

```
*s != 0
```

We can also express this as:

```
*s != '\0'
```

So the loop continues until *s is null. But *s just means "the thing pointed to by s," and s points to the current byte. This simple condition, then, is ultimately just a way of saying:

As long as the current byte is not null...

The integer variable, length, starts at zero and is incremented by one as long as the current byte is not null. The loop doesn't need to do anything else, because the increment expressions (length++, s++) do all the work. When the loop terminates, it produces the string length, which is what we wanted.

Figure 8.2 illustrates how the strlen function works. The pointer, s, starts at the beginning of the string and moves right until the null byte is reached.

163

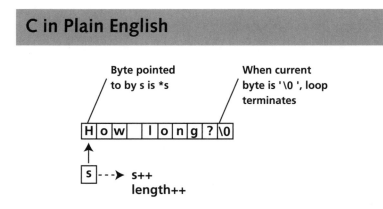

Figure 8.2 *The strlen function in action.*

String Initialization and Declaration

To declare, initialize, and use strings, you need to keep in mind the first cardinal rule of string handling in C:

> **The array dimension of a string determines its maximum length (minus one for the null terminator) and not its current length.**

As simple as this rule sounds, it's the first major obstacle to properly using strings in C. One of the subtleties here is that there is a distinction between the array size of the string—the amount of memory allocated for it—and its current length. The length can never equal or exceed the amount of memory allocated, but the string length can certainly be less than the maximum.

A simple example should help clarify. The following definition allocates 10 bytes to hold string data. The definition uses the string literal "Hello" to initialize the first six bytes of the string (one for each character plus one for the null terminator):

```
char my_string[10] = "Hello";
```

The array my_string does have 10 bytes available to it, but only the first six are currently in use, as illustrated in Figure

8.3. If new data is ever copied to my_string, it can be nine bytes long (allowing one byte for the null terminator). So five is the current length, and nine is the maximum length.

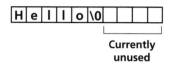

Figure 8.3 *A string with unused bytes.*

This string is genuinely five characters in length, by the way. If printed, the string is not padded with spaces on the right. The printf function stops as soon as it reaches the null byte.

It may strike you that this arrangement is inefficient, because not all bytes are being used. We can get rid of this inefficiency by leaving out the array dimension (10); doing so makes C allocate just enough space to hold the string literal, plus one additional byte for the terminator:

```
char my_string[] = "Hello";
```

Now every byte allocated is used. The compiler allocates exactly six elements for the my_string array, just enough to hold the necessary data (see Figure 8.4).

| H | e | l | l | o | \0 |

Figure 8.4 *A string using all the bytes allocated.*

OK, this is great, you say. No unused bytes. But there's a potential real problem here. The string must never grow in length. This makes the string much too inflexible in programs where you want to copy different values to string variables just as you do with numeric variables.

The problem of maximum string lengths is something you need to consider carefully in C programming. By far the simplest solution is to decide ahead of time the maximum string length you'll ever need and then declare all strings to be of this size. For example, you might realize that each string in your program is intended to be printed on one normal 80-character display line on the screen. In that case, 80 is a reasonable maximum length, so you'd declare all your strings to be this length plus one (for the terminator):

```
#define STR_MAX   81


char string1[STR_MAX];
char string2[STR_MAX];
char string3[STR_MAX];
```

Placing the maximum length in a **#define** directive is good programming practice, incidentally. If you decide to change the string maximum at any point, you need only change one line.

Again, this solution doesn't yield the most efficient use of every byte in your program. But in simpler programs a few extra bytes here and there are rarely a factor. Many sophisticated programs do have to take more clever approaches to allocating and using bytes for strings, and the possible solutions are endless. One answer is to allocate a large **char** array to be used as a common string data area. Whenever a string has to grow in length, it must be reallocated inside the data area and the pointer to it gets a new address. (Moving string data involves the strcpy function, as we'll see in the next section.)

You can also use the malloc function to request more space and place your new string data there. Implementing a solution like that is far from trivial, of course, but the point is that C gives you many options.

In doing operations involving many strings, you're always better off handling pointers to string data rather than copying the string data itself. For example, to sort an array of strings, the best approach is to take an array of pointers to strings, do an alphabetical comparison on the strings pointed to, and then

166

exchange the position of the pointers as appropriate. (The str-cmp function performs the comparison, given two pointers.) The result is an array of sorted pointers to string data. The string data itself should be untouched.

String Copying

Before you attempt to move string data around, you need to learn the second cardinal rule of string handling in C:

> **Because strings are arrays, they can't be directly assigned to variables. You must use a function call or a loop to copy one character at a time.**

This can be a frustrating principle to deal with at first, especially if you've come from the BASIC world. Let's back up for a minute, though; it might seem that assignment of strings is permitted in C:

```
char str[] = "Hello, world.";
```

This is perfectly valid. But consider this statement:

```
str[] = "Goodbye, cruel Earth!";   /* ERROR! */
```

This is illegal. So is this:

```
str = "Goodbye, cruel Earth!";     /* ERROR! */
```

The first statement is valid because it is an initialization and not an assignment. Although both processes use the equal sign (=), this is one of the situations where it is important to distinguish them. The intialization doesn't copy or transfer any data, which is what string assignment would do if supported. The compiler allocates the string data "Hello, world" and then returns the string address; the symbol str is then initialized to this address.

Through a similar logic, the following is legal:

```
char *p;
p = "Hello!";
p = "Goodbye!";
```

What's going on here is that p is a pointer variable, and not an array, and therefore can be assigned different addresses. First, p is assigned the address of the string "Hello!". Then p is assigned the address of the string "Goodbye!". But no string data is being copied here. There are two separate strings; first p points to one, and then it points to the other.

To copy string data from one location in memory to another, you need to call the strcpy library function, which takes two operands, each being the address of a string. The contents of the second are copied to the first, until a null terminator is copied.

Use of this function enables us to copy new data to a blank string. For example:

```
char str[20];   /* Empty string of 20 chars. */

strcpy(str, "Hello!");
```

Although strcpy is a C library function, it's easy to write your own version:

```
char *strcpy(char *dest, char *src) {
    char *save_dest = dest;

    while (*src);
        *dest++ = *src++;
    *dest = '\0';
    return save_dest;
}
```

After all the non-null characters are copied from the source string (src) to the destination string (dest), a null terminator is copied to the next available byte in dest. Finally, the address of dest is returned.

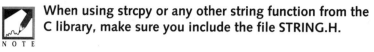 **When using strcpy or any other string function from the C library, make sure you include the file STRING.H.**

In case the distinction between pointer assignment and string copying isn't clear, let's look at more examples—with the help of illustrations. First, consider pointer assignment involving two strings, one longer and one shorter:

```
char *p;
p = "The living end";
p = "END";
```

What's happening is that the pointer p is being made to point to two different strings. This is a pointless sequence of code, incidentally; after the second assignment, all connection to the first string is lost, so it becomes a useless piece of data taking up memory for no reason.

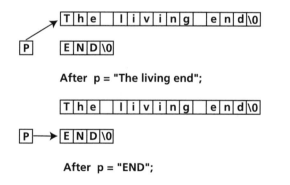

Figure 8.5 *Pointer reassignment.*

This next example uses the strcpy function to move characters around in memory.

```
char *p;
p = "The living end";
strcpy(p, "END");
```

Here the first string is overwritten with the second. In general, the destination string must have a maximum size equal to or greater than the current length of the source string, or you're in danger of corrupting program data.

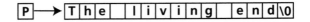

After p = "The living end";

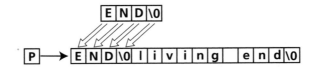

After strcpy (p, "END");

Figure 8.6 *Example of a string copy.*

After this string copy, you'll note that the string pointed to by p has data past the first null character (specifically this data is "living end\0"). This makes no difference; virtually all C functions, such as printf, use the data only up to the first null. The data that comes after the null is effectively chopped off.

Because the strcpy function requires a little more work to use in writing the program, you may be tempted to get lazy and use pointer assignment instead. But you won't yield to temptation when you realize that one operation just can't be substituted for another.

For example, one use for strcpy is in moving string data to a larger string. This would be a good response to a situation in which you accumulate string data in such a way that you are about to exceed the maximum length.

```
char old_string[31];
char *p;
...
```

```
p = (char *) malloc (256);
strcpy(p, old_string);
```

In this example, you get a new string, pointed to by p and initialized with the characters in old_string (which presumably had a maximum size smaller than 256). You can now add new characters to the end of old_string and grow it up to 255 characters, allowing one extra, of course, for the terminator.

But imagine what happens if you use pointer assignment rather than strcpy in the last statement:

```
p = old_string;
```

In this case, at least, the effects are very bad. The pointer p is made to point to the location old_string, so access to the new memory block is lost; now it can never be used or properly freed (leading to memory leaks, a devious bug). Moreover, you can't grow the string data in old_string, as intended. That data still resides in the same old place in memory. Nothing has changed. You simply have another pointer pointing to that same address, for no good reason.

Pointer assignment and string copying have many legitimate uses. In particular, you can often use arrays of pointers to strings rather than arrays of strings; in those cases, sorting an array of pointers is much more efficient than sorting the strings themselves. But in any case, you need to be clear about what your program requires. If you need to move data around in memory, make sure you use strcpy instead of pointer assignment.

This is perhaps the hallmark difference between being a BASIC programmer and being a C programmer. C requires you to think a little more.

Writing a String-Manipulation Function

Once you understand that strings are just arrays of one-byte integers (**char** data type), you can easily write string-manipulation

171

functions. In terms of program logic, strings have just one special property that other arrays do not have: a null terminator to indicate the current length of the string.

The following example changes every letter in a string to uppercase:

```
#include <ctype.h>

char *p;

for (p = string; *p; p++)
    *p = toupper(*p);
```

The toupper macro function is defined in the file CTYPE.H. Regardless of how the character set on your particular system is arranged, this function is written to correctly change any lowercase letter to uppercase. Other kinds of characters are not affected.

You can use a similar loop to convert all the characters in a string to lowercase:

```
#include <ctype.h>

char *p;

for (p = string; *p; p++)
    *p = tolower(*p);
```

Both of these loops act on the string they're given. This approach isn't always satisfactory, because it corrupts the original data. That's not an insurmountable problem, though, because the data can first be copied to another location with strcpy.

Operating on the data you're given isn't always so straightforward. Consider the case of a string-reversing function, which we'll call reversi. It isn't possible to completely reverse a string without having a temporary string to operate on. Fortunately, thanks to the techniques in Chapter 7, we know how to create a temporary string; we just call malloc.

Once the temporary string is created, the reversi function works by finding the last character of the original string, initializing a pointer to the beginning of the temporary string, and then using two pointers moving in opposite directions.

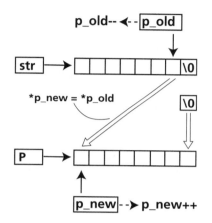

Figure 8.7 *How the reversi function works, using two pointers moving in opposite directions.*

The last two steps of the routine are to copy the contents of the temporary string over to the existing string and free the temporary string.

```
#include    <string.h>
include     <malloc.h>

void reversi(char *str) {
    char *p, *p_old, *p_new;
    int n;

    n = strlen(str);
    p_new = p = (char *) malloc(n);  /* Create temp. */
    p_old = str + n - 1;  /* Point to last char. */
    while (n--) {
        *p_new = *p_old;
        p_new++;
        p_old--;
    }
}
```

```
    *p_new = '\0';    /* Append terminator to string. */
    strcpy(str, p);   /* Overwrite old string. */
    free(p);          /* Free temporary. */
}
```

Note that several address variables are involved here: two for each string. Using this many variables is necessary because the pointer variables p_new and p_old change value as the loop proceeds. The variables p and str continue to point to the starting addresses of the two strings (the string operated on and the temporary) throughout the function and so are used to "remember" the start addresses of the strings.

Other Useful Operations and Functions

The standard C library provided with every compiler has a set of useful functions for manipulating text strings. By calling these functions, you can do almost every operation that other languages support with primitive string operators and string variables. As with strlen and strcpy, these functions are fairly easy to write yourself once you understand the basic architecture of strings in C.

First, however, one fundamental point should be clear: because strings are implemented as arrays, you can access individual characters as array elements. For example:

```
#include <stdio.h>

int c;
char s[] = "Loverly weather we're having, isn't it?";

c = s[6];
putchar(c);
```

The output of this simple example is the seventh character in the string:

```
y
```

This example illustrates a couple of points. First, an individual character is stored numerically and can therefore be represented as **char** (a one-byte integer) or **int**. Characters are stored in the **char** form in arrays, where storage space is at a premium. However, when you use a variable to represent individual characters, it is best to use type **int**. Values are converted to **int** when operated on anyway, and some character-reading functions (such as getchar) read a character and can return a value outside the normal range of **char**.

Another point is that you can use the putchar function, defined in STDIO.H, to print individual characters. A series of calls to putchar can print an entire string, although this is usually less efficient than calling printf or its simpler version, puts (which prints a string as is without any support for formatting).

You can also replace individual characters through array access:

```
s[1] = 'u';
s[2] = 'm';
puts(s);
```

The output of these lines is:

```
Lumerly weather we're having, isn't it?
```

These changes to the string, you should note, don't change the string length. You might want to plunge ahead and replace a word in the string with some other word of different length, but this isn't as trivial as it sounds. To replace an entire word, you need to do the following:

1. Note the beginning and ending position of the word you want to replace.

2. Copy the first N characters to a new string, where N is the beginning position.

3. Append a null terminator onto the new string.

4. Concatenate the replacement word onto the end of the new string.

5. Concatenate the remainder of the original string onto the end of the new string.

To perform these operations, we have to introduce two more string functions: strncpy and strcat (see Table 8.1).

Table 8.1 *String functions strncopy and strcat.*

STRING FUNCTION	DESCRIPTION
strncpy(*dest, src, n***)**	Copy no more than n characters.
strcat(*dest, src***)**	Append src string onto end of dest string, which must have a large enough maximum length to contain the additional characters.

Both of these functions return a pointer to the destination string, as does the strcpy function. This is potentially useful, because it enables you to use the function call within a larger expression, but you can ignore the return value if you choose.

With these two functions in our arsenal, we can now write the string-replacement code. The beginning and ending positions of the word *weather* are 8 and 14, so the following example replaces the word *weather* with the phrase "climatic conditions":

```
include <string.h>

char s[81] = "Loverly weather we're having, isn't it?"
char temp[81];

strncpy(temp, s, 8);
temp[8] = '\0';
strcat(temp, "climatic conditions");
strcat(temp, &s[15]);
```

The last statement concatenates the remainder of the original string—the portion of the string that comes after the word *weather*. This sequence of statements may seem complex, but it can easily be automated by being written as a generalized function. The last line could also be written as:

```
strcat(temp, s+15);
```

You can now copy the results back to the original string and print it:

```
strcpy(s, temp);
puts(s);
```

The output, showing the final look of this string, is:

```
Loverly climatic conditions we're having, isn't it?
```

So far, we've used the standard C library functions strlen, str-cpy, strncpy, and strcat. Other useful functions include str-cmp, which compares two strings and returns a negative, zero, or positive result, depending on the result of the comparison, and strstr, which finds the position of one string inside a larg-er string.

The strcmp function performs an alphabetical compari-son analogous to relational operators you use to compare numbers in C (<, >, ==, etc.). For example:

```
char s1[] = "aaa";
char s2[] = "zzz";
int result;

result = strcmp(s1, s2);
if (result < 0)
    puts("s1 is less than s2");
```

In this context, "less than" means that s1 would precede s2 in a dictionary listing.

The strstr function finds the first occurrence of a sub-string inside another, returning a pointer to the first charac-ter. For example, here's how to find the position of the word *weather* in the previous sample code:

```
char s[81] = "Loverly weather we're having, isn't it?"
char *p;
int pos1, pos2;

p = strstr(s, "weather");
```

More often than not, it's easiest to write programs so that you use the pointer returned by strstr directly. However, the word-replacement example used indexes rather than pointers. You can convert a pointer to an index by subtracting the starting address of the string. Then you can get the index of the first character after weather by simply adding the length of the string "weather":

```
pos1 = strstr(s, "weather") - s;
pos2 = pos1 + strlen("weather");
```

Finally, you can plug these values into the word-replacement algorithm:

```
strncpy(temp, s, pos1);
temp[pos1] = '\0';
strcat(temp, "climatic conditions");
strcat(temp, &s[pos2]);
```

Basic File Operations

Files are an important part of input and output and often involve a lot of work with character strings. There's a lot to say about file operations in C, but reading or writing to a file generally comes down to these basic steps:

1. Include the STDIO.H header file and declare a file pointer of type FILE*.

2. Open the file by calling the fopen function. This function returns a value for the file pointer.

3. Read or write to the file, as appropriate. You can use the file pointer as input to functions such as fprintf, fscanf, fputs, and fgetc, which are analogous to the nonfile functions (printf, scanf, etc.) except that they work on files. The file pointer identifies the file on which to operate.

4. Close the file.

The following example prints the contents of a sample file, DATA.TXT, and converts all the lowercase letters to uppercase as it prints. The program tests for whether or not the file is present. If it is not, the program quits.

```
/* Sample program to print out the entire contents of
   a text file, converting all lowercase letters to
   uppercase. */

#include <stdio.h>
#include <ctype.h>

int main()
{
    int c;
    FILE *fp;

/* Open for reading; "r" specifies read mode. */

    fp = fopen("DATA.TXT", "r");
    if (!fp) {
        puts("Error: DATA.TXT not found.\n");
        return -1;
    }
    while ((c = fgetc(fp)) != EOF)
        putchar(toupper(c));

    fclose(fp);
    return 0;
}
```

One of the new functions here is fgetc. This function gets a character from the specified file (identified by the file pointer fp) and returns the result as an integer. Although the return value of this function is usually in the range of the **char** data type, one of the possible values is EOF, which indicates the end of the file. The value EOF is not guaranteed to be in the **char** range for all implementations of C. For this reason, you should declare the variable c, which gets the value, as an **int** and not a **char**.

This sample program is obviously limited because it has a "hard-coded" file name, DATA.TXT. The program would be much more useful if it allowed the user to enter any file name. The following version prompts the user for a file name at run time and then uses this file name in the fopen function call:

```c
/* Sample program to print out the entire contents of
   a text file, converting all lowercase letters to
   uppercase. */

   This version prompts for the file name.
 */

#include <stdio.h>
#include <ctype.h

int main()
{
    int c;
    FILE *fp;
    char filename[81];

    printf("Enter file name, please: ");
    gets(filename);
    if (strlen(filename) == 0) {
        puts("No file name entered.\n");
        return -1;
    }

/* Open for reading; "r" specifies read mode. */

    fp = fopen(filename, "r");
    if (!fp) {
        puts("Error: file name not found.\n");
        return -1;
    }
    while ((c = fgetc(fp)) != EOF)
        putchar(toupper(c));

    fclose(fp);
    return 0;
}
```

This example introduces another useful library function: a call to the gets input function. This function is vaguely similar to scanf, but it inputs an entire line, stopping not at the first space (as in scanf("%s", filename)) but rather stopping when the user presses **Enter**.

There's still another way to write this function: by getting the file name from the command line. To use this approach, the **main** function must be declared with the argc and argv arguments: argc gives the count of command-line arguments, including the program name; argv is a pointer to an array of pointers. Each pointer in this array points to one of the words on the command line. The pointer argv[0] points to the program name. The pointer argv[1] points to the first command-line argument.

```c
/* Sample program to print out the entire contents of
   a text file, converting all lowercase letters to
   uppercase. */

   This version uses command-line input.
 */

#include <stdio.h>
#include <ctype.h>

int main(int argc, char *argv[])
{
    int c;
    FILE *fp;

    if (argc < 2) {
        puts("Command must include file name.\n");
        return -1;
    }

/* Open for reading; "r" specifies read mode. */

    fp = fopen(argv[1], "r");
    if (!fp) {
```

```
        puts("Error: file name not found.\n");
        return -1;
    }
    while ((c = fgetc(fp)) != EOF)
        putchar(toupper(c));

    fclose(fp);
    return 0;
}
```

Text vs. Binary File Operations

Operations on text files are easy, especially if you have been following all the examples in the book. To print formatted output to the screen, for example, you use printf:

```
printf("The value of n is %d.\n", n);
```

To print this output to a file instead of the screen, you simply open a file for writing and then use fprintf instead of printf:

```
fp = fopen(filename, "w");
...
fprintf(fp, "The value of n is %d.\n", n);
```

The fprintf and fscanf functions use the same syntax as printf and scanf except that the first argument is a file pointer. This pointer identifies the file to operate on.

The use of functions such as fprintf, fscanf, fputs, fgets, fgetc, and fputc presumes that you are working on a text file: a file that is perfectly readable to a human who prints it out. The results of printing a text file should look just like formatted output to the screen.

You could do all your data storage and retrieval with text files. But unless you're dealing strictly with text, reliance on text files can be inefficient. The difference between text files and binary files can be summarized this way: when you use fprintf to print a number to a text file, a number such as –32,000 is converted to a character string and then output to the file. This number uses seven bytes of storage: one for the sign each digit, and one for the null terminator (the comma is not printed).

But in a binary file, data storage is direct. The number –32,000 can be stored in a two-byte signed integer (**short**). Such a number takes only two bytes in a binary file, not seven. This is unimportant in small examples, but think about what happens when a program needs to store thousands of numbers. Moreover, binary files don't involve any formatting of input, so transfer of numeric data is significantly faster.

File operations on binary files look similar in many respects to those on text files. You still have to open the file, use it, and then close it. But when you open a file, you specify an extra character: "b" for binary.

```
/* Open binary file for write operations. */

fp = fopen(filename, "wb");
```

You operate on binary files with three principal functions (see Table 8.2). The first two provide the means to read and write unformatted output. The third function is useful for providing random access to data records.

When you work with binary files, you have to adopt a different approach to program design than you use with text files. The major requirement is that you need to determine exactly how many bytes to read or write at a time (the number read is just the product of the *size* and *count* arguments). One approach is to structure the entire file into uniform-sized data records; **struct** declarations are useful here. You can read the structures sequentially, one at a time, or use the fseek function to provide random access once you know how long the file is.

For example, the following statement reads one record of type movie_review:

```
#include <stdio.h>

struct movie_ratings {
    char movie_name[20];
    char director_name[30];
    int  Roger;    /* 1 = thumbs up, 0 = thumbs down */
    int  Jane;
};

struct movie_ratings my_record;
...
fread(&my_record, sizeof(movie_ratings), 1, fp);
```

Table 8.2 *Binary file operations.*

STRING FUNCTION	DESCRIPTION
fread(*buffer, size, count, file***)**	Reads bytes directly from indicated file (identified by a file pointer). The count argument specifies how many items to read, and size specifies the size of each item. The buffer is the beginning address of the destination of the data.
fwrite(*buffer, size, count, file***)**	All the arguments have the same meaning as in fread except that the buffer is the beginning address of the source of the data to write to the file.
fseek(*file, offset, origin***)**	Positions file pointer relative to origin, which can be SEEK_SET (beginning of file), SEEK_CUR (current position), or SEEK_END (end of file).

After initializing a structure, you can write it to a file in the same way:

```
#include <stdio.h>
#include <string.h>
struct movie_ratings this_movie;
```

```
strcpy(this_movie.movie_name,
    "Pointers from Outer Space");
strcpy(this_movie.director_name,
    "Alfred Hitch Schlock");
this_movie.Roger = 1;    /* thumbs up! */
this_movie.Jane = 0;     /* thumbs down! */

fwrite(&this_movie, sizeof(movie_ratings), 1, fp);
```

See "struct Declarations" in Part II for information on the syntax of declaring, creating, and using structures.

C The Language:

An Alphabetical Reference

Definition

The address operator (&) helps you initialize pointer variables as well as supply an address for a function such as scanf. At the machine level, processors deal with addresses all the time. The difference between C and other high-level languages is that C often makes the use of addresses explicit, whereas other languages do many of the same operations under the covers.

Pointer operations involve both the indirection (*) and the address operators, which can be considered inverses of each other. Indirection means "get the contents at," whereas the address operator means "take the address of." Taking the address of a variable and then getting the contents at that address gets you back to the variable you started with, so *(&var) means the same thing as var.

Syntax

The address operator forms an expression from a single operand:

&*expression*

The expression must be a valid l-value (see "L-values"). In general, this means that *expression* must be a variable of primitive type or pointer type, or a structure, array, or union member having primitive type or pointer type. The easiest way to think about this is that you can always take the address of a simple variable. You can also take the address of a pointer variable (which would result in a pointer to a pointer).

 You cannot take the address of a bit field, although in other respects a bit field is a valid l-value.

N O T E

189

Usage

The address operator occurs only in executable statements
and pointer initialization. The operator produces a constant
address expression. Such an expression is useful for setting a
pointer to point to a simple variable or for passing an
address to a function. For example:

```
int i *ptr = &n;
scanf("%d", &n);
```

When you call scanf, you must supply an address expression. Unlike printf, scanf changes the value of its arguments. The argument must be passed by reference so that
scanf can change its value; passing by reference requires the
use of an address type in C. (The scanf function gets the
location of n, and not just its value, so that it knows where
to copy the data input by the user.)

Aggregates

Definition

An aggregate is a series of constants treated as a single group. Most often, aggregates are used in initialization. Character strings are the most common aggregates and can be used both for initialization and input to a string function such as printf.

Syntax

Each aggregate has one of the following forms:

"string_of_characters"
{ *item, item ...* }

Here the ellipses (...) indicate that *item* is repeated any number of times; each item is a valid constant (and itself may be an aggregate of the appropriate type).

Usage 1: Character Strings

When you use a character string in C code, the compiler creates space for the string, including the null-terminating byte, and returns a pointer to the beginning of the string. You can therefore use a pointer to initialize character strings and pointers to strings, and to pass as arguments where the address of a char is expected. For example:

```
char *p = "Here is a string";
char s[] = "Here is another string";
char big_string[20] = "The end";
printf("Hello there, machine.");
```

In each case, the actual string text is placed in program data and its address is assigned or passed as an argument. Depending on implementation, the last example causes the string to be allocated in memory reserved for constants; the other examples initialize memory reserved for variables. The difference between the first two statements is that p is a variable that may change, whereas s holds a constant address. In the case of big_string, 20 characters are allocated, but only the first eight—including null terminator—are initialized with "The end".

See "String Literals" for more information on character strings.

Usage 2: Set Aggregates

The set-brace syntax ({}) is useful for initializing arrays and structures. If the variable being initialized has a specified size, the number of items in the aggregate may be less than or equal to the size. If no size is specified, the compiler allocates just enough space for the aggregate. For example:

```
/* Last three elements not initialized. */
short nums[6] = {1, 2, 3};
/* ERROR: too many items. */
int nums2[3] = (1, 2, 3, 4, 5);
/* nums3 is 4 ints in size. */
int nums3[] = {99, 7, 28, 58};
```

In the last example, nums3 is exactly four elements long, causing a reference to nums3[6] in an executable statement to result in an error.

As mentioned earlier, a member of an aggregate can itself be an aggregate; this makes sense if you are using it to initialize a complex data type, such as a two-dimensional array or an array of structures. Here, the third member (x) of each structure is left uninitialized, whereas the first two members of each structure are initialized:

```
struct  rectype {
    char *name;
    int age;
    float weight;
};

struct rectype employees[3] = { {"Curly", 30},
    {"Larry", 25}, {"Moe", 35} };
```

192

Definition

An *argument* is a value passed to a function. The concept of argument is very close to that of *parameter*, which is an argument used within the function definition itself. In this book, I've generally used the term argument to refer to both.

For a general introduction to arguments and functions, see Chapter 3, "Anatomy of a C Program Part II: Functions."

Argument Declaration Syntax

Within a function definition, arguments (parameters) are used just like local varaibles. So not surprisingly, they follow almost the same syntax rules.

Within function prototypes and definitions, arguments can be declared with the same syntax as local and global variables. The only variable-declaration syntax elements that cannot appear in an argument declaration are storage class modifiers (**extern**, **auto**, **static**, **storage**) and initializers.

An argument list consists of one or more of the following:

```
[cv] type decl_specifier [, decl_specifier]...
```

The brackets here indicate optional items. The *cv* syntax represents the optional use of **const**, **volatile**, or both.

Each *decl_specifier* can be any of the following (here the brackets around *index* are intended literally:

```
identifier
decl_specifier[index]
*decl_specifier
decl_specifier(argument_list)
```

The last syntax is used for callback functions (see "Pointers to Functions").

Example

The following function declaration takes two integer arguments, a **const** pointer to a character string, and a function pointer:

```
void my_func(int a, b, const char *s, (*f)(void));
```

Definition

Arrays provide a marvelous way to represent large areas of memory and to efficiently process such areas in a loop. Chapter 7, "Pointers and Other Sharp Instruments," introduces the topic; this section provides a summary and discusses some fine points.

C's treatment of arrays is distinctive in a couple of ways. First, the connection of arrays to pointer variables is very close. Second, multi-dimensional arrays are treated as arrays of arrays.

Syntax

An array reference or declaration has one of the following forms, depending on whether it is one-dimensional (the first case) or multidimensional (the second case):

name[*index*]
name[*dim1_index*][*dim2_index*]...

Here the ellipses (...) indicate that [*dim_index*] can be repeated any number of times. The brackets ([]) are intended literally. In declarations, each *index* specifies the number of elements of the array (or the number in the given dimension of the array). In executable statements, valid indexes run from 0 to one less than the *index* in the declaration. Thus, for an array declared "int array[10]", the last element is array[9].

In certain circumstances (described at the end of the next section), *index* can be omitted from the declaration.

Case 1: One-Dimensional Arrays

The connection between pointers and arrays is very close. In many cases, an array name can be used interchangeably with a pointer that points to the array.

195

```
short   x[100]
short   *y = x;
```

Here, x is an array of 100 short integers. The first statement allocates 200 bytes. The second statement allocates room only for y, a pointer; it also intializes y to x, which has the effect of setting y to point to the start of the array. This is because a reference to an array (in this case, x) is translated into the array's starting address.

A reference to y translates into the starting address of the array, as does x. In the following statements, x and y are interchangeable. But bear in mind that x is a constant, whereas y is a variable that can change so that it points to a new address:

```
x[50] = i;
y[k] = j + 5;
*x = 2;
*y = 2;
*(x + 1) = 0;
*(y + 5) = 8
```

The last two statements use pointer arithmetic, which multiplies an integer by the size of the base type (this is called *scaling*) before adding or subtracting to the address. Consequently, the last two statements are equivalent to the following:

```
x[1] = 0;
y[5] = 8;
```

In general, any reference to *name[index]* in an executable statement is equivalent to the following:

(name + index)

Of course, the version that uses brackets ([]) is more convenient.

In a declaration, *index* determines the size of the array; *index* must be a constant. Within an executable statement, *index* can be any valid integer expression—with the caveat that when evaluated it must fall into the range 0 to *size* –1, in which *size* is the index used in the declaration. In the case of x above (100 elements), elements range from a[0] to a[99].

You can actually use an index outside this range; however using an out-of-range index would result in overwriting or reading data outside the array's area in memory, which is guaranteed to cause errors.

A frequent mistake in C programming is to set initial or terminating conditions of a loop incorrectly. This is an easy mistake in part because the maximum index is not equal to the number of elements in the array; it is one less than this number. A correct loop to initialize an array might look like this—notice the initialization and loop condition:

```
for (i = 0; i < NUMBER_OF_ELEMENTS; i++)
    array[i] = 0;
```

In declarations, *index* can be omitted if the size information is supplied elsewhere. This happens in two cases: with initialization by aggregates (see "Aggregates"), in which the initializer determines the size; and in argument declarations where arrays of variable sizes are accepted. For example, consider the following prototype:

```
void array_function(int a[], int *b);
```

Here, a and b are virtually the same type. In each case, my_function expects the address of an integer; it may be a single integer or the first element of an integer array. The size of the array is up to the calling function. Generally the function called will need some way of knowing the array size. This can be communicated in a variety of ways: there may be a programwide standard size, there may be a nullterminator (as is the case with a character string, which is just an array of **char**), or size information may be passed separately in another argument.

Case 2: More than One Dimension

Everything said about one-dimensional arrays also applies to multidimensional arrays. However, the use of more than one dimension adds a few interesting quirks.

Ultimately, all arrays are one-dimensional, because memory itself is one-dimensional: an array is really just a sequence of base elements laid out contiguously in memory (meaning that the array takes up a solid block of memory with nothing interspersed between elements).

For each individual dimension used in declaring the array, the maximum index is always 1 less than the index used to declare an array. Suppose an array, big_matrix, is declared as follows. The total size is 5 * 10 * 10, or 500 elements.

```
double big_matrix[5][10][10];
```

The first element in the array is:

```
big_matrix[0][0][0]
```

The last element is:

```
big_matrix[4][9][9]
```

This may seem strange, but the reason for it is plain: in declarations, each index specifies the *number of elements* and not the *last element*. Simple math tells you that 0, 1, 2, 3, 4 is five elements.

Although memory is laid out one-dimensionally, arrays can be a convenient way to express matrixes and higher-dimensional arrays called for by program logic. The compiler translates a multidimensional array by multiplying each index by the product of all the dimensions *after* the current dimension.

As a two-dimensional array, name[i][j] is translated into:

```
**(name  +  i * dim2  +  j)
```

198

You can think of dim2 as the row size; it's equal to the number of columns and is the second dimension in the declaration. So two-dimensional array references are resolved by multiplying the row number (i) by the row size (dim2) and adding the column number (j).

As a three-dimensional array, name[i][j][k] is translated into:

```
***(name  +  i * dim2 * dim3  +  j * dim2  +  k)
```

C uses row-major order, which means that the last dimension changes most quickly. Suppose that an array is declared as "int 3d[2][2][2];". This defines a 2 * 2 * 2 (eight-element), in which the elements are laid out in memory in this order:

```
3d[0][0][0]
3d[0][0][1]
3d[0][1][0]
3d[0][1][1]
3d[1][0][0]
3d[1][0][1]
3d[1][1][0]
3d[1][1][1]
```

A two-dimensional array is actually an array of arrays, a three-dimensional array is an array of arrays of arrays, and so on. Thus, for a given array definition,

```
int arr[3][5][5];
```

the identifier "arr" is interpreted as an array of three elements (arr[0], arr[1], and arr[2]); each element is itself a 5 * 5 two-dimensional array. Therefore:

- arr is the address of (it *points to*) a two-dimensional array, arr[0].

- arr[0] is the address of a one-dimensional array, arr[0][0].

199

- arr[0][0] is the address of an integer, arr[0][0][0].

Each expression (arr, arr[0], arr[0][0], and arr[0][0][0]) is at a different level of indirection. This is why even after adjusting the address of arr, you have to apply the indirection operator (*) three times to get an integer. The following two expressions, for example, are equivalent:

```
***arr
arr[0][0][0]
```

Definition

In C, assignments perform the usual role of copying data to a location. However, a C assignment has the peculiar quirk of forming an expression itself. This means that you can place assignments inside other assignments or almost any kind of expression.

Syntax

The assignment operator forms an expression from an l-value and a subexpression:

l-value = expression

The *l-value* is typically a variable but can also be a structure-member reference, an indexed array element, or a dereferenced pointer. For more information, see "L-values." The assignment itself evaluates to the value of *expression*— that is, the value assigned.

Examples

The following examples illustrate some simple assignments:

```
a = 1;
a = b * 2;
card[12] = 0;
*p1++ = *p2++;
```

An assignment can be placed inside larger expressions, as in:

```
a = b = c = d = e = 0;
```

For a fuller discussion of how this works, see Chapter 2, "Anatomy of a C Program, Part I."

NOTE Assignment is not the same thing as initialization, even though they look similar. Initialization can be used in variable definitions and must involve a constant expression:

```
int i = 1;
```

True assignments occur outside variable definitions—they are executable statements—and are not restricted to constants. The expression on the right side can be any valid expression, including complex calculations or function references.

Another important thing to remember is never to confuse the assignment operator (=) with the test-for-equality operator (==). Doing so is a major cause of error for first-time C programmers or people whose C skills are rusty.

Definition

Associativity is probably one of those things you had to learn in elementary school. If you were like most people, you forgot about it. However, it rears its head again in C, and for good reasons.

Almost all high-level programming languages have a concept of associativity. Along with a related concept, precedence, it helps determine what the program evaluates in what order. Specifically, associativity determines the order of evaluation of operators that are at the same level of precedence.

In C, associativity of operators becomes an even more important topic, because there are more operators that can be intermixed. And not all of them associate in the same way!

Examples

In simple terms, associativity means that for arimethic operators at the same level of precedence, terms are evaluated left-to-right. For example,

```
x = 1 - a + b;
```

is equivalent to:

```
x = (1 - a) + b;
```

It is not equivalent to the following statement, which would require parentheses to express correctly:

```
x = 1 - (a + b);
```

You can easily check for yourself and see that the results are different for any nonzero value of b.

Although arithmetic operators associate left-to-right (in line with what your math books told you), the unary operators and all the assignment operators associate right-to-left.

This makes sense, if you think about it, because the action of such operators is right-to-left; the right side must be evaluated first. For example,

```
a = b = c = 0;
```

is equivalent to:

```
a = (b = (c = 0));
```

So all three variables are assigned 0. Also, an expression such as *f1(arg) is equivalent to:

```
*(f1(arg))
```

This means that a function is executed and then the indirection operator (*) is applied.

Associativity is only one of the factors determining order of execution. In general, C determines which operators are to be evaluated first by applying principles in this order:

- Operators in parentheses are always applied before operators outside the parentheses. If in doubt, use parentheses to enforce a certain order of execution.

- If operators are at different level of precedence, those at higher levels are evaluated first. Common sense is usually a reliable guide here: arithmetic operations are carried out first (with muliplication and division ranking above addition and subtraction), then comparisons, then logical operations, and assignments last of all.

- Associativity rules are applied last, and only if operators are at the same level of precedence.

For operator precedence, see the table under the topic, Operators.

Definition

The **auto** keyword declares that a variable has automatic storage class—meaning that it is temporary and is allocated on the *stack*, the area of memory reserved for function-call overhead. This means that, in a sense, the variable flashes in and out of existence.

In practice, the **auto** keyword is never necessary, because **auto** is the default for local variables anyway. To be honest, it's included in the language only for the sake of completeness. You will probably go your entire programming career without finding a legitimate need for this keyword.

Syntax

The auto keyword precedes a variable declaration:

auto   *data_declaration*;

The data definition must occur at a local level (inside a function definition or inside a block); such variable definitions are always auto unless declared **extern** or **static**.

Definition

Like a skilled surgeon, you can use bit fields—one of the tools that C provides to pull apart the insides of a byte and extract individual bits. If you read Chapter 5, "Operators: C the Unique," you may realize that such bit surgery is possible with bitwise operators such as & and |. In fact, bit field operations translate directly into bitwise operations when used in programs. The purpose of bit fields is to provide a technique for making bitwise operations easier to understand. Although not all bitwise operations can be expressed with bit fields, those that can be so expressed make for more readable programs.

Syntax

To declare bit fields, declare a structure and qualify members with a bit width, as follows:

struct [*struct_type_name*] {
      unsigned *field1* : *width1*;
      unsigned *field2* : *width2*;
      ...
      unsigned *fieldN* : *widthN*;
} [*struct_variables*];

Here, each *width* is a nonzero integer, which is one or larger. This number, which must be a constant expression, specifies size of the field in bits. The corresponding field is used just like any other structure member except that its range is restricted according to its size. For example, a bit field of size 1 can take only two values: 0 or 1.

 You cannot take the address of a bit field, although in other respects a bit field is a valid l-value.

N O T E

Syntax for Bit Field Access

Bit fields are integer fields and are accessed exactly like other structure members:

structure_var . *member*

Examples

Suppose you need to represent several Boolean values in a small amount of space. You could represent each value with a separate **int** or **char** variable, but this would be wasteful of memory. Using bit fields conserves space. The following example uses bit fields to store each Boolean (1 or 0) value in one bit:

```
struct {
    unsigned shift:1;
    unsigned alt:1;
    unsigned ctl:1;
} shift_state;
```

Now you can easily store a single bit value in each field. The following code accesses these fields just like ordinary structure members, but it is setting and testing individual bit positions:

```
shift_state.shift = 1;
shift_state.alt = 0;
if (shift_state.ctl)
    ctl_function();
```

These statements are roughly equivalent to the following lines of code, which use the three least-significant bits to represent the SHIFT, ALT, and CTL states, just as the previous example does. The difference is that this version does it the hard way.

```
#define SHIFT_MASK  0x1
#define ALT_MASK    0x2
#define CTL_MASK    0x4

int shift_state

shift_state |= SHIFT_MASK;      /* Set SHIFT bit. */
shift_state &= ~ALT_MASK;       /* Unset ALT bit. */
if (shift_state & CTL_MASK)     /* Test CTL bit.  */
    ctl_function();
```

207

The bit field version, you'll probably agree, is somewhat more readable than this version.

Bit fields can be wider than one bit and sometimes are. You should always bear in mind, though, that the width of the field strictly limits the range of that field. A single bit can represent one of two values (0 or 1), two bits can represent four values (00, 01, 10, or 11), and so on.

Suppose you wanted to represent a playing card's identity in as small a space as possible. By the way, this obsession with space may strike you as odd, but there are many cases where space is significant, especially when you're using large arrays or file operations. When you write many data records to a file, saving a few bytes per record can add up to a great deal of saved disk space. As a side benefit, cutting down on the amount of file space can have great impact on program speed.

In any event, it's possible to represent the two components of a playing card in a small space because each component—suit and rank—is restricted to a small range. To pick the size of the fields, we have to review how many possible values there are for each component and compare these numbers to powers of two. Two bits is enough to represent as many as four different values. Four bits is enough to represent as many as 16 values (see Table B.1).

Table B.1 *Number of bits needed to represent suit and rank.*

Field	Number of Values	This is Equal to or Less Than:	Third Column Equals This Power of 2
suit	4	4	2
rank	13	16	4

Suits can be represented in two bits, and ranks can be represented in four bits. The bit field declaration looks like this:

```
struct cardtype {
    unsigned suit:2;
    unsigned rank:4;
} my_card;
```

To make the values easier to work with, let's assign enu-merated values 0–3 to the symbolic constants CLUBS, DIA-MONDS, HEARTS, and SPADES and use the following symbols for rank values: 1 for ACE, 11–13 for J, Q, and K, and face value for the other ranks.

```
enum {CLUBS, DIAMONDS, HEARTS, SPADES};
enum {ACE =1, J = 11, Q, K}
```

The **enum** keyword is just a convenient way to declare con-stants. See "enum Declarations" for more information on the **enum** syntax.

With the bit field structure and the constants all defined, it's now an easy matter to assign settings to a card. Let's look at a couple of examples. First, the ace of spades:

```
my_card.suit = SPADES;    /* SPADES = 3, or 11 binary */
my_card.rank = ACE;       /* ACE = 1 */
```

The value of SPADES is equal to 3, or 11 binary. The value of ACES is 0001 binary (the leading zeros reminding us that the rank is stored in a field four bits wide). Figure B.1 shows how these values are placed in the resulting structure.

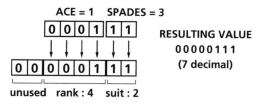

Figure B.1 *Assigning ACE of SPADES to rank and suit.*

Next, let's assign the king of hearts to a card. The following statements assign this value to the my_card structure variable:

```
my_card.suit = HEARTS;    /* HEARTS = 2, or 10 binary */
my_card.rank = K;         /* K = 13, or 1101 binary */
```

209

The value of HEARTS is 2, or 10 binary. The value of K (king) is 13, or 1101 binary. Figure B.2 shows how these values are placed in the resulting structure.

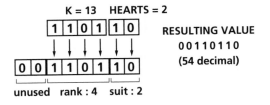

Figure B.2 *Assigning KING of HEARTS to rank and suit.*

As I mentioned, bit fields are convenient ways of representing bitwise operations. The bit field operations for wider fields are less obvious than the operations for fields of only one bit, but the amount of code is not much greater.

When a value is assigned to the suit field, the two corresponding bit positions must first be set to zero—"ANDed out," as it were. Then the new value can be set with the OR operator (|). The following statements assign HEARTS to the suit field:

```
#define SUIT_MASK  0x3    /* 3  = 00000011 binary */
#define RANK_MASK  0x2C    /* 2C = 00111100 binary */

(my_card &= ~SUIT_MASK) |= HEARTS;
```

The case of the rank field is slightly more complicated. Before the bit pattern of K can be combined with the structure, this bit pattern must be shifted to the right two places (two being the size of the preceding field, suit). In other respects, the logic of placing the bits into the proper bit positions in my_card is the same. The following statement executes this bit assignment properly:

```
(my_card &= ~RANK_MASK) |= (K >> 2);
```

210

Clearly, the bit field version is more readable than using bit-wise operators directly. Moreover, the bit field version has the virtue of not requiring you to remember how many places to shift a bit value.

Implementation and Portability

Bit field operations are greatly affected by implementation details. Unless you're writing code that you intend never to run or compile on another system, be careful about making assumptions regarding how bit fields are ordered in physical memory.

When you declare a bit field, almost the only guarantee you have is that it will be allocated in the requested number of bytes. Assuming anything else is usually an unwarranted risk. A typical programming mistake is to assume that bits and bytes in a numeric type are ordered in a certain way— that the first bit field corresponds to the most significant digits, for example, or the least significant.

The problem is that the way one computer arranges bits and bytes in memory may differ from how another computer does it. So you may find that code that runs perfectly well on your system produces mysterious errors on another system. This error is easy to avoid. Simply don't overlay bit fields with other data types (generally done with unions) and then use bit fields to analyze parts of the data.

These issues fall into the general area of portability. This subject is easy to overlook when you're first learning to program—after all, what you're interested in is whether you can get something to run on your own computer! But as you grow in confidence as a programmer and start to learn tricks to squeeze every last bit of speed from your programs, portability becomes an issue. As you write more and more programs you're proud of, it becomes more likely you'll want to recompile them on other systems. So you might as well start forming the right programming habits now.

Bit field implementation, by the way, is a property of compilers and computer architectures and not of individual machines. All systems based on Intel 8086-family processors order bytes in the same way.

Definition

The bitwise operators do just what the word *bitwise* implies: they work on the individual bits of two values. (These values must be some form integer expression, such as **int**, **short**, **long**, **unsigned**, or **char**.) When you use them, you should be serious about wanting to manipulate individual bits. You can use bitwise AND and OR, for example, to form complex logical expressions, but the logical (non-bitwise) operators are recommended for those situations and are more reliable.

Examples

Bitwise operators are most commonly used when you're creating or testing bit masks. See Chapter 5, "Operators: C the Unique" for bit masks used in an example.

Figure B.3 shows how bitwise AND, OR, and XOR (exclusive OR) would operate on sample byte values.

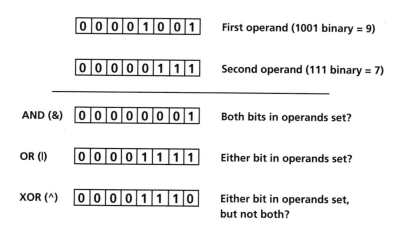

Figure B.3 *Bitwise operators.*

Boolean Values

Definition

Some programming languages have a special Boolean type—a value that can be either TRUE or FALSE. This is a useful concept, because you want to be able to perform comparisons (for example, testing to see whether x is equal to 0) and have the program do something different depending on the true or false value of the result. You may even want to store the true or false value and use it later as part of a complex decision.

C is fully capable of handling true or false values but does not have a special type for them (although you can use the **typedef** keyword to define a special BOOLEAN type if you wish). In any programming language the implementation of a Boolean type is actually an **int**, a **short**, a **char**, or a bit field; C lets you choose the storage most appropriate for the program. It's usually easiest to represent a Boolean value as an **int**, unless you need to pack into a compact structure, in which case **char** (a one-byte integer) or bit fields may be most appropriate.

Syntax Rules

Boolean operations in C follow two rules:

- Control structures consider any nonzero value to be "true." A condition such as (n) is equivalent to the condition (n != 0).

- All comparison and logical (non-bitwise) operators evaluate to 1 if the result of the operation is "true" and 0 if it is "false."

These two rules work together. If a comparison is true, for example, it evaluates to 1, which in turn is considered "true" by a control structure such as an **if** statement. This means that conditions in a control structure work as you would expect:

214

```
/* The statement is printed if a is greater than b. */

if (a >  b)
    printf("a is greater than b.");
```

A strange consequence, is that the numbers 15 and 16 (to take some examples) represent "true" just as the number 1 represents "true." Consequently, a logical expression such as

```
15 && 16  /* Combine 15 and 16 with logical AND */
```

evaluates to 1, although bitwise AND produces a completely different result.

See Chapter 4, "Decisions, Decisions: Control Structures in C," for another discussion of Boolean values and operators.

break Statement

Definition

The **break** keyword exits out of a loop. It's also used to terminate a series of statements for a case within a **switch** statement. This latter use of **break** is probably the most common.

Syntax

The **break** keyword, followed by a semicolon, forms a complete statement:

break;

This statement is valid only within a **switch** statement, a **for** loop, a **while** loop, or a **do-while** loop. The statement causes an immediate exit from the nearest loop. (To break out of several loops, use **goto**.)

Example

Within a **switch** statement, **break** causes control to transfer to the end of the **switch** statement block. Without the use of **break**, control would *fall through* to the next case, meaning that execution would continue sequentially. For example:

```
case 1:
    strcpy(strNum, "One");
    break;
case 2:
    strcpy(strNum, "Two");
    break;
    ...
```

In some cases, it may be convenient to let execution fall through to the next case, so **break** would be omitted. See "switch Keyword" for more information.

Definition

The **case** keyword labels a statement used within a **switch** statement block. As a label, it identifies a specific value you are testing for.

Syntax

The **case** keyword turns a statement into a labeled statement:

case *constant_value*:
      statement

This statement is valid only within a **switch** statement block. A labeled statement is itself a statement; this implies that a statement may be immediately preceded by any number of labels (as in the following example).

The *constant_value* is a constant integer expression. Note that this includes character constants, which are really just integer values.

Example

What's tricky about **case** is that it is only a statement label. Labels don't automatically change the flow of control; this is why each case has to be separated by a **break** statement unless you want execution to fall through. In this example, all five vowels label the same statement block, which exits (**break**) before falling through to the default statement block:

```
switch (c) {
    case 'a':
    case 'e':
```

```
case 'i':
case 'o':
case 'u':
    printf("Character is a vowel");
    break;
default:
    printf("Character is a consonant.");
    break;
}
```

Case Sensitivity

Definition

In C, everything you type is case-sensitive—unless it's inside a comment. Command-line options may or may not be case-sensitive, but that has nothing to do with the language itself.

Case sensitivity simply means that capitalization (or lack thereof) counts. Don't use IF where you mean **if**, for example, or the compiler won't know what you're talking about and will complain accordingly. You should be especially careful about case sensitivity if your background is in BASIC or FORTRAN, languages in which people routinely hit the Caps Lock key without fear of the consequences.

Casts

Definition

A type cast converts a value from one data type to another; for example, you might convert an integer into floating-point data. There are a number of situations in which C will do this for you automatically; a type cast gives you more control.

See "Explicit Type Conversions" for more information.

Definition

The **char** data type is simply a one-byte integer, but typically it is used to store characters: letters, digits, symbols, and so forth—in other words, text. See Chapter 8, "Text Processing," for an introduction to the subject.

Examples

One **char** variable or array element holds a single character, and arrays of characters form character strings. In the case of the latter, you can initialize the character string with a string literal. For example:

```
char letter = 'a';
char name[] = "John Q. Public";
char address[80] = "123 Main Street USA";
```

In the first declaration, a single **char** variable, letter, is declared. In practice, this variable should usually be declared as an integer, because functions that get another character (getc, for example), sometimes need to hold integer values.

```
int letter = 'a';
```

In any case, letter is initialized with a character constant. This constant translates to the numeric code for 'a', which is 97: you can look this up in an ACSII table. (Most personal computers use the ASCII format, although assuming support for ASCII values is not always safe if your code is intended to be ported to different architectures.) Character constants are actually integers.

The preceding declarations of name and address are similar except that they initialize arrays by using character string literals. There is an important difference between single character constants (enclosed in single quotes) and string literals (enclosed in double quotes). A string literal allocates space for every character as well as a null-terminating byte.

221

A string literal also returns the address of the first character, which can be assigned to a pointer or used to initialize an array. A single character constant evaluates to an integer and not a pointer.

The **char** data type is a byte value, so it can hold only 256 different values. Two variations of **char** are:

- **unsigned char**, which ranges from –128 to 127
- **signed char**, which ranges from 0 to 255

The **char** data type without the **signed** or **unsigned** modifier may be signed or unsigned depending on your compiler.

Definition

Character strings hold text, which can be printed, displayed, or written to a file for storage. In C, strings are implemented as an array of bytes (**char** data type), each byte holding a number associated with an ASCII code for a letter or other character. You can also use arrays of **char** for other purposes, since they are basically just numbers.

See Chapter 8, "Text Processing," for more information on the general use of strings. See "String Literals" for details of how text can be represented within a string constant.

Code

Definition

The term *code* is one you'll hear spoken a great deal by C programmers. It's an annoying piece of jargon because it's not always used consistently. The programming world might be better off without it, but it won't go away.

Simply stated, *code* usually refers to the executable statements in your program. But sometimes it refers to everything in the program, including data declarations.

The use of the word *code* is firmly rooted in the history of computers. In the early 1950s, programmers wrote in machine language; at first they didn't have assembly language to write somewhat meaningful statements such as "JUMP TOP_OF_LOOP". This made programming a particularly tedious task (and you thought it was tough now) in which one had to look up the bit pattern to carry out each instruction—the instruction's *code*, if you will. Every processor has its own instruction set that associates certain binary numbers with certain actions: 11001000 might be an ADD instruction, for example, and 10001111 might be a JUMP instruction. To anyone but a chip designer, by the way, these associations will appear to be chosen at random.

(And while we're on the subject, aren't you glad you have a programming language such as C, so you don't have to look up instruction codes?)

When you work with machine-language instructions, it's natural to think of each instruction as a numeric code for a particular action. Machine-language programmers would create punched cards with the instructions on them (code) as well as other cards with numbers to be operated on (data). Since then, programmers have continued to talk about code and data as the two main divisions of their programs. The term *code* has continued to refer to the executable part of the program long after people have stopped writing in machine language.

The jargon is so ubiquitous that it often gets abused. Programmers frequently refer to everything they write and compile as code, even though in other contexts, it refers only to executable statements. Aware of the pitfalls of inconsistency, I've mostly avoided the word, *code* in this book. But it's so natural a part of programmer-speak, you may notice that it's crept into my vocabulary anyway.

Definition

In a computer program, the purpose of comments is to let you place useful remarks in the program listing. These are read by a human, not the compiler. A programmer is free to put any text in a comment. In addition to remarks on how the program works, comments often contain information such as program author, date, and even a copyright notice—unless the programmer is in a silly mood, in which case the comment might contain anything.

Syntax

Comments consist of all text appearing between /* and */. This text forms a part of the program listing or source file, but it is ignored during compilation:

/* comment_text */

The text may span multiple lines:

/* some _text

...

more_text */

Many C compilers, but not all, support the comment-to-end-of-line style comment. Here, the end of a program line terminates the comment:

// comment_text

 The comment syntax has the following exceptions: a begin-comment symbol (// or /*) inside a quoted string does not begin a comment. Also, a begin-comment NOTE symbol inside a comment does not begin a comment. This last statement, though it sounds trivial, has important implications for nesting of comments, which I'll discuss at the end of this topic.

Examples

You can use both multiple-line and single-line comments in code:

```
/* The next two lines of code are data declarations,
   declaring two ints and two doubles. */

int i, j;      /* Indexes into 2-D array */
double x, y;   /* Point coordinates */
```

Comments can be a helpful for explaining the purpose of a loop, a calculation, or an algorithm. But there are two even more obvious places to use them: just before a function definition, to explain the purpose of the function; and on each line that declares or defines variables, to explain the purpose of each variable. For example:

```
/* Factorial function.
   Return the factorial of n: which is the product of
   all numbers from 1 to n. 1 * 2 * 3 * ... * n     */

int factorial(int n) {
    int result = 1;  /* Accumulator of product */

      /* While n not zero, mult. result by n and
         then decrement n. */

    while (n) {
        result *= n--;
    }
    return result;
}
```

Where you place comments is entirely up to you. Just remember that you have to write the comments yourself, and you're usually the main person to read the comments. You may come back to a program six months from now and want to modify or debug it. At that point you may find yourself scratching your head, wondering: what *was* the purpose of that function? So comments can be helpful, especially if well written.

The Problem of Nested Comments

A nested comment is a comment nested inside a larger comment. You might not think there would ever be a need for such a thing, but consider what happens if you want to temporarily take the following code out of the program:

```
int i, j;      /* Indexes into 2-D array */
double x, y;   /* Point coordinates */
```

You don't want to delete this text, only to re-enter it later, so it might seem logical to *comment out* these two lines so that the compiler ignores them:

```
/*
int i, j;      /* Indexes into 2-D array */
double x, y;   /* Point coordinates */
*/
```

The comment now extends from the first line in this example to the fourth line, causing all four lines to be ignored, right? Wrong. The problem is that a comment extends from the first begin-comment symbol (/*) to the first end-comment symbol (*/) encountered thereafter. So, surprisingly, the following is considered a single comment block:

```
/*
int i, j;      /* Indexes into 2-D array */
```

This comment begins on the first line and ends at the *end of the second line*. The compiler then continues on its merry way and attempts to compile the following:

```
double x, y;   /* Point coordinates */
*/
```

228

Here the problems become evident. The statement "double x, y;" gets compiled even though we wanted to exclude it. Furthermore, the end-comment symbol (*/) appears outside a comment, which is wrong and causes a syntax error.

So don't try to comment out any lines of code that already contain a comment. If you do need to temporarily remove some code and don't want to erase it, a more reliable alternative is to use conditional compilation. For example:

```
#if 0
int i, j;      /* Indexes into 2-D array */
double x, y;   /* Point coordinates */
#endif
```

These directives can be nested successfully. See "#if Directive" for more information.

Definition

A compound data type points to or contains a combination of values, in contrast to the primitive data types (**char**, **int**, **short**, **long**, **float**, **double**, etc.), each of which contains a simple value. In general, you can think of the standard data types as building blocks, and compound data types as the structures you build from these types.

By using the **typedef** keyword, you can even name the types you design and then use them in declarations as you would **int** or **double** —just as if your type names were part of the language.

C provides the following principal techniques for creating compound types:

- An *array* is a series of data members, all of the same base type. Members (or elements) of the array can be referred to by a numeric index; this makes arrays easy to size to arbitrary lengths.

- A *structure* is a series of data members, which can be of different types. Each position in the structure has a unique name.

- A *union* is similar to a structure except that the members of a union occupy the same memory location. This is useful when you want to reuse the same area of memory for different uses at different times.

- A *pointer* to a data type can store the address of any variable (or other item in memory) having that type.

See the individual topic ("Arrays," "Structures," "Unions," or "Pointers") for more information. See "Declarations" for a summary of how pointers, arrays, and structures are declared.

Examples

Data types can be defined inside data types to any level of complexity. For example, a structure of arrays of pointers to structures is perfectly valid. A common kind of compound data type is an array of structures. This is, in effect, a table with fixed columns and any number of rows:

```
struct employee_rec {
    char[30]  name;
    char[30]  address;
    char[20]  city_state;
    short   employee_id;
} employee_table[1000];
```

In this example, employee_rec is a structure type, and employee_table is an array of 1,000 of these structures.

You can also create enumerated types, which are values that can range over a subset of integer values. See "enum Declarations."

Compound Statements

Definition

A compound statement is a series of C statements (data declarations or executable code) enclosed in braces. This concept is truly simple. The reason it's *useful* is mainly that it enables an **if** block, a **while** loop, or a **for** loop to contain any number of statements.

Some people also refer to a compound statement as a multiple statement.

Syntax

Anywhere an executable statement can occur, a compound statement can also appear. In terms of C grammar, a compound statement forms a single, unified statement.

```
{
    statements
}
```

The *statements* consist of one or more C statements, and data declarations can be included as long as they precede all executable statements within the compound statement. Generally, each statement is terminated with a semicolon, but that would not be the case if one of those statements were itself a compound statement. Note that a semicolon is not used to terminate the statement block. That's because the closing brace (}) is sufficient for the compiler to know that the end of a compound statement has been reached.

The idea that a compound statement is itself a statement shouldn't be at all confusing, because the concept is taken from English grammar. The statement "First I woke, and then I cried," is made up of two grammatically complete subsentences, but the whole statement makes up one unified sentence.

232

Example

The following **if** statement tests to see whether a value is out of range. If it is, then the two statements within braces ({}) are executed: a statement that prints an error message and a **return** statement. If the value is not out of range, then neither of these statements is executed, and execution skips past the closing brace (}):

```
if (x < 0 || x > 100) {
    printf("x out of range.");
    return -1;
}
```

For more examples of compound statements, see Chapter 4, "Decisions, Decisions: Control Structures in C." This chapter also explains how compound statements can create their own level of scope.

Definition

The conditional operator is one of those C operators that might seem redundant at first. It returns one of two different values depending on the value of a condition; clearly, you can do the same with an **if-else** statement. But the operator is not entirely redundant, and it does add important elements to the language.

You can find at least two practical purposes for the conditional operator: first, it's an effective code-compacting technique, sometimes reducing several lines of **if-else** code to a one-line expression; second, it's the only reliable way to put **if-else** logic into macro functions, because macros are almost always written as expressions and not as complete statements.

Syntax

The conditional operator forms an expression from three smaller expressions:

conditional_expr ? expr1 : expr2

Because the result is an expression (and not a complete statement), it can be placed inside larger expressions.

To evaluate this expression, the program first evaluates *conditional_expr*. If it is nonzero, the value of the entire expression is *expr1*. If *conditional_expr* is zero, the value of the entire expression is *expr2*. The program evaluates either *expr1* or *expr2*, as appropriate, but never both.

Usage

One of the simplest ways to use the conditional operator is to call one of two functions. For example:

```
a == b ? function1() : function2();
```

This is equivalent to the following if statement:

234

```
if (a == b)
    function1();
else
    function2();
```

It's more typical, though, to use the value of the expression by placing it all inside a larger expression. Here, one of two different strings is given as input to a printf statement:

```
printf("The value of n is %s.", n ? "one" : "zero");
```

Presumably, n has been limited to one of two values in this example—one and zero.

In this example, the expression using the conditional operator is:

```
n ? "one" : "zero"
```

If n is any nonzero value, this expression returns a pointer to the string "one". Otherwise, it returns a pointer to the string "zero". To understand this example, remember that when a string literal such as "one" appears in code, the compiler allocates the string data in memory somewhere and replaces the expression with a pointer to this data. Consequently, the conditional expression evaluates to the address of one of two strings ("one" or "zero"), and this pointer value is passed as an argument to printf.

So the entire printf example is equivalent to:

```
if (n)
    printf("The value of n is %s.", "one");
else
    printf("The value of n is %s.", "two");
```

Clearly, the version that uses the conditional operator is more compact.

For more examples, see Chapter 5, "Operators: C the Unique," and "#define Directive."

Definition

The **const** keyword lets you create a variable or argument while ensuring that its value won't change. This keyword modifies a declaration, informing the compiler that it must watch for and prevent all assignments to the item. Initialization, however, is allowed.

Arguments and pointers are particularly useful contexts for the **const** keyword: you can use a **const** pointer argument to prevent data corruption by a function ("Usage 3," below.)

Syntax

When used at the beginning of a declaration, **const** modifies the *type*:

const   *type items*;

Any *items* so declared cannot be the target of an assignment. They can, however, be initialized in the declaration and usually are. If an *item* is a pointer, then anything the pointer points to (such as **item*) cannot be the target of an assignment

The **const** keyword can also be used inside a pointer declaration:

type * **const** *pointer*, ...

Here the ellipses indicate that other items may follow in a declaration. With this syntax, the pointer itself cannot be modified (*item*), but what it points to is not necessarily constant (unless *type* itself is preceded by **const**).

Usage 1: const Variables

The use of **const** with a simple variable is, well, simple. Once a variable is defined with **const**, the compiler flags all statements in which the variable is the target of an assignment.

```
const int id = 12345;   /* This is valid; id may be
                                initialized. */
...
id = 10000;   /* ERROR! attempt to assign new value. */
```

You can also declare compound types, such as arrays and structures, as **const**. All elements or members become **const** items. For example, no member of the **const** array in the following example can be assigned a new value. (You can think of each element as being a **const** integer.)

```
const int magic_nums[] = {10, 27, 4, 53}
...
magic_num[2] = 99;      /* ERROR! */
```

Usage 2: const Pointers

If you're familiar with pointers, you may have thought up a loophole for changing a **const** variable. Perhaps you could get a pointer to point to the variable and then use the pointer to change it:

```
const int id = 12345;
int *p;

p = &id;     /* ???? */
*p = 10000;
```

But C is just too smart to permit this. C does not allow the address of a **const** variable to be assigned to just any old pointer, so the statement that it catches you on this:

```
p = &id;     /* ???? */
```

For the address of a **const** variable to be assigned to a pointer, the pointer must itself point to a **const** type (in this case, **const int**). So the following is legal:

```
const int id = 12345;
const int *p;

p = &id;   /* Valid, because both are "const int"
               types. */
```

But if you then used p to change the value of the variable indirectly, the compiler would flag that as an error:

```
*p = 10000;   /* ERROR; *p cannot change. */
```

Think of p, declared as **const int***, as "a pointer to a constant integer." So *p cannot change, because *p is the integer that p points to. Now p itself can change as often as you like, being made to point to different **const** integers. It can also point to regular integers. But *p cannot be assigned a new value as long as p is declared as **const int***.

If you want to prevent p *itself* from changing, place **const** to the right of the indirection operator (*):

```
int * const p = &i;        /* p cannot change. */
```

Here the pointer p cannot change after being declared and initialized. But the item it points to is of type **int**, so *p can be freely assigned new values. To declare a constant pointer for which neither p nor *p can be assigned a value, use **const** twice:

```
const int * const p = &id;
```

Again, p can be initialized in the declaration, but it cannot be assigned a value in any other assignment statement.

Usage 3: const Argument Types

As pointed out in Chapter 7, "Pointers and Other Sharp Instruments," passing by reference is useful for two reasons:

first, it efficiently passes a variable by placing just the address on the stack; second, it enables the function to change the value of the variable.

But in some cases, you might want the advantages of the first reason while preventing the second from happening. You might want to pass an address but guarantee that the function won't change anything at the address—or, if the item pointed to is an array, you want to guarantee that nothing in the array will be changed.

The way to provide this guarantee is to declare the argument as a pointer to a **const** type. For example:

```
void fnct(const char str[], const double *px, *py);
```

This is a function prototype declaring that the pointer variables str, px, and py cannot be used, through indirection, to assign new values to any data. This is useful information, even in a prototype, because it means that you can call the function with complete confidence that it won't corrupt your data. (Of course, some functions do need to change some arguments and so should not use **const** declarations for those arguments.)

Within the function definition itself, you could always *read* the value of *str, *px, or *py. But any of the following statements would be flagged as errors:

```
*str = 'a';
str[1] = '2';
str[2] = 'z';
*px = 0.0
*py = 98.6;
```

Although all the argument types are **const** pointers, you can pass any **char** and **double** addresses you want. Their types do not need to be **const**. This is a consequence of the following rules:

239

- The address of a **const** item cannot be assigned to a regular pointer (a pointer or argument that is not **const**).

- However, the address of a regular item can be assigned to a **const** pointer.

So the following is perfectly legal:

```
void fnct(const char str[], const double *px, *py);

char str[] = "Nice kitty";
double  x, y;
...
fnct(str, &x, &y);
```

Definition

Just as programs have variables, they also have constants, which are fixed values in the program: simple examples include numbers such as 5 and 1.002. Virtually any useful program uses constants somewhere.

Constants come in three basic kinds: literals, symbolic constants, and **const** variables. The rest of this topic concerns literal constants. Symbolic constants (see "#define Directive") are translated into literals by the preprocessor. Variables declared with **const**, are, strictly speaking, variables; but the compiler prevents assignments to them. The purest form of a constant is a literal constant, which expresses a constant value directly.

Syntax

The different forms of literal constant include integer, floating-point, and string literals:

digits	// integer constant
0*digits*	// integer constant, octal notation (leading zero)
0X*digits*	// integer constant, hexadecimal notation
digits.digits	// floating-point constant
*digits*E*exp*	// floating-point constant with exponent
"*string_text*"	// character string constant
'*character*'	// single character constant

Here, **X** and **E** indicate either an uppercase or a lowercase letter.

Thus, 5 is an integer constant, whereas 5.0 is a floating-point constant. Here are some examples of other floating-point constants:

```
3.1415
12000.5
63e-2
85.66789e12
```

Storage Specification

Constant values are stored in memory in the most efficient way possible, although you can control how they are stored to some extent. On 16-bit systems, an integer is stored as a two-byte signed integer if not outside the two-byte integer range; if outside this range, it must be stored as a long. However, the suffix U forces it to be stored as an unsigned integer regardless of size. An L suffix forces it to be stored as a **long**. (The lowercase versions of these letters can also be used.) The suffix UL forces it to be stored as an **unsigned long**. For example, the following number is stored as a long, even though it is small:

```
7L
```

Floating-point constants are normally stored as double, regardless of value, unless you specify float as the size with an f or F suffix:

```
1.005F
```

Single-character and character-string constants are different, which is why it's important to remember to use only single quotes with character constants. A character constant translates into its ASCII equivalent. For example, '0' is another way of representing the number 48. But its the way a value is used, rather than its numeric value, that determines whether it is a letter or a number. Although you can print the numeric value of a character constant, such constants are usually intended to be used in string operations.

A string constant is an array of type **char**, and has a terminating null byte. See Chapter 8, "Text Processing," for more information, and the topic "String Literals" for some of the more advanced rules applying to strings representation.

Definition

The **continue** keyword jumps to the end of a loop but (unlike **break**) doesn't exit the loop. This is a reasonably simple idea; it's like someone saying, "Go onto the next page, please."

Syntax

The **continue** keyword, followed by a semicolon, forms a complete statement:

continue;

This statement is valid only within a **for** loop, a **while** loop, or a **do-while** loop. The effect is to jump to the bottom of the loop (executing the *increment* expression, if in a **for** loop) and then continue to the next iteration.

Examples

Ultimately, the **continue** statement isn't a necessity but is merely a convenience. You could accomplish the same results by putting a label at the bottom of the loop and then using a **goto** statement. For example, the following code

```
while (expression) {
        statements
        continue;
        statements
}
```

is equivalent to the code shown in Figure C.1.

```
while (expression) {
        statements
        goto bottom_of_loop;
        statements
    bottom of loop:
        ;
}
```

Figure C.1 *Effect of a continue statement*

In Figure C.1, I've added an empty statement—a lone semicolon (;)—for syntactical correctness. At least one statement must follow a label. An empty statement is completely legal and is useful in this situation.

There is one respect in which Figure C.1 is an oversimplification: you wouldn't put a naked **continue** or **goto** inside the loop like this. A **continue** or **goto** is almost always enclosed within an **if** statement. Otherwise, the second set of *statements* would never be executed, and it would have been pointless to have written them in the first place.

In any event, the purpose of the **continue** keyword is get out of the statement block early, without getting out of the loop. For example, the following code prints all the prime numbers between 1 and n. The body of the loop first tests i to see whether it is a prime number and then advances directly to the next value of i if it is not a prime. Otherwise, it prints the results before advancing to the next value of i.

```
for(i = 1, num_of_primes++; i <= n; i++) {
    if (! is_a_prime(i))
        continue;
    printf("%d\n", i);
    num_of_primes++;
}
```

In this example, is_a_prime is a function defined in the program. This function could be defined as follows:

```
#include <math.h>

int is_a_prime (int n) {
    int i, test_val;

    test_val = int(sqrt(n));
    for (i = 2; i <= test_val; i++) {
        if ((n % i) == 0)
                return 0;
    }
    return 1;
}
```

It's certainly possible to write nested loops in C (loops inside other loops). The continue statement always applies to the nearest (most tightly enclosing) for, while, or do loop.

Definition

C supports a variety of data types. The two major categories are primitive data types and compound data types. Primitive data types are ones directly supported by keywords such as **int** and **double**. Compound data types can be created through complex declarations that involve the **struct** or **union** keywords, pointers, or arrays. You can optionally use the **typedef** keyword to provide an alias for a complex type and then use this alias to declare variables just as you would use primitive-data-type keywords.

The rest of this section summarizes the standard data types in C and their minimum ranges. Some implementations of C support extended types, such as 64-bit integers. For more precise information on range and precision, see topics for individual keywords.

C has no primitive string type. Instead, text strings are represented as arrays of **char**.

Table D.1 *Data types in C..*

TYPE	DESCRIPTION	RANGE AND PRECISION
signed char	One byte integer	−128 to 127
unsigned char	One byte integer, unsigned	0 to 255
char	Same as **char** or **unsigned char**,depending on the implementation	
short	Two-byte integer	−32,768 to 32,767
unsigned short	Two-byte integer, unsigned	0 to 65,535
long	Four-byte integer	Approx. −2.147 billion to 2.147 billion

(continued)

246

Data Types

TYPE	DESCRIPTION	RANGE AND PRECISION
unsigned long	Four-byte integer, unsigned	0 to approx. 4.292 billion
int	Same as **short** or **long**, depending on implementation	
unsigned int, or unsigned	Same as **unsigned short** or **unsigned long**, depending on implementation	
single	Four-byte floating point	Approx. plus or minus 3.4 times 10 to the 38th. Seven digits of precision.
double	Eight-byte floating point	Approx. plus or minus 1.7 times 10 to the 308th. 15 digits of precision.

Declarations

Defintion

True to their name, declarations are like declarative sentences in English. They don't exactly tell the processor to do something; they give information about how a variable or function is to be used. Executable statements, in contrast, are more nearly like imperative sentences, commanding an action such as adding numbers or printing a result.

In C, a declaration has one of two purposes: to define a variable or to provide type information to the compiler about something defined elsewhere in the program. The latter category includes **extern** declarations and function prototypes.

Syntax

A declaration forms a complete statement. The possible syntax for declarations is potentially complicated, but it can be basically summarized as below:

[*storage*] [*cv*] *type item* [, *item*]... ;

Here the brackets indicate that something is optional. The ellipses indicate that *item* can be repreated any number of times. The *storage* can be **extern**, **static**, **auto**, or **register**. The *cv* syntax represents **const** or **volatile**.

The critical part of this syntax is *item*, which itself can be simple or frighteningly complex. Each *item* has the following syntax:

decl_specifier [= *initializer*]

The initializer can be any valid constant, including an aggregate in the case of compound types. (See "Aggregates.") The *decl_specifier* is frequently just a variable name, but it may also involve pointer indirection (*), a function call (parentheses), and array brackets ([]), to any level of complexity. In general, the *decl_specifier* can be any of the following:

identifier
decl_specifier[*index*]
*decl_specifier
decl_specifier(*argument_list*)

In decl_specifier[index], the brackets are intended literally."
The *index* is optional; it need not be fixed if the dimension
size is supplied elsewhere (by the calling function or by an
aggregate). If it is supplied, *index* must be a positive, constant integer.

Examples

By applying this syntax recursively, you can make declarations as complex as needed. Some examples should help
clarify. The simplest declaration just declares a variable (in
this case, a variable called "count"):

```
int count;
```

On one line, you can declare as many variables—all of the
same type—as you need. Unless preceded by the **extern** keyword, these declarations are definitions—that is, they actually create the variables.

```
int     count, a, b, c;
double  x, y, z;
```

When defining variables, you can selectively initialize any
variables in the list that you wish. This is a particularly
good idea with local variables, which otherwise are intialized to random values (global variables are initialized to
zero or NULL).

```
int     count = 0, a, b, c = 15, d;
```

Any of the items declared can be an array, a pointer, a function, or compound types made up of these elements:

```
double    a, b, *ptr, c, fn(), arr[50], x, y;
double    matrix[5][5];
long      (*fn1)(), *f2(), *array_of_ptrs[10];
```

Parentheses can be used to determine precedence in interpreting the operators. For example, in the last declaration above, fn1 is a pointer to a function returning type **double**; f2 is a function returning a pointer to type **double**.

Prototypes and Pointers to Functions

In the last line of the preceding example, *f2() is a function prototype and (*fn1)() is a pointer declaration. The way to distinguish these correctly is to consider that if (*fn1)() appears in executable code, the indirection operator (*) is resolved before a function call is launched. Therefore, f1 must be a pointer to a function, whereas *f2() is a function returning a pointer to a **long**.

```
long      (*f1)(), *f2();
```

Let's look carefully at how the operators resolve. First, suppose that f1 is declared along with a function, fnct, that simply returns a **long**:

```
long      (*f1)(), fnct();
```

Because f1 is a pointer, it needs to be initialized to the address of a function:

```
/* After this assignment, f1 points to fnct(), so that
   *f1
   refers to fnct(). */

f1 = &fnct;
```

Now if the expression (*f1)() appears in an executable statement, it is resolved as shown in Figure D.1

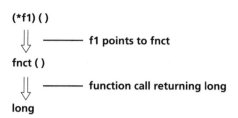

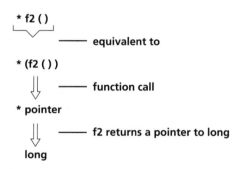

Figure D.1 *Calling a function through a pointer.*

Figure D.1 shows how f1, used in code, is evaluated as a *pointer to a function.* A declaration reflects how something is used in code; therefore, f1's status as a pointer to a function is determined by its declaration. Similarly, if *f2() appears in executable code, it must be resolved as a function returning a pointer, as shown in Figure D.2.

Figure D.2 *A function that returns a pointer.*

So f2 must be an actual function—regardless of its return type—and it must have a function definition somewhere in the program. So far, it has only been declared as a prototype.

To improve type checking, an argument list should be added to the prototype. The argument names (a and b) are optional.

```
long      *f2(int a, int b);
```

Even if the function is intended to be called with no arguments, it should have an argument list: **void**.

```
long      *f2(void);
```

For more examples of prototypes, see Chapter 2, "Anatomy
of a C Program, Part I." Not all functions return pointers, of
course.

If f2 is an actual function, what is f1? Because f1 is only
a pointer, it would be an error to provide a function definition for f1. Instead, f1 must be set to point to something that
is a real function (a_real_function in the following example).
At that point, indirect calls can be made through f1.

```
long  johns = 0;
long  a_real_function(int a, int b);
long  (*f1)(int a, int b);

f1 = & a_real_function;  /* f1 -> a_real_function   */
johns = (*f1)(3, 5);     /* Call function f1 points to. */
...
long  a_real_function(int a, int b) {
    return (a * b);
}
```

Pointers to functions may seem strange, but they definitely
have their uses. See "Pointers to Functions" for further discussion.

Storage Class and Other Modifiers

Each declaration may have one of the following storage class
modifiers:

extern
static
auto
register

And one of the following modifiers:

const
volatile

The use of these keywords can affect the overall meaning of the declaration. If a variable declaration includes the **extern** modifier and does not have an initializer, it is an external variable declaration only; it does not *define* the variable (it does not actually allocate space for this variable in program memory). The variable must be defined somewhere in the program—either in the current source file or in another module to be linked to the program.

```
extern int  cents_less;   /* cents_less defined somewhere. */
```

With **extern**, declarations do define the variable. Be careful here, because a variable of global scope must be defined in only one place. For this reason, **extern** declarations should be placed in header files, and variable definitions should never be placed there. (If you're not using multiple modules, by the way, **extern** is not particularly useful and even header files are not terribly necessary.)

Structures and Type Definitions

The subject of declarations in C is difficult to exhaust because of the considerable flexibility of the language in this area. Two kinds of declarations not mentioned so far include uses of **struct** and **typedef**.

Variables can be declared along with a structure declaration. For example:

253

```
struct  point_type {
   double x;
   double y;
} pt1, pt2, origin = {0, 0};
```

With this structure declared as a type, it can be used in other variable declarations where *type* is called for in the syntax. For example, the following declaration creates four point structures:

```
struct point_type   pt3, pt4, pt5, point_break;
```

For more information on struct syntax, see "struct Keyword."

Finally, another kind of declaration is the **typedef** statement, which associates a complex type with a single identifier. See "typedef Keyword" for more information.

Definition

The **#define** directive has three broad purposes: first, to provide an easy, efficient way to create readable constants (called *symbolic constants*); second, to enable you to write macro functions, which are similar to functions but supported through text replacement at compile time rather than through a run-time call. Finally, the directive can be used to define a symbol for the sake of controlling a condition during compilation (in conjunction with statements such as **#ifdef**).

Syntax

The **#define** statement can be used in any of the following ways:

#define   *identifier replacement*
#define   *identifier(arg1 [,arg2...]) replacement*
#define   *identifier*

Here, the brackets indicate an optional item that can be repeated any number of times. The *replacement* is a series of nonspace characters; however, *replacement* can include embedded spaces if delimited by parentheses or quotation marks. You can use line-continuation (\) to continue beyond one physical line.

Usage 1: Symbolic Constants

Many programs deal with arbitrary or difficult-to-remember numbers. For example, you might have a program that does a lot of trig calculations, and you need to use pi (an important quantity in math equal to approximately 3.14159265). You can define a constant to represent pi as follows:

```
#define PI   3.14159265
```

By convention, symbolic constants are always uppercase. (This distinguishes them from variables.) Of course, the compiler will let you use any name you want.

255

Given this **#define** directive, wherever the word "PI" appears in your program, the compiler replaces PI with the numeral 3.14159265. This happens from the point at which PI is defined to end of the current source file. If you ever change the value of PI—perhaps you decide to use a more precise approximation—you need only change it in one place: the **#define** directive.

 The symbol is not replaced if it appears in a comment, a quoted string, or as part of a larger word (PI inside PIG is not replaced).

A symbolic constant is different from a variable that merely has a constant value, although the two things may at first seem the same. For example, you could define PI as a variable set to this value:

```
double pi = 3.14159265;
```

This data definition allocates a double-precision floating-point number (eight bytes), taking valuable space in the data area used for program variables. Using a **#define** here would have taken no variable space; instead, the compiler's preprocessor replaces each occurrence of "PI" in the program text with "3.14159265." The change is not permanent; it does not overwrite your copy of the program source code. But the effect is the same as if you had typed "3.14159265" everywhere instead of "PI".

An important aspect of symbolic constants is that you can use them for variable initialization. For example, you couldn't do the following if PI itself were a global variable:

```
double angle1 = PI / 2;
```

Symbolic constants are most frequently used for representing arbitrary numbers, such as the maximum string size or size of an array. Typically, you define all such numbers as symbolic constants at the beginning of the program—or in a header file if using multiple modules (because constants have to be defined in each individual module, and a header file ensures that every module gets them). Then, if you ever need to change a definition, you need change it only in one place. For example:

```
#define   ROWSIZE   30
#define   COLSIZE   20
...
int matrix[ROWSIZE][COLSIZE];
int matrix2[ROWSIZE][COLSIZE];
```

The **#define** directive need give no replacment value; in that case, if the symbol is found anywhere, it is replaced with an empty string (no characters); in other words, the occurrence of the symbol is simply removed without replacement, before compilation.

Usage 2: Macro Functions

Macro functions are similar to standard functions but are implemented by the C preprocessor rather than through a run-time call. For example, given the definition

```
#define max(A, B)   ((A)>(B)?(A):(B))
```

the preprocessor replaces the expression "max(i, j)" with the following just before compiling:

```
((i)>(j)?(i):(y))
```

The effect is roughly the same as if you wrote a function named max that returned the larger of two values passed to it. There are few things possible with standard functions that are not possible with macros. The main limitation of macro functions is that they provide absolutely no type checking.

The use of parentheses around each argument in the replacement pattern (as shown in the previous example) is a good idea because it forces evaluation of each argument before the surrounding operators are resolved. Otherwise, if the arguments themselves contain operators, the effect of a macro function can be difficult to predict.

Usage 3: Controlling Compilation

If you use the **#ifdef** or **#ifndef** directive anywhere in the code, then the compiler either reads or ignores certain blocks of code, depending on which symbols are defined. See "#ifdef Directive" for a fuller explanation.

The **#ifdef** and **#ifndef** directives don't care where a symbol is defined, merely that it is defined. You can define a symbol without giving it a replacement value; in that case, if it does appear anywhere, it is replaced with an empty string. However, it is still a valid symbol for the purposes of directives such as **#ifdef**:

```
#define USE_8086
...
#ifdef USE_8086
// Optimize for Intel
...
#endif
```

Most often, symbols that control compilation are specified on the command line; see your compiler documentation for more information.

Definitions vs. Declarations

Definition

The terms *definition* and *declaration* are closely related in C:

- Every definition is a declaration.

- But not every declaration is a definition.

The difference is important. A definition creates a variable—meaning that it actually causes the compiler to allocate space in program memory. Each variable must have a unique definition that occurs once and only once in the program. Other kinds of declarations—**extern** declarations and function prototypes—are not unique and can be included in every module.

The following example is a variable definition. Because the definition creates the variable and allocates space for it, it can also initialize it.

```
int i = 5;
```

Declarations that are not definitions exist only to give scope and type information to the compiler. The two most common examples are **extern** variable declarations and function prototypes. Declarations can also create structures, unions, and types (by using **typedef**). All kinds of declarations can be profitably placed in a header file, especially when you are working with more than one module.

Examples

Here are some examples of declarations that are not definitions:

```
extern int i; /* Integer i defined somewhere, possibly in
                       another module */

void fnct(double x); /* Prototype */
```

NOTE

A #define directive is neither a data definition nor a declaration but is merely an instruction to the preprocessor. Despite the name, a #define directive is much more like a declaration than a definition, because it can safely be placed in a header file.

do Statement

Definition

In working with loops, sometimes you want to ensure that the body of the loop is executed at least once. This is what a **do-while** loop is for. In virtually all other respects, it is the same as a **while** loop—executing as long as a specified condition is true.

Syntax

A **do-while** statement forms one unified statement in C:

do
       loop_body_statement
while (*expression*);

The *loop_body_statement* is frequently a compound statement (see "Example"). Because the entire **do-while** loop forms one statement, it can be nested inside other control structures. The loop continues execution as long as *expression* evaluates to a nonzero (true) value.

Example

The following statements output characters from a file until the end of the file is reached. At least one character is read. In the case of an empty file, this character is an end-of-file character (EOF), which is defined in the file STDIO.H.

```
#include <stdio.h>
...
do {
    c = getc(fp);
    putchar(c);
} while (c != EOF);
```

261

Definition

The **double** data type is a double-precision floating-point number, stored in eight bytes. The related, but smaller, type is **float** (although one would expect it to be "single" so as to correspond better to **double**).

Range and Precision

Approximately plus or minus 1.8 times 10 to the 308th power, with 14 places of precision after the decimal point. Tiny nonzero values can get as close to zero as approximately plus or minus 4.9 times 10 to the –324th power. The type can also hold the value zero precisely.

Syntax

You can declare any number of double-precision floating-point numbers by placing **double** at the beginning of the declaration statement:

[*storage*] [*cv*] **double** *items*;

Here the brackets indicate optional prefixes: *storage* is a storage-class specifier (**auto**, **extern**, **register**, **static**) and *cv* is **const**, **volatile**, or both. The *items* are one or more simple or complex variable declarations.

Example

The following statement defines a simple variable (temperature), an array (daily_temps), and a pointer (ptr_to_float):

```
double   temperature, daily_temps[200], *ptr_to_float;
```

Usage

The **double** floating-point format is generally preferable to **float**, except where storage space is at a premium (such as files, structures, and arrays of structures). It's difficult to compare efficiency of **float** calculations against those using **double**, because different systems implement floating-point operations in different ways. However, math coprocessors typically operate directly on eight-byte floating-point numbers, making **double** at least as fast to operate on as **float**. The recent trend in microprocessors is to support on-board math-coprocessor instructions, having the effect of giving every system a coprocessor.

Definition

The **#elif** directive is useful in conditional compilation when you want to specify a series of alternatives, similar to an **else if** statement. An **#elif** directive specifies a compile-time condition just as an **#if** directive does.

Syntax

The directive specifies a condition that is a constant integer expression:

#elif *constant_expression*

As with the **#if** directive, the *constant_expression* may not include the **sizeof** operator, type casts, or **enum** constants. The expression may include the special **define**(*symbol*) operator, which evaluates to 1 if *symbol* is previously defined and 0 otherwise.

See "#if Directive" for a discussion of conditional compilation as well as complete syntax.

Definition

The **else** keyword provides a way of suggesting an alternative. The **if** keyword executes a statement—or statement block—conditionally; **else** lets you specify what to execute when the condition is not met.

What's useful to know about **else** is that by combining it with a nested **if** statement, you can, in effect, create any number of **else if** clauses, even though there is no "elseif" keyword.

Syntax

The **else** keyword appears in the following syntax:

if (*expression*)
    statement1
[**else**
    statement2]

Here the braces indicate that the **else** clause is optional. Note that either *statement1*, or both, can be a compound statement. If *statement2* is itself an **if-else** statement, you can create multiple alternatives, and are not limited to two.

See "if Keyword" for more information and examples.

Definition

An empty statement (also called a null statement) consists of a lone semicolon:

```
;
```

The statement doesn't do anything, and it certainly doesn't seem to have much purpose. However, it's useful in a few cases—mainly when you need to jump to the very end of a function or loop. Because *some* statement must follow every label, you can't place a label at the very end of a statement block —there must be some statement, and an empty statement is perfectly legal. See "continue Keyword" for an example.

As a consequence of an empty statement being legal, the C syntax is fairly forgiving when you type too many semicolons. For example, the following function definition does not cause an error:

```
double pythagorus(double a, double b) {
    return sqrt(a*a + b*b);;;;;;;
}
```

The function consists of one useful statement followed by five empty statements—none of them serves a useful purpose, but at least they don't cause an error.

endif Directive

Definition

The **#endif** directive is a necessary part of conditional compilation syntax. Anytime you use the **#if** directive or any of its variations (**#ifdef** and **#ifndef**) you have to use **#endif** to end the section of the program that is conditionally compiled.

Curiously enough, the **#if-#elif-#endif** syntax is much closer to the syntax of the IF statement in Visual Basic than it is to anything else in C.

Syntax

The **#endif** directive appears on a line by itself:

#endif

This terminates the syntax that begins with an **#if** directive. See "#if Directive" for a discussion of conditional compilation as well as complete syntax.

Definition

In English, *enumeration* is a fancy word for list—especially a list in which items are counted in a particular order. Similarly, in C, an enumeration is a sequence of items in which each item is assigned an identifying number: 0, 1, 2, 3....

Suppose you want to record whether a card is a club, a diamond, a heart, or a spade. It's inefficient to copy a string every time you want to record this information. It's much easier to assign each suit an arbitrary number (0, 1, 2, or 3) and then consistently use that numbering scheme to represent a suit.

Syntax

An **enum** declaration declares a series of constants and can optionally declare a type and variables:

```
enum [enum_type_name] {
        name_1 [= init_1],
        name_2 [= init_2],
        ...
        name_n [= init_n],
} [variable_declarations];
```

Here the braces indicate optional items.

The effect is to define *name_1* through *name_n* as symbolic constants. Any item in *variable_declarations* is an unsigned integer that is restricted to one of these values. The default value of *name_1* (if not initialized) is 0. The default value of any other name is the value of the preceding item plus 1.

Usage 1: Simple Lists

In general, the use of **enum** is a good alternative to a series of **#define** directives like this:

```
#define   CLUBS      0
#define   DIAMONDS   1
#define   HEARTS     2
#define   SPADES     3
```

The actual values may be irrelevant. In this example, all that matters is the ability to test the constant .

```
card_suit = CLUBS;
...
if (card_suit == CLUBS) {
    /* Get bitmap for clubs */
}
```

Or (as in the game of bridge) the values may be meaningful, but only in terms of the relative ordering (CLUBS is less than SPADES).

In any case, an **enum** declaration creates the same symbol constants with less work:

```
enum {
    CLUBS,
    DIAMONDS,
    HEARTS,
    SPADES
};
```

You can save even more space by putting everything on the same line:

```
enum { CLUBS, DIAMONDS, HEARTS, SPADES };
```

The effect is the same as in the series of **#define** directives. CLUBS is 0, DIAMONDS is 1, HEARTS is 2, and SPADES is 3. But the **enum** version is more convenient. As with the **#define** directives, each of these names is a symbolic constant and not a variable.

Often, a simple list of values starting with 0 is sufficient. Sometimes, however, you might want to start the enumeration at a certain integer value. The following code declares constants for certain number words, assigning to each the value you would expect:

```
enum my_numbers {
    TWELVE = 12,
    THIRTEEN,
    FOURTEEN,
    FIFTEEN,
    TWENTY = 20,
    TWENTY_ONE,
    TWENTY_TWO,
    HUNDRED = 100
};
```

Remember that each constant, if uninitialized, is set to 1 plus the value of the constant before it.

Usage 2: Complex Lists

The simplest applications of **enum** define a series of constants with the values 0, 1, 2, 3..., or possibly 1, 2, 3.... You can create more-sophisticated series of values. One interesting use is in bit masks.

Once a constant is defined, it can immediately be used to specify other values. For example, here the left-shift operator is used so that the first constant sets the rightmost bit and each subsequent constant moves this bit one place to the left.

```
enum file_attr {
    SYS_FILE = 0x01,
    HIDDEN_FILE = SYS_FILE << 1;
    ARCHIVE_FILE = HIDDEN_FILE << 1;
    READONLY_FILE = ARCHIVE_FILE << 1;
};
```

Defining Variables of Enumerated Type

You can give an enumeration a type name and use the type to define variables. For example:

```
enum card_suit {
    CLUBS,
    DIAMONDS,
    HEARTS,
    SPADES
} card1;

enum card_suit card2, pack[52];
```

Here, card1 and card2 are variables of type enum card_suit, and pack is an array of 52 elements of type enum card_suit.

As variables of this type, they can be assigned only the constants CLUBS, DIAMONDS, HEARTS, or SPADES. No other assignment is legal:

```
card1 = CLUBS;
pack[5] = card2 = DIAMONDS;
card2 = 100;  /* ERROR! */
```

Only a few operations are possible with variables of an enumerated type. They can be assigned one of the constants in the **enum** series, they can be assigned values from other expressions of the same type, and they can be compared to other expressions of the same type.

Although an **enum** variable cannot be assigned a regular integer expression (except via an explicit type cast), an integer can always be assigned an enumerated constant:

```
int i = SPADES;
```

271

Definition

An explicit type conversion, or *cast*, gives you complete control over how data is treated. The word *cast* suggests a mold used to reform a substance, changing its form in some way.

(Years ago I used to spell this incorrectly, as *caste*. I was thinking of a rigid social hierarchy in which each data type occupied a special slot. In my imagination, converting data was like moving it to a new caste in society. This may be a colorful metaphor, but the idea of casting, as in molding an object's form, is more accurate.)

Why would you ever want to change thee type of a variable or expression? The truth is, the majority of simple programs have little use for casts. But as you start to work with more-sophisticated types—especially pointers—they become vital.

Syntax

A type cast applied to an expression (often a variable, an argument, or a function return value) forms a larger expression:

(*type*) *expression*

The resulting expression has the same numeric value as *expression* but is converted to the indicated type. Variables and constants in the original *expression* are not affected.

Usage

The compiler handles most of the obvious cases when data needs to be converted. For example, when an integer is added to a floating-point value, the compiler automatically converts the data type of the integer to double-precision floating-point:

```
double  x, y;
int i;
...
x = y + i;   /* i promoted to type double. */
```

You can usually rely on the fact that i would be converted to a **double** in this situation. However, if you wanted to make absolutely sure that this happened (and not rely on the compiler's behavior), you could specify the data conversion this way:

```
x = y + (double) i;
```

But most situations that require type casts involve pointers. Casts are particularly common when you're working with **void** pointers.

Certain library functions (such as malloc) return a **void** pointer. Such a pointer can be used to hold an address; but because its type is **void**, it can't actually be used to access anything. Consider how little sense the following statement would make—if the C language let you do it (which it doesn't):

```
void *p;
short thing;

p = malloc(500);
...
thing = *p;   /* Error! p is void* */
```

What data does *p refer to? You might think that because thing is a short (two-byte) integer, the statement automatically transfers two bytes of data. But it doesn't work that way, because p is **void***. Even though the destination of the assignment is an integer (thing), the program has no idea how you're using the chunk of memory pointed to by p. The expression *p means "the thing p points to." Because p is a pointer to **void**, it doesn't yet point to anything—it's just an address that needs to be recast before being used.

273

This is easy to remedy. You can use the (**short***) data cast to tell the program to treat p as a pointer to short—that is, a two-byte integer:

```
thing = *(short*)p;
```

The data cast (**short***) changes a **void*** expression to a **short*** expression—a pointer to a **short**. The indirection operator (*) gets the contents at this address. The expression

```
*(short*)p
```

is a little misleading the first time you look at it, because the indirection operator seems to be applied twice. Don't be fooled by this; indirection is applied only once. The use of the asterisk (*) inside the parentheses is used only to help specify the type, that's all.

In plain English, what the expression means is, "Use the address in p as a pointer to a short integer; then get that integer." Or more succinctly, "the short integer pointed to by p." (See Figure E.1.)

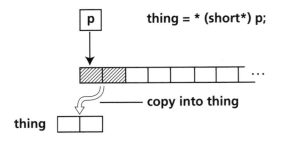

Figure E.1 *Direct copy using (short *).*

As this figure shows, the data copying is direct (there is no conversion), because thing has the same type as the expression "*(short*)p".

Now imagine that the chunk of memory is being used to hold single-precision floating-point data (**float**). In this case, a different data cast is called for:

```
thing = *(float*)p;
```

This statement says, "Use the address in p as a pointer to a floating-point number; then get that number." The data is assigned to thing.

The program gets four bytes of data rather than two. But that's not all. Because the data is floating-point, its format (sign, mantissa, exponent) is radically different from integer format. The program calls a special helper function under the covers, to pull apart the floating-point data and convert it to integer. Any fractional part is dropped in the process. How this magic occurs is not important—it's enough to know it works—but remember that you need to be very clear about what is floating-point and what is not.

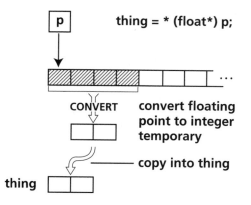

Figure E.2 *Copy using (float *) type.*

As this figure shows, the program converts from floating-point to integer before placing the data in thing. The compiler knows that this conversion must take place because it knows that thing is integer.

You can make the conversion explicit by adding yet another type cast. This other cast isn't required, but it helps document what is going on:

```
thing = (int) *(float *)p;
```

To review, here's how this works:

- p is a nondescript pointer to an address. There's no indication yet of what kind of data it points to.

- The expression (float *)p points to a four-byte floating-point number at this address (changing a **void*** expression to a **float*** expression).

- The expression *(float *)p is the floating-point number itself.

- The expression (int) *(float *)p is the integer equivalent of this floating-point value, after conversion.

As I pointed out in Chapter 7, "Pointers and Other Sharp Instruments," the best way to dynamically allocate memory is to cast the pointer as soon as you get it back from malloc. For example:

```
int *p, i = 10;

p = (int *) malloc (1000 * sizeof(int));
*p = i;
```

The virtue of this approach is that because p is declared as **int***, it contains its own type information so that no further casts are required when doing integer operations.

WARNING

A final caution: as you may have surmised from these examples, it's possible to take any program address and place any kind of information there, or copy any kind of information from that address. You could, for example, move a floating-point value into the middle of an integer array. Doing so would usually be crazy, but the point is that C gives you great control over data handling if and when you ever need it. This is control that probably no other language gives you except for assembly language and C's offspring, C++. But with that control comes responsibility. Once you start using data casts, especially with pointer types, you want to be completely clear in your own mind how you're treating the data and why.

Definition

In general, an expression is any valid combination of variables, constants, and operators. All of the following are statements, but none forms a complete statement, because none is terminated by a semicolon (;).

```
5
x
x + y
f(12.05, a, "Joe Smchoe")
(10 + fnct()) / 25
n++
a = 3 + i
```

You can turn any of these expressions into a statement by terminating with a semicolon:

expression;

The first three examples, however, would not form useful statements unless used in part of a larger expression (such as an assignment or function call).

With few exceptions, an expression evaluates to a single value, which can be used in a larger expression. One exception is a **void** function call, which does not have a return value.

One of the unique aspects of C is that an assignment is an expression like any other and does not automatically form a complete statement unless terminated by a semicolon (;). An assignment evaluates to the value assigned (thus, "a = 5" evaluates to 5), and this value can be reused within the larger expression.

See Chapter 2, "Anatomy of a C Program Part I" for more explanation of assignments, expressions, and statements.

Definition

Complex programs are nearly always split into several different program files (*source files* or *modules*). Doing so allows several different programmers to work at the same time. Even if you're working alone, you might use modules just to make your life easier.

With multiple modules, variables have scope limited to one module unless given an **extern** declaration. This isn't necessary with functions, which are automatically visible to the entire program.

Syntax

The **extern** keyword modifies a data declaration and is placed at the beginning of the statement:

extern *data_declaration*;

What an **extern** declaration says, in effect, is, "The variable or variables are declared somewhere in the program, either in this module or in another."

Usage

To make a variable global to the entire program, define the variable in exactly one module. Then place an **extern** declaration in every module. The following code makes an integer variable, amount, global to the entire program even though it is defined only in the first module:

```
/* MODULE1.C */
extern int  amount;
int  amount = 0;
```

```
/* MODULE2.C */
extern int   amount;

/* MODULE3.C */
extern int   amount;
```

The **extern** declaration is not really necessary in MOD-ULE1.C but does not cause an error. The best way to use **extern** declarations is to place them in a header file and then include the header file in every module by using the **#include** directive. This technique ensures that every module picks up the **extern** declaration.

Any module that does not include the **extern** declaration can have its own variable named amount (although such a confusing practice is not recommended). Such a variable would not be visible to the rest of the program. In fact, it would really be a different variable from the one referred to by other modules.

Example

If no module used an **extern** declaration, then each module would have its own local copy of amount. Changes to amount in one module would have no effect on the variable defined by the other module:

```
/* MODULE1.C */
int   amount;

/* MODULE2.C */
int   amount;
```

Definition

The **float** data type is a single-precision floating-point number, stored in four bytes. Oddly, the longer floating-point type is **double**, even though the shorter, four-byte type is called **float** rather than "single."

Range and Precision

Approximately plus or minus 3.4 times 10 to the 38th power, with six places of precision after the decimal point. Tiny nonzero values can get as close to zero as approximately plus or minus 1.4 times 10 to the power of –45. The type can also hold the value zero precisely.

Syntax

You can declare any number of single-precision floating-point numbers by placing **float** at the beginning of the declaration statement:

[*storage*] [*cv*] **float** *items*;

Here the brackets indicate optional prefixes: *storage* is a storage-class specifier (**auto**, **extern**, **register**, **static**), and *cv* is **const**, **volatile**, or both. The *items* are one or more simple or complex variable declarations.

Example

The following statement defines a simple variable (temperature), an array (daily_temps), and a pointer (ptr_to_float):

```
float   temperature, daily_temps[200], *ptr_to_float;
```

Usage

The **double** floating-point format is generally preferable to **float**, except where storage space is at a premium (such as files, structures, and arrays of structures). It's difficult to compare efficiency of **float** calculations against those using **double**, because different systems implement floating-point operations in different ways. However, math coprocessors typically operate directly on eight-byte floating-point numbers, making **double** at least as fast to operate on as **float**. The recent trend in microprocessors is to support on-board math-coprocessor instructions, having the effect of giving every system a coprocessor.

Definition

A **for** loop is a convenient way to execute a statement block a fixed number of times—for example, when you count to a number or process each element of an array. Like FOR and DO loops in other languages, a C **for** loop can be used in this obvious way. However, the C **for** loop is much more flexible and has many applications.

Syntax

A **for** statement forms one unified statement in C:

for (*initializer; condition; increment*)
     for_loop_statement

The *initializer, condition,* and *increment* are all valid C expressions. The *loop_body_statement* is frequently a compound statement (see "Example"). Because the entire **for** loop forms one statement, it can be nested inside other control structures.

The *initializer* expression is evaluated exactly once: before the loop begins execution. The loop then proceeds just like a **while** statement in which *condition* is the loop condition. The *increment* expression is evaluated at the bottom of the loop. So a **for** statement is almost exactly equivalent to the following syntax:

initializer;
while (*condition*) {
     for_loop_statement
     increment;
}

Note, however, that a **continue** statement, if used, transfers execution to *increment*, and not to the very end of the loop. Aside from this difference, the two loops are identical in their effect.

283

NOTE Don't forget that multiple expressions can be crammed into a single expression by using the comma (,) operator. The initializer expression, for example, can initialize two variables and increment can update two variables:

```
for ( i = 0, k = 1; i < ARRAY_SIZE; i++, j++) {
    ...
```

Example

The following code initializes the first 100 members of two arrays, a and b, so that the first array holds numbers from 0 to 99 and the second array holds even numbers from 0 to 198:

```
for (i = 0; i < 100; i++) {
    a[i] = i;
    b[i] = i * 2;
}
```

Definition

A function is an independent block of code that typically takes care of a specific task. Once a function is defined, you can execute it any number of times from anywhere in the program. (Executing a function is done through a *function call*.) This fact makes functions far and away one of the most essential tools in a programmer's kit.

What's different about functions in C is that the same syntax is used whether or not the function returns a value. Thus, C functions replace all the following in BASIC: functions, procedures, and GOSUB routines. (Functions that do not return a value have the **void** return type.) Another distinctive aspect of C is that all executable statements must be placed inside a function—although **main** (the "main program") is itself a function.

For an introduction to functions in C, see Chapter 3, "Anatomy of a C Program, Part II: Functions." The rest of this topic summarizes the syntax.

Syntax 1: Function Definition

A function definition forms an independent statement block in a program and is *not* terminated by a semicolon(;).

```
return_type name(argument_list) {
        statements
}
```

The *argument_list* includes a series of argument declarations, including both type and name (similar to a prototype, except that the names are not optional). Arguments are separated by commas if there are more than one. The *argument_list* should contain **void** if there are no arguments.

The *return_type* can be a valid type or can be **void**. If the return type is not **void**, then *statements* can include any number of **return** statements to return a value:

return *expression*;

Syntax 2: Prototypes

A function declaration prototype is an item in a declaration:

name(*argument_list*)

A prototype can also be declared alone in its own declaration:

return_type name(*argument_list*);

The *argument_list* is a series of argument declarations, separated by commas if there is more than one:

type item1, *type item2* ...

In a prototype, the argument names are optional and exist principally for documentation purposes. The following prototypes are considered equivalent by the compiler:

```
long fnct(int a, float x, char string[]);
long fnct(int, float, char[]);
```

Syntax 3: Function Calls

A function call forms an expression:

name(*argument_list*)

Here, *argument list* is a list of actual values to be passed to the function. If the function's return type is not **void**, then the function call can be used as part of a larger expression:

```
a = abs(b) + 3;
```

286

Definition

C includes a standard **goto** statement, as virtually all other programming languages do. The danger of using **goto** with wild abandon is that you'll create spaghetti code—programs famous for complex, intertwined connections that are next to impossible to follow (unless you're the computer). Still, **goto** is included because it provides a C programmer with complete control over jumps when needed.

Syntax

The **goto** keyword, along with a target label, forms a complete statement:

goto *label*;

The statement unconditionally transfers control to the target labeled statement, which must be in the same function as the **goto** statement. See "Labels" for more information.

A **goto** statement is occasionally useful as a way of breaking out directly from several levels of enclosed loops. In most cases, the use of **for**, **do**, and **while** loops makes **goto** statements unnecessary.

Header files contain declarations that are useful to one or more source modules. As a rule, header files come in two basic varieties:

- Header files for standard library functions. For example, you should include STDIO.H if doing any kind of input or output, and you should include MATH.H if using one of the math functions from the standard C library. These files provide all the necessary prototypes for using the library functions, and this saves you from having to declare them yourself. It's much easier just to include the file. For example:

  ```
  #include <stdio.h>
  ```

- Header files for your own declarations. If you work with multiple modules, you should throw in prototypes for all your functions, extern declarations for all global variables to be shared programwide, and declarations for other types (typedef, struct, union, enum) that you want to share between modules. This is a much easier approach than having to declare these for every single module. For example:

  ```
  #include "myprog.h"
  ```

This second use is convenient because declarations are not automatically shared between multiple modules. In C, function definitions are the only entities that are automatically visible to the rest of the program. But even functions need a declaration (a prototype) to be included in each individual module.

A particularly helpful aspect of header files is that if you declare things once in a header file and then use the **#include** directive to include this file in each module, you are guaranteeing that things are declared the same way everywhere. This practice prevents the problem of potential errors due to inconsistent declarations in different files.

Some of the items to place in header files include:

- Prototypes for all functions except those that you do not want to share. (these functions should be qualified with the **static** keyword to make them private to their modules.)

- **extern** declarations for all global variables to be shared between modules. Note, however, that in addition to the extern declarations, each individual variable must be defined in one, and only one, module. A good approach is to define all your global variables in the main module.

- **#define** statements for symbolic constants that are used throughout the program as well as for macros.

- **enum**, **struct**, **union**, and **typedef** declarations.

You should never place data definitions or function definitions in header files. These definitions (not to be confused with uses of the **#define** directive, which is completely different) create a variable or a function, and they must be unique. A header file is normally intended to be included by more than one module. Therefore, placing a data definition or function definition in a header file would cause an error because the variable or function would be defined more than once, which C in its wisdom does not allow.

See "#include Directive" for exact syntax rules governing **#include**.

Definition

An identifier is a name you create: this includes not only variable names but also names of functions, structures, symbolic constants, **enum** constants, and user-defined types. For example, in the following structure definition, the names data_record, x, y, and title are all identifiers, whereas **struct**, **int**, and **char** are keywords:

```
struct data_record {
    int  x, y;
    char title[30];
};
```

The difference is that keywords have built-in meanings universal to all C programs, but identifiers have meanings that you (or another programmer) create within a given program.

Syntax

C has three basic rules for forming a valid identifier:

1. An identifier cannot be the same as any C keyword.

2. An identifier must be composed from the following character set:

    - Digits 0 through 9

    - Uppercase and lowercase letters A through Z

    - The underscore (_)

3. The first character must not be a digit.

So the following are all valid identifiers:

```
a
x04
count
xx1
```

290

```
thing27
do_your_own_thing
The_End
BYTE
```

N O T E Although identifiers can begin with an underscore (_), you should avoid that practice. The C compiler defines a number of special symbols (normally hidden from you) that use leading underscores. These are implementation-specific, so they are difficult to anticipate and "program around." But if you simply avoid leading underscores in your own identifiers, you avoid conflicts with these implementation-defined symbols.

Case Sensitivity

All identifiers (as well as keywords) are case-sensitive in C, so bigfoot and BigFoot, for example, are two distinct names. You could use both in a program, although it is not advisable.

Linker behavior can sometimes cause problems. The C compiler is always case-sensitive even though case sensitivity can be switched off by the linker (as is true in Windows programming, for example). This creates a pitfall: bigfoot and BigFoot are considered two different variables by the compiler, but the linker thinks they're the same symbol. The result is that either your program will be wrong or the linker will make a mistake. The solution is to avoid using two names that differ only in case.

Definition

Despite its apparent similarity to the **if** statement, the purpose of the **#if** directive is entirely different from that of the **if** statement. There are two principal uses of the **#if** directive: conditional compilation and temporarily "commenting out" lines. Conditional compilation is useful as a way of maintaining different versions of your program without having to duplicate the parts common to all versions.

An **#if** directive marks the beginning of a conditional-compilation block. If the expression specified by the **#if** directive is nonzero (true), the C preprocessor compiles the statements that follow it, up to the next **#elif**, **#else**, or **#endif** directive.

Syntax

The **#if**, **#elif**, **#else**, and **#endif** directives can appear as follows. Any kind of statement, declaration, or other directive can appear in each *statement_block*:

#if *constant_expression*
statement_block_1
[**#elif** *constant_expression*
statement_block_2]
[**#elif** *constant_expression*
statement_block_3]
...
[**#else**
statement_block_n]
#endif

Here, the brackets indicate optional items; the only mandatory parts of this syntax are the **#if** and **#endif** directives. You can use any number of **#elif** directives but, at most, one **#else** directive, which must follow all **#if** and **#elif** directives.

The C preprocessor evaluates each *constant_expression* until one of the expressions evaluates to a nonzero value. Then the preprocessor compiles the corresponding *statement_block*.

If all the expressions evaluate to zero and if there is an **#else** directive, the preprocessor compiles the statements between **#else** and **#endif** (*statement_block_n*).

Each *statement_block* can contain any kind of C code, including declarations and directives as well as executable statements.

Each *constant_expression* is a C expression made up of constants and operators, but it cannot include the **sizeof** operator, type casts, or **enum** constants. In practice, such constant expressions almost always involve symbols previously defined with **#define** directives. A simple test for equality (==) may be involved. These constant expressions can also use the **define**(symbol) operator, which evaluates to 1 if a symbol is defined, and 0 otherwise.

Usage 1: Conditional Compilation

Conditional compilation allows you to create multiple versions of your program. There are several reasons you might want to do this. You might be writing a program for multiple platforms and find that certain sections of code are not portable—they simply have to be rewritten. You also might want to build both a debug version, which is larger and slower but easier to debug, and a release version, which is more compact. For the debug version, you might want a data dump in the middle of program execution.

Maintaining multiple versions creates a dilemma. If you periodically create new versions of your program by rewriting it, you lose the previous version. You'd have to constantly add and erase the same statements. But if you keep multiple versions of your program around, you eat up extra disk space. Worse, you may encounter change-control problems as the new features added to one version aren't necessarily reflected in the other verions.

The answer to these problems is conditional compilation. For example, my program may have to deal with a variety of coordinate systems for different target computers.

293

Instead of having to rewrite many lines of my program every time I compile for a different target, I need only change one line. First, I define a series of meaningful constants:

```
#define UNSIGNED_INT 0
#define INTEGER      1
#define REAL         2
```

To recompile for a different coordinate system, I need only change one line—the line the defines the value of the symbol COORDSYS. Many compilers support a command-line option that even allows you to specify this define on the command line:

```
#define COORDSYS REAL
```

The rest of the program checks the value of COORDSYS, as needed, to decide what to compile:

```
#if COORDSYS == UNSIGNED_INT
unsigned x, y;
#elif COORDSYS == INTEGER
int x, y;
#elif COORDSYS == REAL
double x, y;
#endif
```

Notice how the use of the **#if** directive is different from that of an **if** statement, despite the similarity. The **if** statement evaluates a condition (which incidentally does not have to be a constant), at run time and takes a different action depending on this condition. The **#if** directive evaluates a condition at *compilation time*— this means that the condition is evaluated before the program ever runs. Based on the condition, different lines of code are compiled, in effect creating a different version of the program.

Usage 2: Commenting Out Lines

Occasionally, you might need to "comment out" lines: remove them temporarily from the program in such a way that it is easy to put them back. One obvious way to do this is to place begin-comment (/*) and end-comment (*/) symbols around the block of code. As I explain in the topic "Comments," however, this approach causes errors if any of these lines themselves have comments. This is the problem of nested comments.

The solution is to use **#if 0** and **#endif** to comment out lines. When the condition for an **#if** directive is the constant 0, the lines are simply never compiled. Whether or not the lines contain comments makes no difference. For example:

```
#if 0
int i, j;      /* Indexes into 2-D array */
double x, y;   /* Point coordinates */
#endif
```

The **#if** directive can be nested to any level. The **#endif** directive associates with the nearest **#if** directive.

if Statement

Definition

One of the more essential parts of any programming language is an **if** keyword or conditional jump of some kind. C is no exception. The C **if** statement is similar to what you may have seen in other languages, with minor syntax differences.

What's different about C **if** statements is that the conditional expression can perform many operations, including assignments. Don't forget, however, that test for equality (==) is different from assignment (=). The former is more common within conditional expressions. If you use assignment in a conditional expression, consider the effect carefully.

Syntax

An **if** statement forms one unified statement in C:

if (*expression*)
      statement1
[**else**
      statement2]

Here the brackets indicate that the entire **else** clause is optional. The statement blocks—*statement1* and *statement2*—are frequently compound statements, using opening and closing braces ({}). Because the entire **if-else** block is itself one statement, it can be nested inside other control structures.

If *expression* is nonzero (true), then *statement1* is executed. Otherwise, *statement2* is executed, assuming that there is an **else** clause. The *expression* can be any valid C expression of integer type. All comparison and logical operators (==, <, >, <=, >=, &&, !!, !, and so on) return either a 1 (true) or 0 (false).

Examples

The following example tests to see whether a number x is in the range 0.0 to 100.0. Note the use of the logical OR operator (||).

```
if (x < 0.0 || x > 100.0)
    printf("x is out of range.\n");
else {
    printf("x is in range.\n");
    return -1;
}
```

In this example, the statements following the **else** are enclosed in braces because they are executed as a compound statement. This is necessary whenever the **if** clause or **else** clause involves more than one statement.

By nesting an **if** statement inside an **else** clause, you can create a virtual "elseif" keyword:

```
if (a < b)
    return -1;
else if (a == b)
    return 0;
else
    return 1;
```

This statement is equivalent to:

```
if (a < b)
    return -1;
else {
    if (a == b)
        return 0;
    else
        return 1;
}
```

297

In this case, the braces are used for clarification of meaning but aren't required. See "switch Keyword" for another way to test for a series of alternatives.

Occassionally, braces are required—not only where compound statements are used but also where the association of **if** and **else** isn't clear. By default, an **else** clause always applies to the nearest **if** statement. Suppose a program follows this logic:

If x equals 0, then
        If y equals 0,
                print "x and y are zero"
Else
        print "x is non-zero"

The *Else* is intended to apply to the first *If* and not to the second. Thus, "x is non-zero" is printed whenever x equals 0—the value of y doesn't matter. In this case, braces are required to clarify the association of the **else** clause with the first **if**.

```
if (x == 0) {
    if (a == b)
        printf("x and y are zero");
} else
        printf("x is non-zero");
```

#ifdef Directive

The **#ifdef** directive is possibly the most commonly used directive for conditional compilation. Consider the following syntax:

#ifdef *symbol*

This means exactly the same as:

#if defined(*symbol*)

So the lines immediately following the **#ifdef**—up to but not including the next **#elif**, **#else**, or **#endif**—are compiled if the *symbol* has been previously defined. The value of the symbol is irrelevant; only the fact that it has been defined is significant. It can even be defined as an empty string, as in the following definition of 32_BIT_SUPPORT:

```
#define 32_BIT_SUPPORT
```

Many compilers support a command-line option for defining such symbols, a practice that allows you to control conditions from inside batch files and make files.

The use of **#ifdef** is appropriate when you want to conditionally compile based on a simple on/off condition. You turn the condition on by defining the symbol.

For a general description of conditional compilation as well as complete syntax, see "#if Directive."

#ifndef Directive

The **#ifndef** directive is occasionally used in conditional compilation. Consider the following syntax:

#ifndef *symbol*

This means exactly the same as:

#if ! defined(*symbol*)

So the lines immediately following the **#ifdef**—up to but not including the next **#elif**, **#else**, or **#endif**—are compiled if the *symbol* has not been previously defined.

The use of **#ifdef** and **#ifndef** is appropriate when you want to conditionally compile based on a simple on/off condition. You turn the condition on by simply not defining the symbol.

For a general description of conditional compilation as well as complete syntax, see "#if Directive." See also "#ifdef Directive."

Implicit Type Casts

Definition

Not all data types are the same. And because they're different, adjustments have to be made when you combine them. Integer data and floating-point data, in particular, have radically different formats. They can't just be added or multiplied together. In the following example, the value of i, an integer, must first be converted to floating-point (**double**) format:

```
int i;
double x, y = 27.555;
x = y + i;    /* Value of i must be converted to double,
                 to match y's format. */
```

What happens is that C applies an implicit type cast, which is equivalent to the following explicit cast:

```
x = y + (double) i;
```

Usage

You can blithely program for a long time, ignoring the fact that C does this—after all, it is automatic. (Other programming languages also do this, by the way.) However, sometimes it's useful to know exactly what the program is doing to your data and how it's stored. The following list is a guide to how and when C implicitly casts data types of expressions. Whenever an expression combines two operands—not involving pointers—the compiler compares them to determine which operand has the type of the lowest rank. The expression of the lower rank is cast to that of the higher rank:

> **double**
>
> **float**
>
> **unsigned long**
>
> **long**

301

unsigned int

int

other integer types (**short, unsigned short, char, unsigned char**)

For example, if an **unsigned int** and an **unsigned long** expression are added together, the **unsigned int** expression is first promoted to type **unsigned long**. Note that the type cast is only applied to the value of the **unsigned int** expression; it doesn't permanently change the type of any variables.

 One consequence of this rule is that all the smaller types (char, for example) are converted to int before being used in any expression. Depending on implementation, the actual size of an int may be two or four bytes.

Pointers have special rules of their own. Assignment of any pointer to a nonpointer type, and vice versa, requires a cast. (Integer expressions, however, can be added to pointers. See "Pointer Arithmetic.")

C lets you freely assign values between pointers: you can assign any pointer or address expression to any pointer of any type. C implicitly converts the type of the source expression. In my opinion, this is sloppiness on C's part and opens up the possibility of inadvertently causing serious errors. C++ corrects this sloppiness. Unless the target of the assignment has type **void***, you to apply a data cast before assigning between any two pointer types.

I recommend that you adopt the practice of C++ programmers, putting in explicit type casts whenever converting between two pointers. For example, the (**float***) cast in the following example makes explicit the conversion between pointer types. In C, this is the same as the implicit cast that the language would have applied for you.

302

```
int i;
float *fp;
...
fp = (float*) &i;    /* (float*) recommended */
```

In general, assignment of an address expression to a pointer of a different base type is dangerous—except when you get a **void*** pointer returned from a function and need to assign it to another pointer.

You should avoid the practice of assignment between pointers of different type unless you're sure you know why you're doing it. Using a pointer of type **float*** to point to an integer, for example, as done here, means that the pointer could subsequently be used to copy floating-point data to an integer address! There are some legitimate situations in which someone might want to do this—for example, pointer casts can be used to suppress the numeric conversion between one type and another—but, in general, you should be wary of assigning or converting one pointer value to another of different type.

See "Explicit Type Conversions" for a further discussion of casting pointers.

Definition

The **#include** directive causes the C preprocessor to read another file into the current source file during the compilation process. In other words, if you use the directive #include <stdio.h>, the effect is the same as if you had typed the entire contents of STDIO.H into your program.

Although any file can be specified with **#include**, the directive is best used with header files—files containing declarations needed by more than one module.

Syntax

An **#include** directive uses one of the following two forms:

#include *"filename"*   /* Project include file */
#include *<filename>*   /*Standard lib include file */

Upon encountering **#include**, the compiler suspends execution of the current file, reads the file specified by *filename*, and continues. All the files read in this manner are compiled as if they were part of one continuous source. So symbols declared in an included file can be referred to in the main source file.

The difference between the two versions of **#include** is that in the *"filename"* version, the C preprocessor searches for the file first in the current directory. Both versions look for the file in the standard include-file directory; on most systems, this directory is indicated by the value of the INCLUDE environment variable or a configuration file that stores such settings. In any case, this should be part of your environment configuration before you run the C compiler.

The general rule is to use the **#include** *"filename"* version for your own header files, which are typically kept in the same directory as the rest of your program files. Use **#include** *<filename>* for standard header files such as STDIO.H.

Included files can be nested to any level. This means that a file read with **#include** can itself have **#include** directives.

Example

The following statement includes the header file STDIO.H:

```
#include <stdio.h>
```

See "Header Files" for more discussion of how **#include** is used.

Definition

The indirection operator (*) is central to pointer operations and is therefore important in C. Basically, the operator means "get the contents at" or "the thing pointed to." So if ptr contains the numeric value 0x2000, *ptr refers to the contents at the address 0x2000 in memory.

When you're first learning C, possibly the most confusing aspect of the indirection operator is that it uses the same symbol as multiplication. But the two operators have nothing to do with each other. Syntactically, you tell them apart by the fact that indirection is a unary operator: it applies to exactly one operand at a time.

Syntax

The indirection operator forms an expression from a single operand:

addr_expression

Here, *addr_expression* is any valid expression with an address type. This is typically, but not necessarily, a pointer variable. It might also be an array name.

When used in an executable statement, the type of the resulting expression is one level of indirection less than the *addr_expression*. For example, if *addr_expression* has type **int*** (pointer to **int**), then **addr_expression* has type **int**. If *addr_expression* has type **float**** (pointer to pointer to **float**), then **addr_expression* has type **float*** (pointer to float).

Usage

In declarations, the indirection operator creates a pointer variable. The operator must be applied to each individual item declared. Consider the following declarations:

```
double  *a, b, *c, (*f)(), *e[50];
```

This statement declares b as a simple variable of type **double**, a and c as pointers to **double**, f as a pointer to a function returning a value of type **double**, and c as an array of 50 pointers to **double**.

In an executable statement, the indirection operator means "the thing pointed to," and it can be applied to any valid address expression. Figure I.1 expresses the relationship between p (a pointer) and *p.

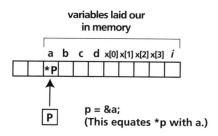

Figure I.1 *Relationship of pointer to *p.*

Although indirection can be applied to any address expression, including any pointer, the value of the address should be meaningful. Applying indirection to an uninitialized or null pointer can cause serious errors at run time. So make sure that you initialize pointers before using them. For example:

```
int *p, i;
*p = 5; /* ERROR: p uninitialized! */
p = &i; /* p now initialized to point to i */
*p = 5; /* This operation copies 5 to i */
```

Initialization, Variable

Definition

Initialization looks a great deal like assignment in C, but it's important to keep in mind the difference between them. They both use a single equal sign (=), but initialization sets a value in the same statement that defines it. Assignment occurs outside the variable definition:

```
int i = 10;   /* i initialized to 10 here. */
i = a + b;    /* i assigned the value a + b */
```

The difference is important, because with gloabl variables, initialization can involve only a constant expression (an expression made up only of constants and operators, no variables). Note, however, that the address of a variable is a constant and so can be used to initialize:

```
int *ip = &i; /* Pointer ip initialized to
                   address of i. */
```

The source of an assignment can be any valid expression, with very few exceptions (the result of a **void** function call cannot be assigned).

```
i = a + b;    /* i assigned the value a + b */
```

It is always a good practice to initialize variables—especially if they are local. Global variables and local **static** variables are intialized to 0 or null. Other local variables are initialized to garbage. Of course, failing to initialize a variable is forgivable if you assign it a value shortly after declaring it.

Local variables are reset to the initial value every time the function (or enclosing block) is executed. But if a local variable is static, it is initialized only once, just as a global variable is.

See "Declarations" and "Aggregates" for more information.

Definition

The **int** data type is an integer that uses the natural integer size of the computer's architecture. This size is usually the processor's register width. For example, in 32-bit architectures, the **int** data type is four bytes in size.

Range

Range varies, depending on whether the size is two or four bytes. When you're using **int** variables, I recommend that you observe the same range as short integers: –32,768 to 32,767.

Syntax

You can declare any number of integer variables by placing **int** at the beginning of the declaration statement:

```
[storage] [cv] int  items;
```

Here the brackets indicate optional prefixes: *storage* is a storage-class specifier (**auto, extern, register, static**) and *cv* is **const, volatile**, or both. The *items* are one or more simple or complex variable declarations.

Example

The following statement defines two simple variables (i and j), an array (id_nums), and a pointer (ptr_to_int):

```
int  i, j, id_nums[10], *ptr_to_int;
```

Usage

The **int** data type presents a paradox: if you want to write portable code, you should assume that an **int** type is no more than two bytes wide. This in effect restricts the range of an **int** to that of a **short**: –32,768 to 32,767. But if you're going to observe this restriction, why not just use **short** all the time instead of **int**? The answer is that on 32-bit systems, operations on four-byte integers are faster than those on two-byte integers.

The general principle is that it's best to select **int** for a type whenever you declare a simple variable used for calculation—assuming it won't go out of the range for a **short**. Reserve **short** for compound data types (such as structures and arrays) where space is at a premium.

Definition

Keywords are a special set of words in C that have universal, preassigned meanings. You cannot give any of your own functions or variables names that conflict with these words. You cannot give your own variable the name **if**, for example, because in C this word has special meaning to the language.

When you first program in C, there's a small chance you might accidentally pick a name conflicting with a keyword. It isn't worth trying to memorize the list of keywords to avoid this problem. If it does happen, you'll get a strange syntax error message about a word you thought was a valid name at that point, you might consider whether you accidentally picked a keyword for a variable name.

One advantage of C is that the list of keywords is kept small compared with most other programming languages. This fact gives the language a cleaner, more streamlined quality and reduces the chance of identifier/keyword conflicts. Table K.1 lists the standard keywords in C.

Table K.1 *C Keywords.*

auto	double	int	struct
break	else	long	switch
case	enum	register	typedef
char	extern	return	union
const	float	short	unsigned
continue	for	signed	void
default	goto	sizeof	volatile
do	if	static	while

One of the differences between C and other languages such as BASIC is that many things involving a keyword in BASIC (PRINT, for example) are replaced by a standard library function in C. If you chose, you could easily replace the implementation of one of these functions, supplying your own function definition. (But note that many activities,

311

such as printing, require knowledge of how to call the operating system if you're going to implement them yourself.) The standard library functions have no special status except that they are supplied with the compiler.

l-values

Definition

An l-value is something you can assign a value to. The *l* in the name refers to the fact that the item can appear on the *left* side of an assignment.

 It isn't necessary that you master the nuances of this topic unless you're really interested. The bottom line is N O T E **this: C compilers, depending on the implementation, often talk of l-values in the error messages they report. In such cases, you probably mistyped something on the left side of an assignment.**

Usage

This concept, which tends to be a little more cut-and-dried in other programming languages, takes on interesting subtleties in C, largely because of pointers. The simple cases, though, are just like those in other languages. Clearly, the following sort of statement makes sense. It says to put the name 5 into the variable named amount:

```
amount = 5;
```

But the next statement makes no sense, because you cannot put 5 into another constant:

```
27 = 5;   /* ERROR! Can't do this. */
```

Because 27 is a constant, it cannot appear on the left side. It is not an l-value.

Examples

So what is an l-value? The most common example is a simple variable of primitive type—for example, "amount" in the first example, which is a simple variable of type **int**—Another case is an individual element of an array:

```
double rates[100];
rates[10] = 7.8;
```

Here, rates[10] is an l-value. Broadly speaking, an l-value is any expression that corresponds to a specific location in program memory reserved for variables. This includes the following:

- Simple variables of primitive type (**int**, **char**, **long**, **double**, and so on).

- Members of structures, unions, and arrays, or any compound type, in which a path is fully specified to data of primitive type. For example, rates[10] in the preceding example is an l-value because it refers to a particular integer.

- A pointer variable. In terms of how they are stored and manipulated, pointers are very nearly integers, although they have some special attributes.

- Dereferenced pointers or address expressions, resulting in an expression of primitive type or a pointer type.

The last two categories are the interesting ones, because they are what makes C different. Using pointers, casts, the address operator (&), and pointer arithemetic, an address expression can be arbitrarily complex. If this expression is then dereferenced, resulting in an expression of primitive type, it can be used as an l-value.

That's a lot to digest, although the idea is simple enough once you understand it. The most trivial case is a single, dereferenced pointer variable:

```
int i, *ip;

ip = &i;
*ip = 7;
```

There are two assignments here, and each has a legitimite l-value. In the first assignment, ip is a pointer variable, so it may be assigned an address or pointer of the same base type (**int**). The expression &i is the address of an integer and so matches in type.

In the second assignment, a pointer to an integer is specified (ip) and then dereferenced (*ip). It is therefore an l-value. This is a simple case of a dereferenced pointer as l-value:

```
*ip = 7;
```

L-values become interesting when you use a complex expression and then dereference it. Suppose an integer and an array are defined as follows:

```
int my_array[20], i;
```

The following is a valid address expression. The program takes the address of my_array, adds i, and adds the constant 3, doing the appropriate scaling for each addition (see "Pointer Arithmetic").

```
my_array + i + 3
```

You cannot place this expression on the left side of an assignment even though it is a valid address:

```
(my_array + i + 3) = new_val;   /* ERROR! */
```

But you can use the indirection operator to instruct the computer to place a new value *at* this address:

```
*(my_array + i + 3) = new_val;
```

Array names (my_array, for example) evaluate to the address of the first element and are almost equivalent to pointer variables. One basic difference is that pointer variables can be assigned new values any time, but array names are constants. The following assignment is not valid, because a constant is on the left side:

```
my_array = 1000;
```

This statement, if allowed, would attempt to change the address that my_array represents. It would say that the array is at the location 1000 in memory. That's not a valid operation, because it would be a direct contradiction of fact, just as the assignment "27 = 5" is a contradiction of fact. You can, however, use indirection (*) to assign a new value *at* the address that my_array represents (the address of the first element):

```
*my_array = 1000;
```

This statement puts 1,000 into the first element of my_array.

Incidentally, "my_array = 1000" is a contradiction in fact because my_array has already been allocated in program memory and its address is fixed. But as I've mentioned, pointer variables can hold different addresses at different times and so are legitimate l-values (even when not dereferenced).

Labels

Definition

A statement label serves the same purpose in C as it does in other languages. A label is like a line number, giving **goto** statements specific locations to jump to. But unlike line numbers, statement labels can have meaningful names, making them easy to use.

Labels also work with a **switch** statement. This aspect of C grammar throws most people at first, because it means you usually need to put **break** between each case.

Syntax

A labeled statement forms a statement in C and has one of three forms:

identifier: statement
case *constant_expression: statement*
default: *statement*

Note that a statement must follow the label, even if it is an empty statement (a lone semicolon).

Because a labeled statement in C forms a single, unified statement, you can apply the syntax recursively to precede a statement with any number of labels. However, this is rarely done except with **case** labels, where it can be useful.

Usage 1: Target of goto Statements

The most familiar use of labels is in the first syntax, which gives a statement a meaningful name:

```
start_calculations_here:
    a = x + y / 2;
```

It's irrelevant to the C compiler whether the label itself and the rest of the statement are on the same physical line. This fact gives you leeway in spacing.

317

A statement labeled this way can be the target of a **goto** as long as the **goto** and the statement are in the same function. For obvious reasons, no two statements in the same function can be labeled with the same *identifier*.

Blocks of code that use **goto** statements are usually better written as **if-else** blocks, **while** loops, **do** loops, or **for** loops.

Usage 2: Case and Default Labels

Within a **switch** statement block, you can label statements with **case** and **default** to serve as targets for execution:

```
case 5:
    strcpy(num_str, "five");
    break;
...
default:
    strcpy(num_str, "unknown");
    break;
```

A **switch** statement tests an expression and jumps to the **case** that matches the expression (or **default**, if no cases match).

The **break** statement is necessary because **case** and **default** are just labels. A label does not change the flow of control, but only serves as a target. Execution starts at the appropriate **case** or **default** statement and continues until one of two things happens: the end of the statement block is reached or a **break** statement is executed.

See the topics "case Keyword," "break Keyword," and "switch Statement" for examples.

Definition

The **long** data type is a four-byte integer. The ANSI C standard requires only that a **long** be at least four bytes, but **long** is exactly four bytes wide in the vast majority of implementations.

Range

Approximately plus or minus two billion: –2,147,483,647 to 2,147,483,647, to be exact.

Syntax

You can declare any number of long integers by placing **long** at the beginning of the declaration statement:

```
[storage] [cv] long   items;
```

Here the brackets indicate optional prefixes: *storage* is a storage-class specifier (**auto**, **extern**, **register**, **static**) and *cv* is **const**, **volatile**, or both. The *items* are one or more simple or complex variable declarations.

Example

The following statement defines a simple variable (population), an array (pops), and a pointer (ptr_to_long):

```
long   population, pops[200], *ptr_to_long;
```

Usage

On 32-bit operating systems, a **long** is equivalent to an **int**. However, if you're writing programs that might be ported to different systems, you can't assume that an **int** will be as large as a **long**. Therefore, if there is any chance that a variable will fall outside the range of a **short** (–32,768 to 32,767), declare it as a **long**.

319

Definition

C has three loop structures: **while, for,** and **do-while**.

Loops are at the heart of programming. Computers would not be one millionth as useful without loops in some form. The idea behind loops is simple: it's just the idea of saying go back to step one (or step two, or three, or whatever).

Example

A trivial example is printing all the numbers between 1 and 1,000, a tedious and boring task. If you have to tell the computer to print each individual number, "Print 1, then print 2, then print 3...," you might as well do the job yourself.

Programming starts to become most useful when you realize that you don't have to direct every individual move but can instead set a general pattern of action in motion by writing a loop. The beauty of this is that it's five steps rather than 1,000:

1. Set i to 1.

2. Is i greater than 1,000? If so, exit.

3. Print i.

4. Add 1 to i.

5. Go back to step 2.

In C, this program logic could be equally well expressed as either a **while** loop or a **for** loop. First, the **while** loop:

```
i = 1;
while (i <= 1000) {
    printf("%d\n", i);
    i++;
}
```

The **for** loop does the same thing but is more concise:

```
for (i = 1; i <= 1000; i++)
    printf("%d\n", i);
```

For more explanation of loop syntax, see Chapter 4, "Decisions, Decisions: Control Structures in C" or the topics "do Keyword," "for Keyword", and "while Statement".

Mistakes in Loop Writing

Despite the simplicity and elegance of the idea of loops, they offer one of the most common areas for programmer error. Often, loops go wrong because you didn't correctly set initial or terminating conditions.

This is particularly likely when arrays are involved. Array indexes in C run from 0 to size –1, where size is the number of elements. Therefore, when you write a loop that accesses each member of the array in turn, initialize the index to 0 (not 1, as you would in most other languages). The loop should continue as long as the index is *less than* the number of elements. Once the index is equal to the number of elements, the loop should terminate, because the highest index is one less than this number.

The following is an example of a correctly written loop that initializes every element to 10:

```
#define ARRAY_SIZE   1000

int i, numbers[ARRAY_SIZE];

for (i = 0, i < ARRAY_SIZE; i++)
    numbers[i] = 10;
```

Definition

With few exceptions (such as Windows programming and writing code for libraries), every program must have a **main** function—the function that's always executed first. Although **main** is restricted in terms of its arguments and return type, it behaves in almost every respect like a standard function and must observe the same rules

Syntax

The function definition for **main** can take either of the forms shown in Figure M.1.

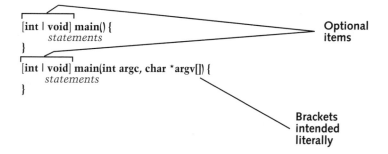

Figure M.1. *The function definition for main can take either of these forms.*

Here, the expression [**int** | **void**] indicates that **main** can be qualified by the **int** or **void** return type, but not both. (By default, **main** has a return type of **int**, which means that **main** should return a value.) However, in the case of ***argv[]**, the brackets are intended literally.

Note that, as with other functions, the function definition of **main** is not terminated by a semicolon (;), which would cause a syntax error.

Case 1: main with No Arguments

Writing a **main** function with no arguments is simple. A **main** function can have local variables and complex statements just like other functions, but in many programs all the **main** function does is to call the other principal functions in the program and let them do all the work.

In the following example, **main** is defined with a void return type, so no return value is expected (a return value would require use of the **return** statement):

```
void main () {
    init_vars();
    prompt_for_input();
    print_results();
}
```

Case 2: main with Arguments

If you're expecting command-line input entered on the command line, you can use the special *argc* and *argv* arguments to get at this input from within the program. In many programs, in fact, the principal work of **main** is to access these arguments and then call other functions.

For example, suppose you wrote a DOS or console application called SORT.EXE, which accepts two command-line arguments: the name of an input file and the name of an output file:

```
sort  datafile.txt  results.txt
```

The *argc* argument contains the total number of items on the command line (in this case, 3). The *argv* argument is an array of pointers. In this case, it would be an array in which the first three elements point to one of the strings—"sort", "datafile.txt", and "results.txt"—and in that order.

Main Function (continued)

In the following example code, the program prints an error message and exits if two command-line arguments were not entered:

```c
int main(int argc, char *argv[])) {
    if (argc != 3) {
        printf("Bad number of arguments.\n");
        printf("Syntax: sort inputfile outputfile.\n");
        return -1;
    }
    ...
```

Modulus Operator (%)

Modulus operator is the name that many C manuals use for what I call the remainder operator. Whatever name it goes by, the function of this operator is to divide one integer by another and return the remainder of the division. A typical use is determining whether a number is even or odd, or whether it's exactly divisible by four.

See "Remainder Operator" for more information.

The C operators are summarized here in two tables. For an introduction to some of the stranger operators in C, see Chapter 5, "Operators: C the Unique."

Table O.1 summarizes operators by level of precedence. The unary operators are those applied to only one operand. For example, x - y uses the subtraction operator, but -5 uses unary minus (-) to change 5 into a negative number.

Table O.1 *Precedence of C operators.*

OPERATORS	ASSOCIATIVITY
() [] . -> ++ (postfix) -- (postfix)	left to right
++ -- ! ~ **sizeof** (*type*) + (unary) - (unary) & (unary)	right to left
* / %	left to right
+ -	left to right
<< >>	left to right
< <= > >=	left to right
== !=	left to right
&	left to right
^	left to right
|	left to right
&&	left to right
||	left to right
?:	right to left
= += -= *= /= %= <<= >>= &= ^= |=	right to left
,	left to right

Table O.2 gives a brief description of each operator. Operators not separated by a solid line are at the same level of precedence.

Table O.2 *Descriptive summary of C operators.*

Operator	Description	Associativity
()	Function call, as in *fnct(args)*	left to right
[]	Array indexing, as in *array***[index]**	
.	Structure-member reference: *struct.member*	
->	Pointer-member reference: *structptr.member*	
++	Postfix increment	
--	Postfix decrement	
++	Prefix increment	right to left
--	Prefix decrement	
!	Logical NOT	
~	Bitwise NOT (one's complement)	
sizeof	Width of type or expression, in bytes	
(type)	Explicit type cast	
+	Unary plus, specifies positive number	
-	Unary minus, specifies negative number	
&	Address-of operators	
*	Pointer dereference	
* /	Multiplication and division	left to right
%	Remainder operator	
+ -	Addition and subtraction	left to right
<< >>	Left and right bitwise shift	left to right
< <= > >=	Tests for less than, less than or equal to, etc.	left to right
==	Test for equality	left to right
!=	Not-equal-to test	left to right

327

OPERATOR	DESCRIPTION	ASSOCIATIVITY
&	Bitwise AND	left to right
^	Bitwise exclusive OR (XOR)	left to right
|	Bitwise OR	left to right
&&	Logical AND (uses short-circuit testing)	left to right
||	Logical OR (uses short-circuit testing)	left to right
?:	Conditional operator: *exp1* ? *exp2* : *exp3*	right to left
=	Assignment	right to left
+= -=	Addition/subtraction and assignment	
*= /=	Multiplication/division and assignment	
%=	Remainder operator and assignment	
>>= <<=	Left/right shift and assignment	
&= ^= |=	Bitwise AND, XOR, OR and assignment	
,	Comma operator: evaluate both of *expr1* , *expr2*	right to left

328

Parameters

Many C manuals use *arguments* and *parameters* as interchangeable terms. In this book, I've stuck almost exclusively with *arguments*, avoiding *parameters* because it complicates the discussion. The latter is a perfectly legitimate term, but it's sometimes difficult to distinguish between arguments and parameters. The two concepts are the two sides of the same coin.

Parameters are arguments, looked at from the standpoint of the called function rather than the caller. To be entirely correct technically, the word *arguments* should be applied during a function call, so that 3 and 5 in the following example are arguments:

```
hyp_length = pythagorus(3, 5);
```

In contrast, the parameters are the variables that represent the arguments in the function definition. This means that a and b in the following code are parameters:

```
double Pythagoras(double a, double b) {
    return sqrt(a * a + b * b);
}
```

The distinction is useful here but can be difficult to maintain when you're examining a function call. Is the data placed on the stack arguments or parameters? It's usually not worth arguing about.

Definition

Under the covers, pointers are nearly the same as integers, and you can add or subtract them. For lack of a better word, such operations are called *pointer arithmetic*. It's an important subject in C because it is the basis for array indexing. Pointer arithmetic has some quirks of its own, which make perfect sense when you consider how pointers are used.

Syntax

The following operations are valid for *addr*, an address expression (such as a pointer, array name, or &variable), and *integer*, an integer expression.

```
addr + integer    /* address-expression result */
addr - integer    /* address-expression result */
addr - addr       /* integer result */
```

The result of the first two operations is an address expression; the result of the third is an integer.

These operations are scaled, meaning that *integer* is multiplied by the size of the base type of *addr* before being added or subtracted. In the *addr - addr* syntax, the pointers must be of the same base type. The difference in the addresses is divided by size of the base type.

 Addition assignment (+=), subtraction assignment (-=), and increment and decrement operators are all supported in a similar fashion, so that addr += integer, for example is valid.

Examples

Suppose that my_array and ptr are declared as follows:

```
long  my_array[20];
long  *ptr = my_array;
```

Both my_array and ptr are address expressions, and each has the base type **long** (long integer), which is four bytes in size. So the scaling factor is four. The expression

```
ptr
```

points to the first element of my_array; let's say that this is the address 0x1000 (addresses are usually represented in hexadecimal notation). The following expression evaluates to the address 0x1004, because the integer, 1, is first multiplied by four and then added to ptr:

```
ptr + 1 = (numeric value of ptr) + 1 * sizeof(long)
        = 0x1000 + 1 * 4
        = 0x1004
```

So this expression points to the second element of the array.

Similarly, the next expression evaluates to the address 0x1008, because the integer, 2, is multiplied by four:

```
ptr + 2 = (numeric value of ptr) + 2 * sizeof(long)
        = 0x1000 + 2 * 4
        = 0x1008
```

And this expression, in turn, points to the third element of the array. Figure P.1 illustrates how this works:

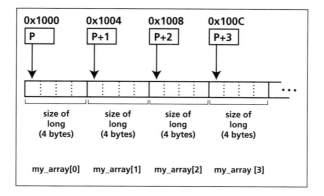

Figure P.1 *Pointer addition.*

331

This process of scaling—multiplying the integer by the size of the pointer's base type—makes sense because ptr, in this case, points to items of type **long**, and not just to individual bytes. In these expressions, the integer is scaled by whatever the size of the base type is—eight bytes for **double**, for example; possibly more for structures. Only **char*** and **void***—pointer types do not involve scaling (because **char** is one byte in size).

Incrementing ptr is the same as adding 1:

```
/* Equivalent expressions: each increases the
   address stored in p by 4. */

ptr = ptr + 1;
ptr++;
```

In either case, the number 1 is multiplied by four (assuming that the base type has a width of four) and then added to the numeric value stored in ptr. If ptr points to a position in an array, adding four is the same as saying, "Point to the next element of the array."

Indexing and pointer arithmetic are closely linked. When the expression my_array[10] appears in executable code, it is equivalent to:

```
*(my_array + 10)
```

In fact, the compiler translates the expression my_array[10] into this expression.

Definition

Most C programs make heavy use of pointers (a pointer is a variable containing an address). The importance of pointers in C is that they provide the only ways to do the following: pass by reference, manipulate strings, or use dynamically allocated memory. Moreover, once you've been around pointers for awhile and learn to use them cleverly, they open up new possibilities for writing fast, compact programs and manipulating data. Pointers combined with the right type casts allow you to do almost anything.

For a general introduction to the subject, see Chapter 7, "Pointers and Other Sharp Instruments." This section summarizes some of the finer points of pointer syntax and use. You might also look at the topics "Pointer Arithmetic" and "Pointers to Functions" for specific information about those areas.

Syntax

The pointer indirection operator (*)—not to be confused with multiplication, which is a binary, not a unary, operator—means "the thing that *ptr* points to":

```
*ptr
```

If this expression appears in an executable statement, it refers to the contents of the address stored in *ptr*. So if **ptr* is an integer, *ptr* is a pointer to an integer, and vice versa. The rest of this topic explores the implications of this syntax.

Pointers and Address Expressions

Numeric values can be used to represent many things: the number of cents in your checking account, the population of your state, a position within an array. Some special kinds of expressions represent addresses—that is, numerically indexed locations within the computer's own memory. These *address expressions* look a lot like integers; they are usually stored in either two or four bytes, depending on system architecture. But address expressions have a number of special restrictions and uses.

Suppose that the following variables are declared, and one of them (ptr) is initialized to point to the start of the array:

```
int *ptr, my_array[100], i;

ptr = my_array;
```

All the following are valid address expressions. The variable my_array, when it appears without an index, is interpreted as the address of the first element.

```
ptr            my_array            &i
```

These expressions hold the address of an integer, and all have type **int***. There is an important difference between these expressions: ptr is a variable, whereas the other two expressions are constants. So only ptr can be assigned a new value. For example:

```
ptr = &i;       /* Assign address of i to ptr. */
ptr = my_array;  /* Assign address of start of array to
                    ptr. */
```

Pointer arithmetic allows you to add or subtract integer values to address expressions: the result is another address expression. (See "Pointer Arithmetic.") Both of the following represent addresses:

```
ptr + 1
array + 7
```

Only a restricted set of operations is permitted with address expressions. You can add integers to them, as done here. You can assign them to a pointer variable. You can also

334

apply the indirection operator (*) to access the contents at the location. The result is an expression of the base type. In this case, because the expressions ptr, array, and &i all have the type **int***, the resulting type is **int** (integer).

```
*ptr
*array
*(array + 7)
*(&i)          /* This is the same as i itself. */
```

These expressions, which are integers, can be used wherever an integer variable can be used. For example:

```
*ptr = 5;              /* Put 5 into the int pointed to
    by ptr. */
i = *ptr + 10;         /* Put 15 into i. */
*(&i) = 1;             /* Put 1 into i. */
*(array + 7) = 100;    /* Put 100 into array[7]. */
(*ptr)++;              /* Increment the int pointed to
                          by ptr;
                          parens necessary because ++ has
                          higher precedence than *. */
```

The variable ptr has another interesting twist. Because it is a variable and not a constant, it has its own address in memory. Consequently, you can take the address of ptr itself:

```
&ptr
```

The result is a constant expression of type **int****, a pointer to a pointer to an integer.

Pointer Initialization

In addition to the differences noted above, there is one other crucial difference between ptr, a pointer variable, and a constant address expression such as my_array and &i: ptr must be either initialized or assigned an address before being used:

```
ptr = my_array;
```

If ptr is not explicitly given a value, its use represents a potential danger to the program. (This is one of the things that gives C a bad name among some people; but you just have to learn how to handle your pointers!) Specifically, consider this innocent-looking couple of statements:

```
int p;
```

```
*p = 5;
```

The second statement copies the value 5 to the location pointed to by p. The problem is, what does p point to? If p is global, it is initialized to 0 (NULL). If it is local, it contains some random address. In either case, the statement moves data to an invalid address in your computer's memory. If you're not running on a system with protected memory, then your statement could overwrite basic operating system code! This is why C programs that misuse pointers often cause the whole system to come crashing to a halt. You'll have to reboot, and any unsaved data from other running programs is lost.

N O T E Many compilers have a "check for null pointer" feature, which puts in code to check for an error at run time whenever a pointer with a value of 0 (NULL) is used to read or write data. This is useful, especially when you're first using C, and it stops the program before it does real damage. For this check to be effective, though, you must initialize all pointers to 0, except those initialized to a valid address. Pointers that contain random values escape detection until it's too late.

Another thing that can save you from having to reboot is an operating system that uses protected memory. Your program will be abruptly terminated and will not be allowed to infect the rest of the system with its random memory operations. Of course, you shouldn't rely on the system to police you like this.

So it's important to initialize pointers. Often, a pointer is declared that is to be assigned an address later. You may want to indicate that, for whatever reason, the pointer is not valid yet and not to be used. In any case, the way to initialize a pointer with no current address is to initialize it to NULL:

```
#include <stdio.h>

int *p = NULL;
```

NULL, in turn, is a symbolic constant defined in the file STDIO.H. NULL is defined as follows:

```
#define   NULL   ((void*)0);
```

As you can see, NULL is just the value zero, cast to a pointer type. C programmers frequently make good use of NULL as an indicator that the pointer is not yet assigned a value. Because NULL is equivalent to zero (false), you can test for it in expressions such as the following:

```
if (p)                  /* If pointer NOT null, */
    *p = new_total;   /*   use pointer.        */
else
    /* Pointer not valid; go initialize it. */
```

This kind of "fail-safe" logic uses a test to ensure that the pointer p points somewhere before using it. You don't need to do this if you've just assigned a value to p or have reason to be certain p is initialized to a valid address. However, many programs use NULL as a possible value for pointers, indicating that the pointer is not yet ready to use.

Global variables are automatically initialized to zero (NULL) values by default. This applies to pointers as well. Local, nonstatic variables are more troublesome because they can contain random values if not initialized, so take care to initialize local pointers.

Initialization and Aggregates

A pointer can be initialized to any constant address expression. Note that the name of an array is a constant expression that translates into the address of the first element.

```
int n, ages[10];

int *ptr1 = &n;    /* Point to n */
int *ptr2 = ages;  /* Point to 1st element of ages */
int *ptr3 = NULL;  /* Init to (void*)0 */
```

One of the differences between pointers and arrays is that an array definition allocates many bytes of storage, whereas a pointer definition allocates only enough room for one pointer—usually two bytes wide on 16-bit systems and four bytes wide on 32-bit systems (or longer, depending on special considerations such as memory model or use of a **far** pointer).

Consider the following definitions:

```
char s[] = "Hello!!";
char *p = s;
```

Here, the definition of s[] allocates eight bytes: one for each character and one for a terminating null byte. The definition of p allocates space for just one pointer (this is four bytes on a 32-bit system).

However, the following definition intializes a pointer through the use of an aggregate. You can do this with string literals, as done here, or with other kinds of aggregates. In either case, the declaration allocates space for the aggregate data and then returns the address of this data. That address is then assigned to the pointer.

```
char *p = "Goodbye";
```

In this case, the definition allocates eight bytes for the string data, plus four for the pointer, for a total of eight bytes.

Figure P.2 illustrates how these definitions allocate data.

C symbol Data

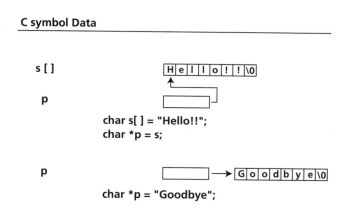

char s[ ] = "Hello!!";
char *p = s;

char *p = "Goodbye";

Figure P.2 *Effect of pointer definitions on data allocation*

When s[] and p are declared separately, as in the first case, the identifier s is always available as a constant, pointing to the start of the string. In the second case, the only access to the string data is provided through p, the pointer. If p is later assigned a new address, then access to the string data may be permanently lost. (It's still there in memory, but there's no way to refer to it.)

The first approach, it should be noted, does not result in the allocation of any more program data; its only drawback is that it creates more symbols for the compiler to deal with. The choice of which approach to use should be guided by the logic of your particular program.

Definition

Pointers to functions (function pointers) provide an amazing capability: the ability to call another program or function and say "call me back at this address." Your own function—the *callback* function—can then modify some aspect of the other function's or program's behavior. This kind of capability has great usefulness in many advanced applications: object orientation, terminate-and-stay-resident software, and programming for graphical user interfaces such as Microsoft Windows, to name just a few.

The concept may strike you as terribly abstract in the beginning, so in this topic I'll use a simple example—the qsort library function—and take it slowly.

Syntax

A pointer to a function (function pointer) is declared with the following syntax. You also use this syntax to call the function pointed to, in an executable statement:

(*function_ptr)(arguments)

You can specify a function address with *function* or &*function*. Note the absence of parentheses following the name, which means that the function is not actually being called:

function_ptr = function;
function_ptr = &function;

Example

One of the many useful functions in the C standard library is the qsort function, which sorts any array that you pass it. The function uses the quick-sort algorithm for sorting.

But the qsort function doesn't know how to compare the elements. One person might use qsort to sort an array of

340

integers, whereas someone else might use it to sort an array of strings. How does qsort judge which of two elements is "greater" than the other?

The answer is that you must write a function that actually does the comparison. The qsort function calls your function back every time it needs to compare two elements.

The prototype for the qsort function is:

```
void qsort(void *base, size_t num, size_t width,
    int (*compare)(const void* p1, const void* p2));
```

The first element is a pointer to your array (**void*** means that qsort doesn't assume any particular type of array). The second and third arguments contain the number of elements and the size of each element. The **size_t** type is an alias for **unsigned int**.

The last argument, compare, is not a real function name; it is just a pointer name. You can call your comparison function anything you wish. Then you pass along the address of this function to qsort. This argument is the strangest of declarations—an argument declaration that is actually a function prototype!

```
int (*compare)(const void* p1, const void* p2)
```

This prototype says that your callback function must take two pointers and return an integer. Note that the types in the last set of parentheses qualify arguments *of your callback function,* and not qsort itself. The arguments of the callback are **const** arguments, so your callback function must not use the arguments to modify any values. (See "const Keyword.")

Let's say that you want to sort a simple array of integers:

```
int a[] = {27, 1, 100, 5, 63, -3, 7, 0, -11, 8};
```

You need to write a callback function that returns 1, 0, or –1, depending on whether the first argument is greater than, equal to, or less than the second argument, respectively. This is easy to do with integers:

```
/* cmp: Integer comparison function:
   Return 1 if *p1 > *p2,
          0 if equal,
         -1 if *p1 < *p2
*/

int cmp(const void *p1, const void *p2) {
    int i, j;
    i = *(int*)p1;
    j = *(int*)p2;

    return (i > j ? 1 : (i == j ? 0 : -1));
}
```

The type cast, **(int*)**, is necessary for using the **void*** pointers. See "Explicit Type Conversions" for an explanation of this kind of C code.

Now that the callback function has been written, you call qsort to sort the array, passing the address of the callback as the fourth argument:

```
qsort(a, 10, sizeof(int), &cmp);
```

When you make this function call, qsort uses the first three arguments for information on the array. The last argument gives the address of your callback function.

This procedure creates an interesting flow of control between your program and the qsort library function (see Figure P.3).

Within qsort, the code to execute your callback function might look like the fragmant shown next. This is sample C code from a possible implementation of qsort. Here the function is called through compare, the function-pointer argument as it appears in the declaration. Remember that compare is a pointer passed to qsort by qsort's caller, so the actual callback function will be different for every program.

```
if((*compare)(ptr_elem1, ptr_elem2) > 0)
    swap(ptr_elem1, ptr_elem2, width);
    ...
```

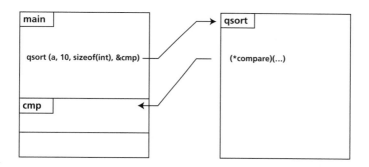

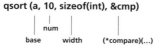

Figure P.3 *Use of a callback function*

Because you use the function pointer, compare, to call your function, qsort lets your code do the actual comparison between any two elements. Determining which elements to compare is qsort's job.

With any luck, the subject of pointers to functions hasn't yet overwhelmed you. It's simply a way of calling a yet-to-be-determined function or a function supplied by another program or process. An expression such as "(*compare)" is a stand-in, of sorts, for a function supplied elsewhere. In calling qsort, you're saying, "Call me back at this address." This gives C a flexibility undreamed of in most programming languages.

343

Definition

The word *precedence* means the order in which things are done. Despite its anti-egalitarian ring, the term doesn't imply any value judgement. Assignment, for example, has a very low precedence, but that doesn't mean that it's less important than any other operation. It simply makes sense to do it last.

Sometimes you'll need to look up precedence of operators (see "Operators"), but general familiarity with C combined with common sense usually clears things up. Precedence follows the rules of elementary and high-school math, so multiplication and division have higher precedence than addition and subtraction. For example, consider the following expression:

```
a * a + b * b
```

This is equivalent to:

```
(a * a) + (b * b)
```

You can immediately recognize the precedence of operators in the majority of cases if you remember this general order:

1. The unary operators, such as *, &, ++, and —, have the highest precedence, as do tightly binding operations such as indexing ([]) and structure or member references.

2. Next come the arithmetic operations: addition, multiplication, and so on.

3. Then come comparison operations: >, <, ==, and so on. This is reasonable, because arithmetic calculations typically are performed, and then results are compared.

4. All the logic operations come next. Comparison operators produce true or false values, and then

logic operations, if used, usually combine results. Of these, the bitwise versions have higher precedence than the logical (non-bitwise) versions.

5. The assignment operators (= and its cousins +=, *=, /=, and so on) are nearly lowest in precedence.

6. The comma operator (,) is lowest of all, because it has the effect of evaluating two expressions as if they were separate statements.

The conditional operator (?:) ranks above assignment but below logical operations. This makes sense because the conditional operator is generally used to produce one of two values, which is then assigned to a variable. Naturally, the assignment is carried out only after the result is determined.

Precedence in C is occasionally tricky at the highest level—but mastering this is just a matter of gaining familiarity with the language. Most notably, increment and decrement *postfix* (example: n++) have the highest precedence, along with function calls, indexing ([]), and structure references (struct.member). Consequently, the common expression

```
*p1++ = *p2++
```

is evaluated as if it were written this way:

```
*(p1++) = *(p2++)
```

This, in turn, is essentially the same as the following series of statements:

```
*p1 = *p2;      /* Copy item pointed to by p2. */
p1++;           /* Then point to next elements. */
p2++;
```

If in doubt, consult the table of precedence in "Operators." Beyond that, when precedence gets to be tricky or difficult to predict, it's always a good idea to make certain of the

345

order of evaluation by using parentheses. Making a mistake in precedence is impossible if you correctly use parentheses to state explicit order of execution.

When operators surrounding an item are at the same level of precedence, associativity (left-to-right or right-to-left) determines which operations are carried out first.

Primitive Data Types

Definition

A *primitive data type* is one of the data types provided directly by C. These types include **char**, **int**, **short**, **long**, **float**, **double**, and the **unsigned** variations of the integer types (all except **float** and **double** are integers). These types are the building blocks upon which you can develop more complex types. (See "Compound Data Types.")

Examples

The subject of primitive data types is important in C, because certain operations are valid only on primitve-type variables and pointers. For example, you cannot assign an array directly to another array. Instead, you have to operate on the individual elements, which may be of a primitive type. This also extends to strings, a fact that is a stumbling block for people coming from a BASIC background:

```
char str1[80];
char str2[] = "Hello, goodbye."

str1 = str2;    /* ERROR! Invalid assignment. */
```

The individual elements of str1 and str2 have type **char**, which is a primitive type, so you could do the following:

```
str1[0] = str2[0];
```

The strcpy function uses a series of such operations to copy one string to another. You need to include STRING.H to call this and other string functions.

```
strcpy(str1, str2);
```

See "Data Types" for a summary of all the primitive data types.

Definition

There is no built-in PRINT command or keyword in C, but you can print data by calling the printf function included in the standard C library provided with every C compiler. You need to include the STDIO.H header file before calling printf so that it's properly declared. This book does not cover most library functions, but I discuss printf because it's so universal.

Syntax

A call to the printf function has the following syntax:

#include <stdio.h>

printf(_format_string_, _arguments_**);**

Each of the arguments is a value corresponding to a format specifier in the _format_string_ (a null-terminated character string). Each argument is a numeric value or pointer, as appropriate. The **printf** function returns the number of arguments printed.

printf Formats

Table P.1 summarizes the format specifiers that can appear in _format_string_:

Table P.1 _Format specifiers for format_string._

SPECIFIER	DESCRIPTION
%c	Print a single character (on most systems, the ASCII table is used to interpret values).
%d, %i	Print as a decimal integer.
%u	Print as an unsigned decimal integer.
%o	Print integer in octal format.

SPECIFIER	DESCRIPTION
%x, %X	Print integer in hexadecimal format.
%e	Print floating-point in exponential format. Example: 1.273110e+01
%E	Same as %e, but use capital E: 1.273100E+01
%f	Print floating-point in standard format. Example: 12.73110.
%g	Print floating-point in %e or %f format, whichever is shorter.
%G	Same as %g, but use capital E.
%s	Print null-terminated character string; argument is interpreted as a pointer to this data.
%p	Print pointer value in hexadecimal format (similar to %x).
%%	Print a literal percent sign (%).

Format Modifiers

When you call printf (especially to print floating-point numbers), you may want to control how many characters are printed. The printf syntax lets you modify the meaning of each format in the following ways, in which c represents a format character:

%[-]*min*c
%[-]*min*.*precision*c

Here the brackets indicate that the minus sign (-) is optional. If included, it indicates that the data is to be left justified within the print field.

The *min* modifier is a decimal number indicating size of the print field. For example, the following format specifies a decimal integer printed into a field at least five characters wide:

%5d

349

The *precision* modifier is also a decimal integer. Its meaning depends on the format:

- Maximum number of characters printed in a string format (%s).

- Number of digits after the decimal point in a floating-point number (%f, %e, etc.).

- Minimum number of digits in an integer (%d, %i, etc.).

Example

Suppose the following statement appears in a program:

```
printf("The %s temperature is %5.4f.", "Alaskan", 25.7);
```

When the program is run, the output you'll get is:

```
The Alaskan temperature is 25.7000.
```

Definition

The **register** keyword requests that a variable be allocated in one of the processor's registers, if possible. In the early days of C, this was one of the things that most impressed some programmers. Because of optimization technology, this keyword is now considered relatively unimportant.

If you've programmed in assembly language, you know what a register is. If not, suffice it to say that registers are special memory locations residing inside the processor. Values are routinely moved in and out of registers all the time. If an intensive amount of calculation is going to be done with a particular variable, a program can be made significantly faster by reserving a register for the exclusive use of that variable.

Syntax

You can modify a variable declaration by preceding it with the **register** keyword, which is one of the storage class specifiers.

register *declaration*;

The items declared should be of an integer or pointer type.

Example

In the following example, the variable i is used intensively for array manipulations—being accessed in potentially thousands of operations in a row—and is therefore placed in a register:

```
void init_array(int a[], size, data) {
    register int i;

    for (i = 0; i < size; i++)
        a[i] = data;
}
```

351

The use of the **register** keyword is not binding on the compiler; it is actually only a suggestion, or hint, about how registers should be allocated. With the advent of improved optimizing technology, many current C compilers make their own sophisticated judgments about how best to allocate register usage. Therefore, if the program would profit by reserving a register for a variable, a good optimizing compiler is probably doing this anyway, making the keyword a bit superfluous.

Some compilers, in their arrogance, simply ignore this keyword altogether. With older compilers, however, use of **register** can make a difference. In any case, it never hurts to use it.

Definition

The remainder operator, also called the modulus operator, returns the remainder when one integer is divided by another integer. For example, 7 divided by 2 is 3 with a remainder of 1, so the expression 7 % 2 evaluates to 1.

Syntax

The remainder operator (%) forms an expression from two integer subexpressions:

quantity **%** *divisor*

The syntax is the same as division (/) except that the remainder, not the quotient is the result.

Usage

The remainder operator has any number of uses, but a common use is to determine when an integer is exactly divisible by another integer. For example, the following function determines whether a number is odd or even. It returns 1 if the number is even, and 0 otherwise.

```
int is_even(int n) {
    return (n % 2 == 0);
}
```

In general, if a number n is exactly divisible by a divisor d, then n % d evaluates to 0.

In Chapter 5, I used the remainder operator to print a space after every fourth digit:

```
for (i = 1; i <= 16; i++, input_field <<=1) {
    putchar((input_field & 0x8000) ? '1' : '0');
    if (i % 4 == 0)
        putchar(' ');
}
```

353

return Statement

Definition

The **return** statement causes a function to immediately return control to its caller. Optionally, it can return a value. It's similar to **return** or "exit function" statements in other languages.

Syntax

The **return** statement, which appears in one of the following two forms, is a complete statement in C:

```
return expression;
return;
```

The first version should be used in any statement that does not have a **void** return type. (By default, the return type of any function, including **main**, is **int**.) The function immediately returns with *expression* as its return value; this means that the entire function call evaluates to the value of *expression*. The type of *expression* should match the return-value type of the function. If not, the compiler implicitly converts the type.

The second version should be used only in functions with **void** return type, in which case its use is optional. The only purpose of **return** in this case is to exit early from a function. Such a statement generally appears inside an **if** or **switch** statement.

Example

In the following example, the factorial function uses the **return** statement to report the results of its calculation. If the function is called with an argument of 4, it executes **return** *expression* in its last statement, with *expression* equal to 24. This means that the function call factorial(4) evaluates to 24.

354

```
i = factorial(4);    /* i gets the value 24. */
...
long factorial(int n) {
    long result = 1;

    while (n)
        result = result * n--;
    return result;
}
```

Definition

There's no built-in INPUT command or keyword in C, but you can input data by calling the scanf function included in the standard C library. You need to include the STDIO.H header file before calling scanf so that it's properly declared. This book does not cover most library functions, but I discuss scanf because it's so universal.

The scanf function does not print a prompt message. You need to do that separately, using printf.

Syntax

A call to the scanf function has the following syntax:

#include <stdio.h>

scanf(*control_string, arguments***);**

Each format specifier in the *control_string* determines how to read and interpret data; the function reads text, converts it, and then copies data to the address indicated by the corresponding argument. For example, if the format calls for integer input (%d or %i), the corresponding address should give the address of an integer (for example, &n).

scanf Formats

Table S.1 summarizes the format specifiers that can appear in *control_string*:

Table S.1 *Format specifiers for scanf.*

SPECIFIER	DESCRIPTION
%c	Next character input (even a white space) copied to **char** destination.
%d, %i	Decimal integer input converted to numeric value and sent to integer destination (but %i accepts octal input with 0 prefix and hexadecimal input with 0x prefix).

SPECIFIER	DESCRIPTION
%u	Same as %d, but destination is an unsigned integer.
%o	Integer input interpreted as octal; destination is integer.
%x, %X	Integer input interpreted as hexadecimal; destination is integer.
%e, %f, %g	Floating-point input, in any format supported by printf. Note that if the destination is of type **double,** format needs to be qualified with "l", as in "lf".
%s	Characters copied to string destination until non-white space encountered.

All the arguments to scanf msut be address types. Typically, this means combining a variable with the address operator (&). However, the name of a string is already an address type, so you should not use the address operator in that case. For example:

```
#include <stdio.h>

int   id;
char string[256];

printf("Enter name and id number: ");
scanf("%s %i", string, &id);
```

Format Modifiers

Between the percent sign (%) and the format character, an "l" can appear, indicating that the format is "long." This is necessary in the case of arguments with a destination of type **double**, which will not get correct data unless "l" is used to indicate the type. For example:

```
double  x, y, z;
float   flt_var;

scanf("%lf %lf %lf %f", &x, &y, &z, &flt_var);
```

357

You can also use "h" (short) and "l" (long) to modify integer formats. It's a good idea to use these modifiers if a variable is specifically declared **short** or **long** rather than **int** (which just uses a default size).

Other Characters in the Control String

Aside from format specifiers, other characters in the control string are usually not important. Blank spaces and tabs are simply ignored. Other text characters (not preceded by %) are expected to match the input verbatim, so that scanf("abc%n") skips past the input "abc" and then reads an integer.

This last feature of scanf—reading past fixed characters—may not sound very useful, but it is helpful sometimes with its sister function, fscanf. The fscanf function is nearly identical to scanf except that it reads input from a file. In a data file, a pattern of fixed text characters may be embedded in the file. You may need to read past the fixed characters to get to the numeric data.

WARNING There are number of common mistakes with scanf. By far the most common is to forget that arguments must be addresses. This can be a nasty error, because it causes data to be sent to a random address. The following statement can cause unpleasant results for your program:

```
scanf("%d", id_num);
```

If id_num is an integer, make sure that you give its address to scanf:

```
scanf("%d", &id_num);
```

Another common mistake is to forget that the proper input format for arguments of type double is "%lf", and not "%f". Forgetting this will cause your program to get values that seem to come from outer space.

Scope

Definition

Scope is an attribute of variables, and it refers to how much the program knows about a particular variable. The variable is said to be *visible* over that section of the program.

Examples

This all sounds abstract and fuzzy without examples. A simple example is a local variable. Because it's defined within a function, a local variable can be used only within that function. A variable defined inside a statement block (compound statement) has even smaller scope. It is visible only within that block.

```
void my_func(int n) {
    int i, j;

    for (i = 0; i < MAX_SIZE; i++) {
        double x_coord, y_coord;
        ...
        }
}
```

Here, the scope of i and j is functionwide. The scope of x_coord and y_coord is restricted to the compound statement within the **for** loop. Outside this block, a reference to x_coord or y_coord would be an error.

Global variables have scope throughout the current module (or possibly farther, if **extern** declarations are used). The syntax for a global variable definition is identical to that of a local variable; the difference is simply that global variable declarations are placed outside of function definitions.

See Chapter 6, "A Few Words About Scope," for more information and examples.

The **short** data type is an integer that is two bytes (16 bits) wide. Although the ANSI C standard states only that the size of a **short** be at least two bytes, the vast majority of C compiler implementations—especially on personal computers—use exactly two bytes.

Range

–32,768 to 32,767.

Syntax

You can declare any number of short integers by placing **short** at the beginning of the declaration statement:

[*storage*] [*cv*] **short** *items*;

Here the brackets indicate optional prefixes: *storage* is a storage-class specifier (**auto**, **extern**, **register**, **static**), and *cv* is **const**, **volatile**, or both. The *items* are one or more simple or complex variable declarations.

Example

The following statement defines a simple variable (cake), an array (id_nums), and a pointer (ptr_to_short):

```
short  cake, id_nums[10], *ptr_to_short;
```

Usage

Although **short** and **int** are equivalent types on many systems, the **short** type is best reserved for situations when space is at a premium: for example, in a structure written out to a file or repeated many times in an array. The **int** type is defined as the natural size for a given system and may be either two or four bytes, depending on what would be optimal for the system to use in calculations; **int** is generally the better choice for simple variables.

Statement

Definition

A statement is the fundamental unit of execution in C. Declarations are also statements.

The term *statement* is a concept of grammar in C, just as it is in ordinary language. You don't really need to know what the parts of speech are called in a language in order to speak the language—although it doesn't hurt, and might conceivably help. The practical knowledge is what's important, even in C.

Mainly, you need to know is that statements are usually terminated with a semicolon (;) unless they are compound statements (using braces) or function definitions. The relationship between expressions and statements in C is very close: append a semicolon to any expression and it becomes a statement.

Syntax

The following list summarizes all the executable statements in C. The most common category is the first: expressions. In C, an expression can contain assignments and all kinds of function calls. In other languages, assignments and some kinds of function calls (procedures) are considered types of statements.

This syntax is totally recursive. For example, a compound statement contains any number of statements, each of which can itself be a compound statement.

Each executable statement in C is one of the following.

- Expression statements, consisting of an expression terminated by a semicolon:

  expression;

- Compound statements, consisting of braces enclosing one of more statements:

  { *statements* }

- Null statements, consisting only of a semicolon. Such statements do nothing but are syntactically valid; one useful example is a labelled null statement at the very end of a function to serve as a target of a **goto**.

  ;

361

- Jump statements, which transfer control of the program to another location. These include:

  break;
  continue;
  return;
  return *expression***;**
  goto *identifier***;**

- **if** statements; in this syntax, brackets indicate that the **else** clause is optional:

  if (*expression*)
     statement
  [**else**
     statement]

- **switch** statements; see "switch Statement" topic.

- Loops, including **while**, **do-while**, and **for** statements; see the individual topics.

Any statement can be given a label, making it a target for a **goto** (or, with **case** and **default** labels, a target within a **switch** statement). The forms of labeled statement are:

identifier: *statement*
case *constant_expression:* *statement*
default: *statement*

Not all lines of code in a C program are executable statements. Many are declarations, which may define a variable, state that it is an **extern** variable, define a new type (**enum**, **struct**, **typedef**, or **union** declaration), or prototype a function. Some program lines may also be taken up by directives and comments.

Function definitions and directives are not terminated by semicolons, but type declarations and definitions are.

This last rule may seem arbitrary and hard to remember, but it makes a lot of sense. A function definition needs to be clearly differentiated from a function prototype, which can look quite similar. The fact that a function definition is not terminated by a semicolon is helpful to the compiler (but a function definition will *contain* statements that are terminated by semicolons).

Definition

The **static** keyword is one of the storage-class keywords that modify declarations. In practice, **static** has two useful applications: first, to extend the lifetime of local variables so that they retain their values; second, to prevent functions from having external scope. That these two uses are both supported by the same keyword, **static**, is one of the strange quirks of C that you have to live with.

Syntax

To make a local variable into a static variable, place **static** in front of the variable's declaration:

static *declaration*;

All the variables defined in the *declaration* take on static storage class. This gives them the same lifetime as the program itself. The lifetime of the variable extends past the function so that the variable has the same value when the function is called again. (It retains its value between function calls.)

Usage

A static local variable is like a global variable in every way except that a static local variable is accessible only to the function (or statement block) where it is declared. Such a variable is initialized just once—with a default value of zero if you don't initialize it yourself—and retains its value between function calls.

As a simple example, you could declare a variable that is incremented every time a function is called. Because it's **static**, it retains its value between function calls. This might be a useful tool in debugging:

```
int calculate_it(double a, double b) {
    static int number_of_calls = 0;
```

363

```
printf("The number of calls is: %d\n",
    ++number_of_calls);
...
```

Because number_of_calls is incremented at the beginning of the function, it keeps a running total of the number of calls to this function. If this variable were not declared **static** it would be initialized to 0 every time. But static variables are initialized only once.

 A goal of some programs and operating systems is to have functions that are "reentrant": supporting multiple instances of calls to the function in which none of the instances interferes with any other. This is a requirement of recursive functions, for example. Reliance on local static and global variables can make reentrancy fail, because what one instance of the function does with a static variable can affect all the other instances.

Static Functions

The other practical use of **static** is to qualify function definitions. By default, a function is visible not just to the current module (source file) but also to all the modules linked together to form the program. If you place **static** at the very front of a function definition, the function is not visible outside the current module. This isn't done often, but it can be useful as a way of modularizing your code so that only select data and functions are shared between different modules. Most programmers who want this kind of modularization migrate to C++.

Storage Class

Definition

The storage class of an item determines how it is stored in memory and whether it is linked to other modules—assuming you are writing a multiple-module program. For example, an **auto** variable (almost any local variable) is allocated on the stack along with function-call information, and the **auto** variable is destroyed as soon as the function terminates. A **static** variable is fixed at a specific place in memory, hence the name "static." Storage class, in theory, is separate from scope (the visibility of an object), although some kinds of storage class specifications do, in practice, limit or alter scope in some way.

Syntax

Storage class in C is always specified by placing a storage class keyword (**extern,** for example) at the beginning of a declaration:

```
extern int amount;
```

Table S.2 shows the four kinds of storage class.

Table S.2 *Storage class specifiers.*

STORAGE CLASS	DESCRIPTION
auto	Default for local variables; allocates variables on the stack, for temporary storage.
extern	Default for functions. Object recognized in this and all other modules.
register	Requests that register be reserved for data object.
static	Default for global variables. Object is allocated in program data area and has same lifetime as program.

For more information, see the topic for the particular keyword.

Definition

A string literal consists of text enclosed in quotation marks; you can use it as constant data in your program, just as you can numerals (27, 3, 100, etc.). When a string literal appears in your program code, the compiler allocates space for it and replaces the string expression with the address of this data. Therefore, you can use string literals in contexts (such as the printf function) that expect an address to **char** data.

Syntax

You form a string literal by enclosing text in double quotation marks ("):

"text"

When the compiler reads a quotation mark (except in comments), it interprets the characters that follow the mark to be part of the string literal until the next quotation mark is reached, which ends the string.

Special Characters in Strings

The following characters have special meaning inside a string:

- The backslash (\) is an escape character and is not read as a normal character. To specify a literal back-slash, use two consecutive backslashes (\\).

- The character sequence \n represents a newline character.

- The characters \x, where x is a constant number, place the numeric value x directly into the string. (To see what equivalent character this produces, consult the appropriate table for your system—this is the ASCII table on most systems.) You can use \0 to embed null (zero) values.

366

- The characters \" represent an embedded double quotation mark. A single quotation mark (') can be embedded freely.

- The backslash, at the end of a line, is a line-continuation character. The compiler continues to read each character it encounters into the string, except the backslash and the physical end of line (newline) that it is reading past. (See example for clarification.)

Here's an example

```
char *path_name = "C:\\WINDOWS\\SYS";
char *silly_string = "\"Get out the veto pen,\" said \
Bill."
```

The strings path_name and silly_string, when printed on-screen, look like this:

```
C:\WINDOWS\SYS
"Get out the veto pen," said Bill.
```

Definition

A structure in C is what's often called a record or user-defined type in other languages: it's a set of data items of different type, organized together for the convenience of the program. In practice, you'll usually find structures in one of two situations: first, file operations, in which units of data (records) are written out to files in a fixed format; second, linked-list operations in which structures—connected by pointers—form in-memory lists, networks, or trees.

Declaration Syntax

The syntax for a structure declaration is:

struct [*struct_type_name*] {
    declarations
} [*struct_variables*];

Here, brackets are used to indicate optional items. Note that, unlike a function definition, a structure declaration is always terminated by a semicolon. Each of the *declarations* is a variable declaration, following the standard rules of syntax.

Declaration Example

The usual boring example given for structures is an employee record (although I suppose it isn't so boring if you're depending on employee-recordkeeping software that prints your paycheck). Let's use a different example: a recordkeeping system for a couple of friendly movie reviewers: Roger and Jane.

```
struct movie_ratings {
    char movie_name[20];
    char director_name[30];
    int  Roger;      /* 1 = thumbs up, 0 = thumbs down */
    int  Jane;
};
```

368

Here, each movie_ratings structure records information on one film: the name of the movie, its director, Roger's rating, and Jane's rating.

This declaration creates only a structure type, movie_ratings, and not any actual structures.

Structure Variable Syntax

If the structure is given a *struct_type_name*, the structure type can then be used to declare variables in subsequent declarations using the following syntax.

struct *struct_type_name struct_variables*;

Structure Variable Example

Now that we have a structure type—movie_ratings—we can use it to create actual records for movies:

```
struct movie_ratings current_movie, my_movie;
struct movie_ratings years_ten_best[10];
struct movie_ratings *p_oscar_pick;
struct movie_ratings *get_oscar_pick(void);
```

The second declaration creates an array of 10 movie_ratings structures: one for each of 10 movies. The third declaration creates a pointer. When Roger and Jane go back over existing movies to select an Oscar pick, the pointer p_oscar_pick is set to point to the chosen structure. Using a pointer to select a movie review is much more efficient than copying the data to an entirely new structure. For example:

```
p_oscar_pick = &my_movie;
```

The fourth declaration is a prototype of a function that returnins a pointer to the Oscar-pick structure.

Structures Members: Syntax

The following syntax is a reference to a member of a structure:

structure_variable . *member_name*

Here, *structure_variable* is any valid reference to a structure; for example, this could be a simple structure variable or a member of an array of structures.

Pointers to structures are so common that C also supports the following syntax:

ptr_to_structure -> *member_name*

This is really the same as de-referencing the pointer, then referring to the member:

(*ptr_to_structure*) . *member_name*

Structure Members: Example

Let's build an example that ties together all the syntax elements shown so far. This is a simple example, because all it does is to print one record. A more realistic example might read a series of such records from a file and print them all.

```c
#include <stdio.h>

struct movie_ratings {
    char movie_name[30];
    char director_name[30];
    int  Roger;      /* 1 = thumbs up, 0 = thumbs down */
    int  Jane;
};

void print_movie(struct movie_ratings *p_film);

void main() {

/* Create a movie structure. */

    struct movie_ratings this_movie;
```

```
/* Set the fields of the structure, then print. */

    strcpy(this_movie.movie_name,
        "Pointers from Outer Space");
    strcpy(this_movie.director_name,
        "Alfred Hitch Schlock");
    this_movie.Roger = 1;    /* thumbs up! */
    this_movie.Jane = 0;     /* thumbs down! */
    print_movie(&this_movie);
}

void print_movie(struct movie_ratings *p_film) {
    printf("Film: %s\n", p_film->movie_name);
    printf("Dir.: %s\n", p_film->director_name);
    printf("Roger went thumbs %s.\n",
        p_film->Roger ? "up" : "down");
    printf("Jane went thumbs %s.\n",
        p_film->Jane ? "up" : "down");
}
```

Note that the print_movie function accepts a pointer to a
structure and not the structure itself. Consequently, only
two or four bytes of data are passed to the function rather
than the 60 or 70 bytes that would be placed on the stack if
the structure were passed by value. You can pass structures
by value with some implementations of C, but doing so is
usually not the best way, because it's so inefficient.

So the print_movie function just gets a pointer to an
existing structure. The structure-pointer operator (->) refers
to a member in the structure pointed to in statements such
as these:

```
    printf("Film: %s\n", p_film->movie_name);
```

The program, when executed, prints the following output:

```
Film: Pointers From Outer Space
Dir.: Alfred Hitch Schlock
Roger went thumbs up.
Jane went thumbs down.
```

371

Structures Referring to Structures

As soon as a structure is declared, it becomes recognized as a valid type within the rest of the module. Subsequent structure declarations can refer to the structure, as in the following declarations:

```
struct Point {
    double x;
    double y;
};

struct Polygon {
    struct Point P[MAX_POINTS];
    long    line_color;
} box1, box2, triangle;
```

Here, each structure of type Polygon contains within it an array of Point structures. If MAX_POINTS is 20, then the memory occupied by each Polygon structure is in excess of 20 * 16 (the size of a Point structure), which is 320 bytes. Compound data types can grow to a large size quickly.

Linked Lists

Linked lists and in-memory trees could easily be the subject of a book or even a whole set of books. I introduce them briefly here, just to suggest the flavor of how structures are used by advanced C programmers. Linked lists are extremely useful, because you can allocate them dynamically and therefore avoid having to deal with preset limits (as you do with arrays). Moreover, if you extend the linked list concept you can create binary trees and any number of other network-like structures.

You can define a pointer to contain almost any data type, including a pointer to another structure. What's surprising is that this can be a pointer to *another structure of the same type*. This kind of structure self-reference is legal only as long as it is done through pointers.

For example, we can create a linked list of Point structures by first declaring a structure like this:

```
struct Point {
    double x;
    double y;
    struct Point *next;
};
```

The member called "next" provides the link to another Point structure. Figure S.1 shows how any number of structures can be linked through this mechanism. The last record should be initialized to point to NULL; that way, you can test the "next" pointer for a NULL value to see whether a structure is the last in the list.

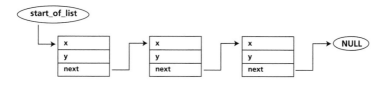

Figure S.1 *Linked lists of structures.*

A feature of linked lists is that the structures do not need to be next to each other in memory or part of the same array. They can be allocated through separate calls to malloc.

For example, suppose that you have a pointer to a current structure, ptr_old_point. You can allocate a new point and hook it to the end of the list with the following code. Note the use of the type cast.

```
/* Create new point and get back a pointer. */

ptr_new_point = (struct Point *)
    malloc(sizeof(Point));

/* Hook up new point to the old point. */
```

```
ptr_old_point->next = ptr_new_point;

/* New point has no "next" point yet, so init its
   "next" field to NULL. */

ptr_new_point->next = NULL;
```

Figure S.2 illustrates each of these three steps. I've limited this to a simple operation. Through operations similar to this, you can create complex linked-list programs complete with insertion, deletion, and searching procedures. There are a number of books that spell out these procedures explicitly, but I always felt it was more fun to figure them out without help. When you analyze how pointers and structures work, inserting and deleting list elements is not mysterious.

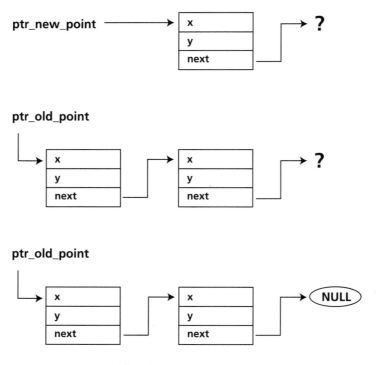

Figure S.2 *Adding a new structure to the end of a list*

Definition

The **switch** statement (**switch-case**) provides an efficient way to respond to a set of alternatives. The statement tests a particular expression—usually a variable—and jumps to different locations depending on the value.

If you think this sounds like a series of **if-else** statements, you're right, because anything you can implement with **switch** you can implement with **if** and **else**. However, when **switch** can be used it is helpful, because it results in cleaner, more compact, easier-to-read programs.

Syntax

A **switch** statement forms one unified statement in C:

```
switch (expression) {
case constant_expression_1:
        [statements]
case constant_expression_2:
        [statements]
...
case constant_expression_n:
        [statements]
[ default:
        statements ]
}
```

Here, brackets indicate optional items. You can have any number of **case** statement labels, and there is no minimum number. The action of the **switch** statement is to evaluate the *expression*, and then jump to the **case** label with the value that matches the result (or **default**, if none of the labels has a matching value).

In each block of statements, the last statement executed should usually be a **break** statement; otherwise, execution falls through to the next case. The reason **break** is needed is that the **case** keyword is just a label and not a statement, and it does not alter the flow of control. The **switch** statement jumps to one of the labeled statements, but from there execution continues normally unless interrupted with **break**.

Examples

Suppose you have a program that prints a number not as "1," "2," or "3," but as "one," "two," "three," etc. One way to do this is with a series of **if else** statements:

```
if (n == 1)
    printf("one\n");
else if (n == 2)
    printf("two\n");
else if (n == 3)
    printf("three\n");
```

You can get the same functionality from a **switch** statement, which is leaner and a little easier to follow:

```
switch (n) {
case 1:
    printf("one\n"); break;
case 2:
    printf("two\n"); break;
case 3:
    printf("three\n"); break;
}
```

In terms of run-time efficiency, the **switch** version will be at least as optimal as the **if else** version and possibly a little faster, depending on the compiler implementation. The **switch** version tests the value of n only once, after which it jumps directly to the appropriate label. The **if** version has to test n repeatedly and keeps jumping to the next **if** after each test fails.

The flow of execution "falls through" when the **break** statements are omitted. To see how this works, first suppose that you have the following test program. (The putchar function is a macro defined in STDIO.H that prints a single character to the standard output device.)

```
#include <stdio.h>

void print_val(int n);

void main() {
    print_val(1);
    putchar('\n');
    print_val(2);
    putchar('\n');
    printf_val(3);
}
```

If the print_val function consists of the **switch** statement introduced earlier, the program prints the following result:

```
one

two

three
```

But suppose that print_val uses **switch** without any **break** statements:

```
void print_val(int n) {
    switch (n) {
    case 1:
        printf("one\n");
    case 2:
        printf("two\n");
    case 3:
        printf("three\n");
    }
}
```

In that case, the program prints this strange result:

```
one
two
three
```

```
two
three

three
```

In the case of n equal to one, the control of execution jumps to the statement labeled case 1 but does not stop there. Execution simply continues right past the next **case** labels. This fact may seen annoying, but it makes C more flexible. There might be times you want to combine the action of different cases. For example:

```
switch(c) {
    case 'y':
        printf("sometimes ");
    case 'a':
    case 'e':
    case 'i':
    case 'o':
    case 'u':
        printf("is a vowel");
        break;
    default:
        printf("is a consonant");
        break;
}
```

This **switch** statement uses a couple of tricks. First, the 'y' case falls through to the other cases so that it prints the word "sometimes" and keeps on going. Second, the vowel cases are all combined. In terms of C syntax, the second printf statement is a labeled statement with five labels, which is perfectly valid.

If the test expression is 'y', this **switch** statement prints the following result:

```
sometimes is a vowel
```

Figure S.3 summarizes the flow of control in this statement:

```
switch(c) {
    case 'y':
        printf("sometimes ");
    case 'a':
    case 'e':
    case 'i':
    case 'o':
    case 'u':
        printf("is a vowel");
        break;
    default:
        printf("is a consonant");
        break;
}
```

Figure S.3 *Flow of control in a* **switch** *statement.*

The C switch statement does not support testing string values, because strings are arrays, not simple variables. If you need to supply a series of alternative actions depending on a string value, the only way to do this is to use a series of if else statements and use the strcmp function to test for equality. For example:

```
if (strcmp(str, "one") == 0)
    n = 1;
else if (strcmp(str, "two") == 0)
    n = 2;
...
```

NOTE

379

Definition

The **typedef** keyword is one of those keywords that C could theoretically do without, but it's a great convenience when you know how to use it.

A **typedef** declaration takes a complex type declaration and represents it with a single name. This name can then be used to define new variables, exactly as keywords such as **int**, **char**, **short**, **long**, and so on. Use of **typedef** can reduce the amount of program text to enter; moreover, as long as you are clear about what your types are, using **typedef** can be an aid in making complex declarations simpler and easier to understand.

Syntax

A **typedef** declaration looks almost like a variable declaration except that it is preceded by the word **typedef**:

typedef *declaration*;

When preceded by **typedef**, a *declaration* does not define variables but instead declares an alias for a complex type. Each identifier not previously defined becomes a type name.

Example

A description of **typedef** syntax will almost certainly seem too abstract without examples. Remember this basic rule: to define a type, write a declaration as if you were defining a variable of that type; then precede everything with **typedef**.

For example, you could define a character string holding 80 characters this way:

```
char big_string[80];
```

This statement creates a character string named big_string, allocating 80 bytes in the program data area. To declare the character string as a type, precede this same declaration with the **typedef** keyword:

```
typedef char big_string[80];
```

Now big_string is not a variable but is instead a type name; it defines exactly the same type that big_string would have if **typedef** were not present. Therefore, this declaration defines a string type having 80 characters.

Here, big_string is used to create four strings, each 80 characters in size:

```
big_string    s1, s2, s3, s4;
```

Here, big_string is used just like **char** or **int**, so this is a valid variable definition. This definition is equivalent to the following:

```
char          s1[80], s2[80], s3[80], s4[80];
```

Not only is big_string useful in variable definitions, but it also becomes a valid type name in all contexts, including function return values and explicit type casts. (Of course, in the latter case, the compiler has to know how to convert data to the indicated type or the conversion is not valid).

An interesting and useful technique is to use the name big_string within even more complex declarations. For example:

```
big_string    s1, *p, array_of_strings[10];
```

This declaration defines the following variables:

- s1 is a character string holding 80 characters.

- p is a pointer to a character string (note that its type is **char***, and not **char***).

- array_of_strings is an array of 10 elements —each of *those* elements is a character string holding 80 characters. This definition therefore allocates 800 bytes of program data.

381

You can even reuse a name declared with **typedef** inside another **typedef** declaration. For example, here the new type is named array_of_string_type:

```
typedef  big_string array_of_string_type[10];
```

typedef and Structures

Using **typedef** with structure declarations is a nice convenience, and seasoned C programmers do it all the time. Suppose you have declared a structure:

```
struct Point {
    double x;
    double y;
};
```

You can use Point as a new type, but you have to include the **struct** keyword every time you use Point, which is annoying.

```
struct Point p1, p2, p3;
```

But by declaring the structure type with **typedef**, you can avoid having to use the **struct** keyword when you define variables. For example:

```
typedef struct Point Ptype;

Ptype    p1, p2, p3;
```

You can even combine **typedef** with a structure declaration, as done here:

```
typdef struct Point {
    double x;
    double y;
} Ptype;
typdef Ptype *ptr_to_Point;
```

Now you can define new variables by using either "struct Point" or "Ptype". The example also declares the type ptr_to_Point, which can be used to define pointers to structures.

In a final extension of the **typedef** technique, you can declare a pointer structure type before declaring a structure and then use the pointer, type as a "next" pointer as described in "struct Declarations (Structures)":

```
typdef struct Point *Ptype_ptr;

typdef struct Point {
    double x;
    double y;
    Ptype_ptr next;
} Ptype;
```

typedef and #define Directives

For a long time I ignored the **typedef** keyword, because I assumed that the **#define** directive made **typedef** redundant. This is true only in part. There are some situations in which the use of **#define** will produce the same results as **typedef**, but there are many times when it will not. For example, suppose you define an integer pointer type:

```
typedef int *p_int;

p_int    p1, p2, p3;
```

The second statement creates three pointers: p1, p2, and p3. Suppose you attempted to use **#define** the same way:

```
#define p_int int*

p_int    p1, p2, p3;
```

This creates only one integer, p1, because after the C preprocessor replaces p_int, the statement becomes:

383

```
int*    p1, p2, p3;
```

This is equivalent to:

```
int     *p1, p2, p3;
```

And this statement does not make pointers out of p2 and p3. Therefore, using **typedef** is by far the more reliable way of defining a new type.

Definitions

Not all data is equal. Some variables hold one byte of information, others hold four, and still others hold eight or more. A variable's *type* determines how much information it holds and what its format is—integer format, for example, being radically different from floating point.

C is a more strongly typed language than some languages (BASIC, for example), but it is not quite as strongly typed as Pascal. C's offspring, C++, has stronger type restrictions than C in some cases: for example, C++ does not permit one pointer value to be assigned to another without an explicit type cast.

One of the distinctive features of C is that it permits you considerable freedom in converting data between different types. You can use explicit type casts to control, force, or even suppress data conversions. You should know exactly what you're doing when using type casts, particularly when they involve pointer types.

C's types include **char**, **short**, **int**, **long**, **float**, **double**, and **unsigned** variations of these. See "Data Types" for statics on each type.

See "typedef Declarations," "struct Declarations (Structures)," and "union Declarations" for information on declaring new types from existing types.

Definition

Unions are often difficult for people to understand when they're first learning C, in part because unions have nearly the same syntax as structures but serve a different purpose.

Simply stated, a union allocates several different data members *at the same address*. You may object that if several variables occupy the same address, writing to any one of them overwrites all the others. This is true. But this is no problem when you want to use the same area of memory for different data formats at different times.

The example in this topic presents a relatively simple situation, illustrating how a union might be useful in an advanced program.

Syntax

The syntax for a union declaration is:

union [*struct_type_name*] {
        declarations
} [*union_variables*];

Here, brackets are used to indicate optional items. Note that a union declaration is always terminated by a semicolon, unlike a function definition. Each of the *declarations* is a variable declaration, following the standard rules of syntax.

Although the union syntax is nearly identical to that of structures, union declarations rarely appear alone. Instead, union declarations are usually nested inside a larger type—usually a structure (as shown in the "Example" section that follows).

The rest of the union syntax echoes that for structures. In particular, you refer to members the same way:

union_variable . member

Example

Suppose you want to create a "variant" data type similar to the one supported in most versions of Visual Basic. A variant data type can hold data in different formats—integer, string, floating point, and so on.

The variant data type needs to store data in a variety of formats; but at any given time, it only needs to use *one* of these formats. It can hold either integer or floating-point data, for example, but it doesn't need to hold both an integer and a floating-point at the same time. Logically, then, the same data area could be reused for both.

You could use a simple structure, allocating one member of each kind of data and not worrying about reusing memory space. This would work, but it would be wasteful of memory.

Here is an efficient structure to implement a variant data type. It contains a nested union as its second member:

```
struct variant {
    short type;
    union {
        short c;
        long  i;
        char  *s;
        double f;
    } data;
};
```

The two members of the structure are type and data. The second member (a union) has four members: c, i, s, and f.

All the union members overlap in memory, starting at the same address. Figure U.1 shows illustrates the memory layout for a variable of type variant, whose address (for the sake of example) starts at 0x1000. The example also assumes that pointer size is four bytes, although on some systems it is two.

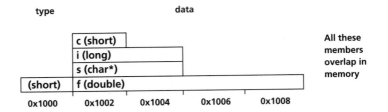

Figure U.1 *Memory layout of the variant type.*

Clearly, writing to any of the union members corrupts the data residing in all the other members. But the variant structure is not designed to use more than one of these members at a time.

Given this structure/union declaration, you could assign values to a variant by writing out both the data type and the data itself. For example:

```
enum { CHAR, INT, STR, FLOAT};

struct variant v1, v2;

v1.type = FLOAT;
v1.data.f = 27.5;

v2.type = STR;
strcpy(v2.data.s, "Hello");
```

Here, the **enum** keyword is used to provide a set of constants (CHAR is 0, INT is 1, STR is 2, and FLOAT is 3). Their only significance is that they indicate different formats. CHAR, INT, STR, and FLOAT could be fixed at any values as long as they were different from each other.

The example shows that the data path to a member must be fully qualified (see Table U.1).

388

Table U.1 *Referring to member of a uniuon within a structure.*

REFERENCE	DESCRIPTION
v1	A structure.
v1.data	A union within that structure.
v1.data.f	A member of the union within the structure. This is a reference to primitive data of type **double**.

You can write a generic function that prints the value of a variant structure depending on the current format:

```
void print_var(struct variant v) {
    switch(v.type) {
        case CHAR:  printf("%c", v.data.c); break;
        case INT:   printf("%i", v.data.i); break;
        case STR:   printf("%s", v.data.s); break;
        case FLOAT: printf("%f", v.data.f); break;
    }
}
```

Definition

The **unsigned** keyword is a modifier that helps to create a series of types in C. You can place **unsigned** in front of any integer type (**char**, **int**, **short**, or **long**) to create a type containing unsigned data. When **unsigned** is used alone, it means the same as **unsigned int**.

An **unsigned** data type has no plus or minus sign; it therefore can't contain negative numbers—it contains only positive numbers and zero. In exchange for giving up negative numbers, you can represent twice as many positive numbers. For example, the range of **short** is –32,768 to 32,767, whereas the range of **unsigned short** is 0 to 65,535.

Types and Ranges

Table U.2 summarizes the ranges of different integers, including **unsigned** types. Note that except in the case of **char**, an integer type is signed unless preceded by **unsigned**.

Table U.2 *Signed and unsigned integer ranges.*

TYPE	RANGE
signed char	–128 to 127
unsigned char	0 to 255
short	–32,768 to 32,767
unsigned short	0 to 65,535
long	–2,147,483,648 to 2,147,483,647
unsigned long	0 to 4,294,967,295
int	Same as **short** or **long**, depending on the system
unsigned int	Same as **unsigned short** or **unsigned long**, depending on the system
unsigned	Same as **unsigned int**

Conversions and Unsigned Data

Although C lets you intermix signed and unsigned data freely, you should be careful about the effects of conversion and type casts when unsigned types are involved. Surprisingly, the following small program prints two different results:

```
#include <stdio.h>

void main() {
    int i1, i2;

    i1 = (signed char) -2;
    i2 = (unsigned char) -2;
    printf("The value of i1 is %d.\n", i1);
    printf("The value of i2 is %d.\n", i2);
}
```

The output of this program is:

```
The value of i1 is -2.
The value of i2 is 254.
```

In a nutshell, program produces this result because the same data is interpreted differently, depending on whether the type that holds it is signed or unsigned. In the case of a one-byte type (**char**), the bit pattern 1111 1110 represents either –2 (signed) or 254 (unsigned). Through a process known as *sign extension*, this bit pattern becomes 1111 1111 1111 1110 when –2 is assigned to an integer variable (i1). The bit pattern becomes 0000 0000 1111 1110 when 254 is assigned to an integer variable (i2).

Unsigned data is by far the easier of the two cases to understand. With an unsigned data type, the largest number possible is all ones: 1111 1111 when stored in one byte. This quantity is 255, and it is *zero-extended* when converted to a larger type. For example, 255 becomes 0000 0000 1111 1111 when stored in two bytes.

Signed types use *two's complement* arithmetic to represent negative numbers. Under this scheme, the leftmost bit determines the sign: a one in the leftmost position means that the number is negative. Consequently, the upper half of an unsigned range becomes negative in a corresponding signed range. (In other words, the values 128 to 255 in an **unsigned char** type become the negative range, –128 to –1, in a **signed char**.)

In the two's complement scheme, you represent a negative number as follows:

1. Perform bitwise negation on the corresponding positive number.

2. Add one.

For example, to get –1, you first take the bitwise negation of 1 (0000 0001) to produce 1111 1110. Adding one produces 1111 1111. So 1111 1111 represents –1.

Similarly, –2 can be produced by taking the bitwise negation of 2 (0000 0010) to produce 1111 1101. Then add one. So 1111 1110 represents –2.

What's tricky about signed numbers is that you can't simply tack on leading zeros as you can with unsigned numbers and expect to get the same quantity. For example, –1 is represented as all ones no matter what the width of an integer, so (strange as it seems) 1111 1111 and 1111 1111 1111 1111 represent the same number. Signed data is converted to larger sizes through sign extension, which works as follows:

1. Examine the leftmost bit.

2. If the leftmost bit is 0, add leading zeros to convert to the larger type.

3. If the leftmost bit is 1, add leading ones to convert to the larger type.

Figure U.2 shows how -2 and 254 are sign-extended and zero-extended.

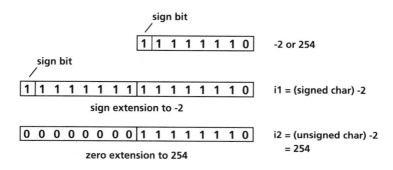

Figure U.2 *Conversion of signed and unsigned data.*

With typical processors, signed operations are performed at virtually the same speed as unsigned operations. In particular, most processors have built-in support for operations such as sign extension. The choice between signed and unsigned types, then, should rest entirely on what kind of data you need to store, because the processor can handle both types with equal efficiency.

Signed and unsigned types are often interchangeable, but the difference is significant in the following situations: in a printf or scanf format character (%u always prints an unsigned value); in assigning to a larger integer type, as done here; and in multiplication and division.

One of C's unique features is that it enables you to write functions that take any number of arguments—so that the function might be called with one argument during one function call and ten arguments in the next. To write these functions, you need to use a series of macro functions declared in STDARG.H.

Declaration Syntax

Functions with variable argument lists are declared and defined as others are, except that ellipses follow the last argument:

[*type*] *function_name*(*arguments*, ...)

Here the ellipses (...) are intended literally. The *arguments* are any number of standard C argument declarations, separately by commas if there are more than one.

Writing the Function Definition

To write a function that takes multiple arguments, first include the STDARG.H header file:

#include <stdarg.h>

You can then use the following definitions and macros to access the variable argument list. These are the arguments passed to the function after the last of the standard arguments.

MACRO OR DEFINITION	DESCRIPTION
va_list *arg_ptr;*	Defines argument pointer (*arg_ptr*), which is used to read the variable argument list.
va_start(*arg_ptr, last_arg*);	Initializes argument pointer to start of the variable argument list; *last_arg* is the last argument in the standard argument list.
value = va_arg(*arg_ptr, type*);	Gets the current argument (which must have specified *type*) and advances to the next argument.
va_end(*arg_ptr*);	Terminates reading of the argument list.

Example

The following function prints out all the integers passed to it, and then prints the total. The first argument (which is a standard argument) specifies how many integers follow it.

```c
#include <stdio.h>
#include <stdarg.h>

void print_ints(int num_of_args, ...)
{
    int total = 0, i;
    va_list  ap;

    va_start(ap, num_of_args);
    while(num_of_args−) {
        i = va_arg(ap, int);
        printf("%d\n", i);
        total += i;
    }
    printf("Total is %d.\n", total);
    va_end(ap);
}
```

If you call this function with the following statement

```c
print_int(3, 20, 35, 15);
```

you get this output:

```
20
35
15
Total is 70.
```

Definition

Almost any programming language has some kind of variable, which is just a place to store information that may change. A variable is a named storage location within the program. C doesn't differ very much from other languages in this respect except that it has some special types of variables that other languages lack (most notably, pointers).

Syntax

One difference between C and BASIC is that you must declare each variable before you use it, without exception. C is much like Pascal in this regard, although the syntax is somewhat different. (The C syntax is a bit simpler.) C variable declarations are formed by entering a type name—for example, **int** for integer or **double** for double-precision floating-point—followed by any number of variables, separated by commas:

```
int     a, b, c;  /* Variables a, b, c, of type int. */
double  x, y, z;  /* Variables x, y, z, of type double. */
```

Global declarations appear outside any function; the variables declared have scope from where they are declared, onward to the end of the module. Local variables appear within a function or compound statement. They must preceed all executable statements in the same block. (C++ has relaxed this particular restriction, by the way.)

Most variable declarations are also *definitions*—meaning that they create the variable and allocate space for it. The principal exception is **extern** declarations, which don't create a variable but instead say that it is defined somewhere (possibly in another module).

For more information on variable-declaration syntax, see "Declarations."

Definition

What all the uses of **void** have in common is that they suggest the condition of emptiness or nothingness. C (along with its offspring, C++) is possibly the only language to have *nothing* as a type. Yet **void** is a practical keyword, and ultimately it's no stranger than the number zero is in arithmetic.

Usage

The best way to understand **void** is to understand the three contexts in which it is used:

- In function prototypes and definitions, **void** can appear by itself in the argument list to indicate that the function takes no arguments. This is helpful information and less ambiguous than simply leaving the argument list blank. In a prototype, a blank argument list would mean that there might be arguments but they aren't specified yet:

```
int update_global_vars(void);
```

- In function prototypes and definitions, a **void** return type indicates that the function does not return a value. This makes the function like a procedure or subroutine in another language. Again, **void** is useful, because if the return type were omitted it would be assumed to have **int** (and not **void**) return type.

```
void print_results(int count, double area, x, y);
```

- In pointer declarations and type casts, **void*** is the generic pointer type. A pointer of type **void*** can hold an address but cannot be dereferenced until it is first cast to another type. The reason **void*** is useful is that certain functions (such as malloc) accept or return an address without a specific type. Having a **void*** type indicates a generic address, whose use will vary depending on the function's caller.

```
void *pv;   /* generic pointer */
```

If you want to be fanciful, you can think of **void** as being the most existential or Zen-like of C keywords. But don't let **void** intimidate you. It's there to serve useful, miscellaneous purposes. The designers of C reused the same word, **void**, for each of these situations rather than let additional keywords proliferate. This is in keeping with the philosophy of C: its compact and concise quality, from which stems much of its elegance.

Definition

In a beginning-to-intermediate program, you'll probably never use **volatile**. Its use is confined mainly to systems programming and to programs that interact with the hardware.

The word *volatile* suggests something unstable and uncontrollable. In computer terms, a volatile object is one that can be changed without warning by an outside agent: the system clock, for example, or a memory-mapped video buffer, or a semaphore used for inter-process communication. Such objects, if not handled in a special way by the program, are likely to cause errors.

Example

The compiler normally assumes that data never changes except as a result of a statement in your own program. The compiler can therefore place a value in a register and leave it there, not having to go out and access memory. For example, consider the following statements:

```
x = object;
y = object;
z = object;
f(object);
```

Under normal circumstances, the compiler can produce optimal code by placing object in a register, generating assembly-language code like this:

```
MOV   reg, object
MOV   x, reg
MOV   y, reg
MOV   z, reg
PUSH  reg
CALL  f
```

The problem is that if object is volatile, its value may have changed between the first instruction and the last. In that case, each time object is referred to, the program should go out to memory and retrieve its value again:

```
MOV   reg, object
MOV   x, reg
MOV   reg, object
MOV   y, reg
MOV   reg, object
MOV   z, reg
MOV   reg, object
PUSH  reg
CALL  f
```

This less optimal code is necessary for something that inter-acts with the rest of the system (for example, a semaphore used to communicate with other processes). By declaring an object **volatile**, you tell the compiler it has to handle the object with added care. It can't assume that the value of the object hasn't changed between instructions.

The following example declaration declares two **volatile** data items—x and y—and one volatile pointer, *p_sys_object. The pointer itself doesn't require special handling, but each access of data through the pointer (using *p_sys_object in an executable statement) requires a new memory access.

```
volatile int  x, y, *p_sys_object;
```

Syntax

The syntax of the **volatile** keyword mirrors in every respect that of the **const** keyword, so see the "const Keyword" topic for details. For example, you can't assign the address of **volatile** object to a pointer unless that pointer also has a **volatile** base type (echoing the rules for **const**).

Paradoxically, a variable may be both **const** and **volatile**:

```
extern const volatile int  *p_to_sys_clock;
```

This declaration states that an outside agency (the hardware in this case) may alter what this pointer points to without warning but that the program code must not change this value. The hardware can change the value, but the program can't.

As a consequence of syntax rules, such a pointer value cannot be assigned to another pointer unless that pointer is also declared **const volatile**.

while Statement

Definition

A **while** loop is the fundamental loop structure in C; you can write any other control structure by using a **while** loop (although in some cases the result would be cumbersome). Simply stated, a **while** loop executes a statement or statements as long as a specified condition is true.

Syntax

A **while** statement forms one unified statement in C:

while (*expression*);
    loop_body_statement

The *loop_body_statement* is frequently a compound statement (see "Example"). Because the entire **while** loop forms one statement, it can be nested inside other control structures. The loop repeats execution as long as *expression* evaluates to a nonzero (true) value.

Example

The following statements output characters from a string until the end of the string is reached. The end of a string is indicated with a null (zero) value so that the test expression, *p, is equal to zero when the end of the string is reached. The **while** statement considers zero a false condition and so stops.

```
#include <stdio.h>
...
p = string;
while (*p) {
    putchar(*p);
    p++;
}
```

402

The **while** statement is not terminated with a semicolon in this case because it ends with a compound statement. This code is a good candidate for a **for** loop; it also could have been written more concisely as:

```
#include <stdio.h>
...
p = string;
while (*p)
    putchar(*p++);
```

Index

#define directive, 260, 289, 383
#elif directive, 264, 292, 294
#endif directive, 267, 292, 294
#if directive, 292-295
#ifndef directive, 300
#include directive, 18, 31-32, 304-305

A

Addition, 327
Address expressions, 306, 314-315, 333-335
Address operator (&), 145-146, 189-190, 327, 334
Address types, casting, 274-277
Address variables
  see Pointers
Addresses, passing, 140-141, 146
Aggregates, 191-194, 338-339
Aliases, type, 380

Alternatives, selecting from, 92-96
AND operations, 105-107, 116, 213, 238
ANSI C, contrasted with non-ANSI, 9-10
argc, 181-182
Argument declaration, 193-194
Argument lists, empty, 63-64, 397
Arguments
  command-line, 181-182, 323-324
  const, 238-240
  defined, 41
  passing, 59-60, 62
  variable number of, 394-395
argv[], 181-182
Arithmetic operators, 327
Arithmetic, pointer, 330-332
Arrays, 195-200
Arrays
  and pointer arithmetic, 332
  copying between, 151-152
  creating, 148-149

405